Incarceration Nation

The United States incarcerates more of its citizens than any other country in the world. At a time when the public, politicians, and pundits struggle to understand how this came to be, *Incarceration Nation* offers the most comprehensive account of the rise of mass incarceration ever. Peter K. Enns turns conventional wisdom on its head. For decades scholars have argued that conservative politicians like Barry Goldwater and Richard Nixon led the development of the carceral state. The author shows that Goldwater, Nixon, and even Democratic President Johnson were responding to an increasingly punitive public. Enns analyzes why the public became so punitive and why it has had such a commanding influence on criminal justice policy. Just as striking, the focus on the public's punitiveness – and evidence that it has been declining – offers a critical path forward for those seeking to reform the criminal justice system.

Peter K. Enns is associate professor in the Department of Government at Cornell University and executive director of the Roper Center for Public Opinion Research. He is also team leader of the Cornell Institute for Social Science Theme Project on the Causes, Consequences, and Future of Mass Incarceration, and he is a former faculty director of Cornell's Prison Education Program. His research has been funded by the National Science Foundation and the Russell Sage Foundation and has appeared in journals such as the *American Journal of Political Science, British Journal of Political Science, Journal of Politics, Perspectives on Politics*, and *Public Opinion Quarterly*. He edited (with Christopher Wlezien) *Who Gets Represented?*

Incarceration Nation

How the United States Became the Most Punitive Democracy in the World

PETER K. ENNS

Cornell University

Susan,
Thank you for your continued support of the Roper Center @ Cornell!

[signature]

June 2016

CAMBRIDGE
UNIVERSITY PRESS

CAMBRIDGE
UNIVERSITY PRESS

32 Avenue of the Americas, New York, NY 10013-2473, USA

Cambridge University Press is part of the University of Cambridge.

It furthers the University's mission by disseminating knowledge in the pursuit of education, learning, and research at the highest international levels of excellence.

www.cambridge.org
Information on this title: www.cambridge.org/9781316500613

© Peter K. Enns 2016

First published 2016

Printed in the United States of America by Sheridan Books, Inc.

A catalog record for this publication is available from the British Library.

Library of Congress Cataloging in Publication Data
Names: Enns, Peter (Peter K.), author.
Title: Incarceration Nation: How the United States became the most punitive democracy in the world / Peter K. Enns.
Description: New York, NY: Cambridge University Press [2016]
Identifiers: LCCN 2015040741| ISBN 9781107132887 (hardback) |
ISBN 9781316500613 (pbk.)
Subjects: LCSH: Imprisonment–United States–History. |
Criminal justice, Administration of–United States–History. |
Corrections–United States–History. | United States–Politics and government.
Classification: LCC HV9466.E56 2016 | DDC 365/.973–dc23
LC record available at http://lccn.loc.gov/2015040741

ISBN 978-1-107-13288-7 Hardback
ISBN 978-1-316-50061-3 Paperback

To Melissa
With all of my thanks, appreciation, and love.

Contents

Acknowledgments

Many people have shaped this book, but none more than Mary Katzenstein. Mary, who is my colleague and a founder of Cornell's Prison Education Program, encouraged me to start this project, and she continues to shape my thinking on the topic to this day. I am exceedingly grateful for Mary's influence and support. Marc Mauer, the executive director of the Sentencing Project, was another early influence. Marc met with me in 2009, and his interest and suggestions served as critical catalysts for this book. Since these initial conversations, I have steadily accumulated a long series of additional debts that have made this book possible.

This book could not have been written without the year I spent as a visiting scholar at Princeton University's Center for the Study of Democratic Politics (CSDP). Not only did that year offer time to work on this research, but CSDP and Princeton's Politics Department offered a lively and intellectually engaging atmosphere to develop this research. While I was at CSDP, Michele Epstein, Martin Gilens, Jon Kastellec, Amy Lerman, Devah Pager, Markus Prior, and the other CSDP Fellows, Miriam Golden, Isabela Mares, Monika Nalepa, and Jeff Segal, offered friendship and support. My research has also benefited immensely from generous support from the Russell Sage Foundation (RSF). Jim Wilson has been especially supportive, and the results in Chapter 6 could not have been completed without the RSF. Financial support from Cornell University came from a LaFeber Research Grant, a Houston I. Flournoy Fellowship, and the Brett De Bary Mellon Writing Group: Immobility, Surveillance, and Detention.

I am also grateful to Cornell University's Institute for the Social Sciences and its support of the Theme Project on the Causes, Consequences, and Future of Mass Incarceration in the United States. My team members on this project, Maria Fitzpatrick, Anna Haskins, Julilly Kohler-Hausmann, and Chris Wildeman; our research assistant, Alyssa Goldman; ISS directors Kim Weeden and Dan Lichter; and Lori Sonken and Anneliese Truame have been incredibly helpful. Other colleagues and former colleagues at Cornell – both within the Department of Government and beyond – have also provided crucial input and support. These individuals include David Bateman, Tamar Carroll, Gustavo Flores-Macias, Chris Garces, Armando Garcia, Desmond Jagmohan, Michael Jones-Correa, Sarah Kreps, Adam Levine, Andrew Little, Joe Margulies, Suzanne Mettler, Jamila Michener, Kevin Morrison, Emily Owens, David Patel, Tom Pepinsky, Jim Schechter, Jon Schuldt, Rob Scott, Anna Marie Smith, Jessica Weeks, and Ben Yost.

I was fortunate that the students in my undergraduate course on Public Opinion and Representation read the introductory chapter and gave me valuable feedback. This book also benefited immensely from outstanding research assistance. Kailin Koch and Nikhil Kumar provided research assistance that was central to Chapters 3 and 5, respectively. And Delphia Shanks-Booth and Julianna Koch's research assistance was instrumental for the Chapter 6 analysis. This book would also have been impossible without the Roper Center for Public Opinion Research, which is now at Cornell University.

I have had the good fortune to present the research that went into this book at many universities and conferences. I am grateful to scholars and seminar participants at Columbia University's Population Research Center, George Washington University, McGill University, Princeton University, Stony Brook University, Syracuse University, Temple University, the University of North Carolina at Chapel Hill, the University of Pittsburgh, the University of Wisconsin-Madison, the Annual Meeting of the American Political Science Association, and the Annual Meeting of the Midwest Political Science Association. Many other individuals have provided valuable suggestions, feedback, and support throughout this project. Jamie Druckman's consistent enthusiasm and encouragement have been especially helpful. I am also indebted to Alyssa Goldman, Mary Katzenstein, Sarah Lageson, Willie Marshall, Shadd Maruna, Steve Raphael, Chris Uggen, and Chris Wildeman, who all read and commented on a final draft of the manuscript. Their comments, suggestions, and encouragement are enormously appreciated. Others who have influenced this work include Jason Barabas, Traci Burch, Shawn Bushway, Bill Franko, Amanda Geller, Marie Gottschalk, Michael Hagan, Seth Hill, Jon Hurwitz, Will Jennings, Greg McAvoy, Megan Mullin, Dave Peterson, Mark Ramirez, Bob Shapiro, John Sides, Stuart Soroka, Isaac Unah, Vesla Weaver, and John Zaller. I thank Mark Ramirez for providing presidential rhetoric data used in Chapter 4. I am also grateful to Robert Dreesen, the Senior Editor at Cambridge University Press, and to Brianda Reyes, also at Cambridge.

Of course, I actually began accruing debts before this project began. I could not have written this book without the graduate training I received while earning my PhD in political science at the University of North Carolina at Chapel Hill. My research has been positively influenced by my many graduate school friends and by all of the professors I encountered at UNC. I am especially grateful to my dissertation committee, Mike MacKuen, Marco Steenbergen, Jim Stimson, George Rabinowitz, and Paul Kellstedt. Jim Stimson's mentorship has been especially valuable. His influence on my research could not be overstated. This is not the book I thought I'd write when I left graduate school. I hope it passes muster. Chris Anderson, Paul Kellstedt, and Chris Wlezien have also been hugely influential mentors. I cannot thank them enough.

I have also benefited immensely from the support of my family and friends – both near and far. Special shout outs go to James and Josh in Princeton, Jon, Kenny, Will, Nick, T.R., and Dan in Ithaca, Adam and Corinna in Copenhagen, Fernando and Dakota in Chicago, Brian and Marybeth in Allentown, Ryan, Evan, and Lex in the Bay Area, Craig, Patty, Mike, and Vince in Kingsburg, Eamonn and Colleen in Chapel Hill, Kevin and Marcela in Pittsburgh, Jody, Marc, Paige, and Scott in NYC, Wendy and Jon in LA, Jenny in Richmond, Ryan in Atlanta, and Mark, Evan, and Toddd.

I

Introduction

Few nations – and no democracies – punish lawbreakers as energetically as the United States.

James A. Morone (2009, p. 921)

On November 4, 1995, Leandro Andrade walked into a Southern California Kmart. Andrade – who had several past criminal convictions – was about to commit a crime that would lead to a prison sentence of twenty-five years to life. Two weeks later, still a free man, Andrade struck again. This time, the target was a Kmart just three miles to the west of his previous crime. His plan was identical and would result in another sentence of twenty-five years to life. In two weeks, Andrade had attempted to steal nine VHS tapes: *The Fox and the Hound, The Pebble and the Penguin, Snow White, Casper, Batman Forever, Free Willy 2, Little Women, The Santa Clause,* and *Cinderella*. The total cost of the movies was $153.54. The actual cost to Andrade was fifty years to life.

Two years earlier, Andrade's actions would not have been noteworthy. At both Kmarts he was caught in the act by a store security guard – the videos never left the store. Considering his criminal record, in 1993 Andrade would have faced a maximum possible sentence of three years and eight months.[1] More likely, the punishment would have been less. However, under California's 1994 Three Strikes law, two counts of petty theft with a prior carried consecutive sentences of twenty-five years to life. The Three Strikes law, which had been overwhelmingly endorsed by 72 percent of California voters, increased the maximum sentence from under four years to an indeterminate life sentence with no possibility of parole for fifty years.

---

[1] California Penal Code §1170.1(a) (1999). See Chemerinksy (2003) for a detailed overview of Andrade's legal case.

Gary Ewing also found the high cost of shoplifting with a prior in California. Ewing walked out of a golf pro shop with three clubs concealed in his pants. The "limp" these clubs caused was a clear giveaway. Like Andrade, Ewing was caught in the act. Also like Andrade, Ewing faced California's Three Strikes law. Because this was his third strike, the punishment for stealing three golf clubs was a life sentence with no possibility of parole for twenty-five years.[2]

Although these are extreme examples of the punitive nature of California's Three Strikes law, they are not without comparison. In 2010, 32,392 individuals were imprisoned in California with their second strike. Another 8,764 were incarcerated with their third strike. Of the second strikers, 883 were in for petty theft. And like Andrade and Ewing, an additional 341 individuals faced a potential life sentence for stealing items valued at $950 or less.[3]

Of course, California is not the only state to legislate harsh sentences. After police found half a kilogram of cocaine hidden in the attic of her Florida home, Stephanie George was sentenced to *life without parole*. George claimed that she was unaware that her former boyfriend had hidden the drugs in her home. Her former boyfriend testified that he had paid her to store the cocaine. The judge concluded that his hands were tied. He told Ms. George, "your role has basically been as a girlfriend and bag holder and money holder but not actively involved in the drug dealing, so certainly in my judgement it does not warrant a life sentence." Yet life without parole was the sentence he was required to deliver. The judge later recounted, "The punishment is supposed to fit the crime, but when a legislative body says this is going to be the sentence no matter what other factors there are, that's draconian in every sense of the word" (Tierney 2012*a*, p. A1).

The judge in Robert Riley's case also expressed reservations about the severity of the punishment he was required to hand down. The judge wrote, "It gives me no satisfaction that a gentle person such as Mr. Riley will remain in prison the rest of his life" (Zlotnick 2008, pp. 49–50). Robert Riley had two felony drug convictions that stemmed from arrests outside Grateful Dead shows. His third conviction occurred in Iowa for conspiring to distribute LSD. The amount of LSD was minuscule. But the blotter paper it was on weighed more than 10 grams. This weight and the previous convictions meant a mandatory life sentence without parole (Tierney 2012*b*, Zlotnick 2008).

Of course, these four individuals represent just a tiny fraction of the 7 million people under the supervision of the US justice system (Glaze 2011). Yet their stories help illustrate an important fact: by almost any measure, the US legal system is one of the most punitive in the world. Controlling for the crime rate

---

[2] See Beale (2013) for a detailed discussion of Ewing's case.

[3] In 2012, Californians voted to revise the Three Strikes law so that a life sentence can be imposed only when the new felony conviction is "serious or violent." See Domanick (2004) for a history of California's Three Strikes law. The California incarceration data come from "Second and Third Striker Felons in the Adult Population," March 31, 2011. Department of Corrections and Rehabilitation, State of California, Data Analysis Unit, Estimates and Statistical Analysis Section, Offender Information Services Branch.

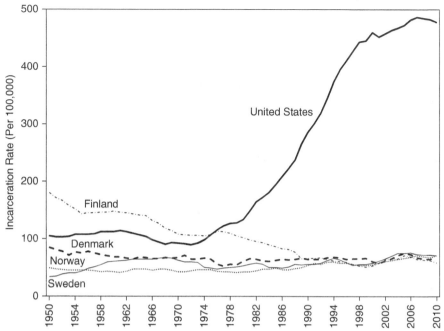

FIGURE 1.1. The annual incarceration rate for the United States, Finland, Norway, Denmark, and Sweden from 1950 to 2010.

Source: Nordic Criminal Statistics 1950 to 2010, Stockholms universitet, Table 15; United States: Sourcebook of Criminal Justice Statistics Online, Table 6.28.2010.

and the population size, the United States hands down longer sentences, spends more money on prisons, and executes more of its citizens than every other advanced industrial democracy (Amnesty International 2012, Blumstein, Tonry, and Van Ness 2005, Cowen 2010, Farrell and Clark 2004).[4] Furthermore, the difference between the United States and comparable countries is substantial. Per capita, the United States spends almost twice as much on prisons as England or Canada (Farrell and Clark 2004). More shocking, the proportion of individuals serving life without parole in the United States is approximately *180 times* greater than in England. Canada's Criminal Code (Section 745) does not allow life sentences without parole.

It is equally important, however, to remember that the US prison system has not always been such an outlier. In fact, during the 1950s and 1960s, the US incarceration rate was not especially remarkable. Consider Figure 1.1, which

4 In 2011, the United States ranked fifth in the world in the number of executions, behind China, Iran, Saudi Arabia, and Iraq. Of the thirty member countries of the Organization of Economic Cooperation and Development (OECD), Japan and South Korea are the only other two countries that allow the death penalty, and South Korea has not executed anyone in more than ten years (Amnesty International 2012).

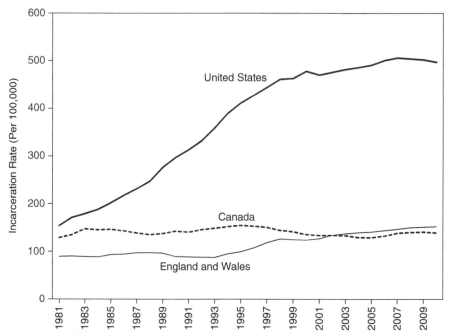

FIGURE 1.2. The annual incarceration rate for the United States, Canada, and England and Wales from 1981 to 2010.

Source: Canada: Statistics Canada, Canadian Centre for Justice Statistics, Corrections Key Indicator Report for Adults; England and Wales: Offender Management Caseload Statistics 2009 and 2012, Ministry of Justice Statistics Bulletin, Table 7.5; United States: Sourcebook of Criminal Justice Statistics Online, Table 6.28.2010.

reports the annual incarceration rate for the United States, Finland, Norway, Denmark, and Sweden from 1950 to 2010. Given the extensive scope of their social welfare policies, these Scandinavian countries are rarely grouped with the United States (Arts and Gelissen 2002). Yet, during the early years shown in the figure, the US incarceration rate was roughly on par with these countries, falling between Denmark and Finland. The US incarceration rate did not begin to pull away until the 1970s. Today the differences in incarceration rates are massive.[5]

Figure 1.2 compares the US incarceration rate with the incarceration rates of Canada and England and Wales from 1981 to 2010. Despite similarities in their

---

5 The US incarceration data in Figures 1.1 and 1.2 represent the incarceration rate for those sentenced to more than one year. While this offers the closest comparison to the data from other countries, we must remember that the series understates the overall incarceration rate, which includes individuals in jail with shorter sentences.

economies and social welfare policies (Esping-Anderson 1990, Hall and Gingerich 2009, Korpi and Palme 1998), only the United States has experienced a dramatic rise in its incarceration rate during the past three decades. In the early 1980s, the US incarceration rate already exceeded that of Canada and England, but not dramatically.[6] However, by 2005, the US incarceration rate was almost five times the rate in these countries. The growth of the US carceral state is without comparison. The United States now incarcerates a higher proportion of its population than any other country in the world (Walmsley 2009).

This book aims to understand the unparalleled expansion of the US prison system. We will see that objective conditions, such as the crime rate, matter. But the most important factor will turn out to be growing public support for "tough-on-crime" policies. In short, the public's increasing punitiveness – and the criminal justice system's responsiveness to this punitiveness – is critical to understanding mass incarceration in the United States. Thus, this book's title, *Incarceration Nation*, does not just refer to the fact that the United States incarcerates more vigorously than any other country. We are the *Incarceration Nation* because the public has been a catalyst for this outcome. Before this chapter ends, I will detail the many ways public opinion can influence criminal justice policy – and the incarceration rate in particular. However, prior to theorizing the relationship between public opinion and mass incarceration, the next section discusses the staggering social, economic, and political consequences of maintaining the world's most prolific prison system. In addition to illustrating the broad implications of mass incarceration, this discussion highlights the puzzling aspects of US prison expansion.

1.1 THE HIGH COSTS OF MASS INCARCERATION

Perhaps not surprisingly, it costs a lot to keep one out of every thirty-three adults under the supervision of the criminal justice system (Glaze 2011). The Bureau of Justice Statistics estimates that in 2008, federal, state, and local governments spent almost $250 billion for police, corrections, and judicial activities.[7] To put this value in perspective, in 2008, this amount represented about 40 percent of the total US national defense budget, about five-and-a-half times what the federal government spent on unemployment compensation, and more than seventeen times what the government spent on foreign aid.[8]

State and local governments foot most of this bill. Furthermore, because most state constitutions require balanced budgets, the rise of the carceral state has replaced spending in other areas. California Governor Arnold

---

[6] The incarceration rate for Canada in Figure 1.2 is slightly inflated relative to the other countries because these values are based on the adult population as opposed to the total population.

[7] Criminal Justice Expenditure and Employment Extracts Program (CJEE), Table 1 (cjee08fn01.csv). The actual estimated amount was $246.7 billion.

[8] Historical Tables: Budget of the US Government, Fiscal Year 2012, p. 71. Foreign aid refers to international development and humanitarian assistance.

Schwarzenegger drew attention to this pattern in his 2010 State of the State Address. The governor explained:

> The priorities have become out of whack over the years. I mean, think about it. Thirty years ago 10 percent of the general fund went to higher education and 3 percent went to prisons. Today, almost 11 percent goes to prisons and only 7.5 percent goes to higher education.[9]

Governor Schwarzenegger's comments imply that in order for the state to maintain its incarceration rate – which had more than quadrupled in the previous three decades – Californians were compromising other government programs and services. This tradeoff is not unique to California. During the past three decades, almost every state increased the proportion of its budget devoted to corrections and decreased the proportion dedicated to higher education.[10]

Of course, the costs of mass incarceration extend far beyond government expenditures. Scholars have repeatedly documented the significant social costs to those incarcerated, their families, and their communities (e.g., Clear 2007, Travis, Western, and Redburn 2014). Perhaps most obviously, incarceration can have a devastating effect on individuals' ability to earn a living. Upon leaving prison, the obstacles to employment are substantial. Most of those incarcerated have low education levels when they enter prison. Minimal to no job training opportunities in prison means that the formerly incarcerated typically reenter society even less equipped to meet the expectations of employers. The stigma many potential employers attach to prison and the fact that many jobs do not hire individuals with a prior conviction further reduce employment options.[11] Additionally, because of their criminal records, many former inmates are ineligible for health and welfare benefits, food stamps, public housing, and student loans (Forman 2012). The challenges of reentering society with few employment opportunities and limited access to public services are often further exacerbated by debt that has accrued while in prison. It is increasingly common for former inmates to be greeted by thousands of dollars in child support and legal fees from their time behind bars (Beckett and Harris 2011, Katzenstein and Nagrecha 2011).[12] Importantly, these financial concerns do not just affect those who have been convicted and sentenced. The fiscal strains that these individuals face weigh heavily on their families and communities.

Rising incarceration rates have also corresponded with substantial health costs. Those who have been incarcerated are significantly more likely to suffer

---

9 www.govspeech.org/pdf/19694d.pdf
10 Data from the Tax Policy Center State and Local Finance Data Query System.
11 See, for example, Pager (2003, 2005, 2007), Pettit and Western (2004), Raphael (2014), Wakefield and Uggen (2010), Western, Kling, and Weiman (2002), and Uggen (2008). Uggen et al. (2014) show that even an arrest for a low-level crime that does *not* lead to a charge or conviction affects employment prospects.
12 See Katzenstein and Waller (2015) for an important overview of the many exorbitant fees, including fees for telephone calls, medical services, and food, that inmates often must pay.

from mental *and* physical health problems.[13] Because of the increased risk of exposure to infectious disease, the American Red Cross will not accept blood from an individual who spent more than seventy-two consecutive hours during the previous year "detained or incarcerated in a facility (juvenile detention, lockup, jail, or prison)."[14] Of course, as with financial strains, those incarcerated are not the only ones affected by the health risks associated with incarceration. As Massoglia (2008*a*, p. 66) concludes, "Given the detrimental impact of incarceration on health and the high number of inmates released yearly, the penal system may have a transformative effect on aggregate health and the health care system." Perhaps less well known, correctional officers also face increased physical and mental health risks. Research consistently finds evidence of elevated levels of stress, burnout, depression, and PTSD due to the challenging work environments that correctional officers face, and correctional officers (as well as police and sheriff patrol officers) are among the professionals with the highest occupational injury rates. Thus, we must remember that those who work in the criminal justice system also experience its consequences.[15]

The high costs of incarceration are also borne by the children of those who are incarcerated. Not surprisingly, the research shows that it is hard on kids when they have a parent in prison. Haskins (2014), for example, finds a direct negative relationship between paternal incarceration and children's educational preparedness. Research also shows that children with an incarcerated parent are more likely to experience homelessness and foster care (Berstein 2005, Foster and Hagan 2007). Notably, as the US incarceration rate increased through the 1970s, 1980s, 1990s, and 2000s, more and more children have had to face the many challenges that stem from having an incarcerated parent.[16]

Punitive policies also carry political consequences. Some of these consequences are automatic. In forty-eight states, for example, convicted felons lose the right to vote.[17] In eleven states, the loss of vote is permanent. That is, even after completing their prison sentences and after completing parole or probation, ex-felons never regain the right to vote (Uggen, Shannon, and Manza 2012). This disenfranchisement holds real electoral consequences, and these

---

[13] See, for example, Liebling and Maruna (2011), Massoglia (2008*a,b*), Schnittker and John (2007), and Schnittker, Massoglia, and Uggen (2012).

[14] www.redcrossblood.org/donating-blood/eligibility-requirements/eligibility-criteria-topic#lifestyle

[15] Highlighting the scope of mental health concerns, in 2009, the New Jersey Governor's Task Force on Police Suicide found that between 2003 and 2007 the suicide rate among male corrections officers was two-and-a-half times greater than that of the same-aged men in the population (also see Stack and Tsoudis 1997). The same report found that the suicide rate for other law enforcement officers was 1.1 times the same-aged men in the population. Also see The Bureau of Labor Statistics (2013), Finn (2000), and Rogers (2002).

[16] For additional research on the substantial negative effects of parental incarceration on children, see Johnson and Waldfogel (2002), Wakefield and Wildeman (2011, 2013), Wildeman, Haskins, and Muller (2013), and Wildeman, Wakefield, and Turney (2012).

[17] Maine and Vermont do not take away the right to vote from convicted felons.

consequences have increased as the incarceration rate has expanded (Manza and Uggen 2006). For example, using the most conservative estimates of voter turnout, Manza and Uggen (2004) conclude that if Florida allowed ex-felons to vote in 2000, Al Gore would have won Florida – and thus the presidential election – by more than sixty thousand votes. In addition to the effects of these voter laws, recent research finds broader effects of the criminal justice system on political behavior. As the incarceration rate has grown, police stops, arrests, court appearances, and other interactions with the criminal justice system have become the most salient contact with government for an increasingly large segment of the population. Weaver and Lerman (2010) have shown that these interactions have a profound influence on individuals. In particular, they find that contact with the criminal justice system – even contact that does not result in jail or prison time – leads to significantly lower levels of voting, participation in civic groups, and trust in government (also see Burch 2013 and Lerman and Weaver 2014*a*).

Another important cost associated with the expansion of the prison system is the increased probability of incarcerating innocent people. The National Registry of Exonerations at the University of Michigan Law School has identified 1,621 individuals who have been exonerated since 1989.[18] Astonishingly, 520 of these exonerated individuals had been sentenced to death or to life in prison.[19] Equally concerning, the majority of wrongful convictions do *not* result in exoneration. Thus, these numbers are likely to vastly understate the actual number of wrongful convictions. Recognizing this growing concern, fifteen district attorney offices have established wrongful conviction units tasked with reviewing convictions of those imprisoned.[20]

In sum, whether we consider the *economic, social*, or *political* costs, maintaining the world's highest incarceration rate carries important consequences. These consequences include tradeoffs in the services offered by local, state, and federal governments, diminished economic and health conditions among the incarcerated, their families, and their communities, wrongful convictions, and changes to some election outcomes. Just as important, we must remember that the social and political consequences of mass incarceration are *not* borne equally by all segments of society. Those with low incomes or low education levels face the highest probability of incarceration. Additionally, although millions of white Americans have been imprisoned in recent decades, racial minorities are the most likely to be imprisoned. African Americans represent 12 percent of the adult population and Hispanics represent 13 percent of the population. Yet these two groups constitute 60 percent of the incarcerated

---

[18]   www.law.umich.edu/special/exoneration/Pages/about.aspx
[19]   www.law.umich.edu/special/exoneration/Pages/detaillist.aspx?View=faf6eddb-5a68-4f8f-
        8a52-2c61f5bf9ea7&SortField=Sentence&SortDir=Desc
[20]   See, for example, Gerber (2015).

population (39 and 21 percent, respectively).[21] In addition to (and perhaps because of) being disproportionately represented in prison, every cost described earlier – such as limited employment, greater health risks, and political alienation – has been shown to be more dramatic for racial minorities.[22] It is easy to see why Michelle Alexander refers to mass incarceration as *The New Jim Crow*.

Just as striking as the dramatic costs and unequal consequences of the current criminal justice system, most scholars conclude that the benefits of rising incarceration rates for crime reduction have been limited, at best. There is broad consensus that the rising incarceration rate reduced the crime rate to some extent. At a minimum, the fact that large numbers were incapacitated behind bars meant that there were fewer people who could commit a crime. In his extensive analysis of the relationship between incarceration and crime rates, Western (2006) estimates that the prison boom reduced the rate of serious crime by 2–5 percent in the 1990s. Levitt's (2004) analysis, by contrast, suggests that the growth of the carceral state accounted for about a third of the reduction in crime during this period. Most estimates fall somewhere between these two values (e.g., Donohue 2009). Interestingly, although Levitt's (2004) estimates of the crime-reducing effect of incarceration are among the highest, from a cost-benefit perspective, he provides three reasons for why incarceration is *not* the most efficient way to reduce crime. First, Levitt estimates that dollar for dollar, spending on police yields a greater crime reduction than spending on prisons. Second, he highlights some of the social costs discussed earlier. Finally, he points out that the marginal benefit of crime reduction likely decreases as more people are incarcerated because the most violent and active criminals are likely to be among the first who are imprisoned. Indeed, Johnson and Raphael (2012) estimate the crime reduction effects of incarceration between 1991 and 2004 to be less than a third of the size of the effects between 1978 and 1990 (see also Useem and Piehl 2008). Thus, the general consensus is that rising incarceration rates have had some influence on crime rates, but even the most favorable estimates suggest that the incarceration rate exceeds the optimal crime reduction level.

Another perspective argues that current incarceration rates may *increase* criminal activity. The concern is that incarceration can have a criminogenic effect, socializing inmates toward heightened criminal activity. To study this possibility, Gaes and Camp (2009) took advantage of a change in how the California Department of Corrections and Rehabilitation assigned inmates

---

[21] Adult population estimates based on the US Census Bureau (www.census.gov/compendia/statab/cats/population.html). Incarceration data based on the *Sourcebook of Criminal Justice Statistics* (www.albany.edu/sourcebook/pdf/t6332008.pdf).

[22] See, for example, Clear (2009), Johnson and Raphael (2009), Lee et al. (2015), Mauer (2011), Pager (2005, 2007), Schnittker, Massoglia, and Uggen (2011), Wakefield and Uggen (2010), Western (2006).

to high (level III) or low (level I) security facilities. Between November 1998 and April 1999, adult male inmates in California were classified under both a proposed new classification system and the old classification system. Furthermore, after receiving both classifications, a random process was used to determine whether the inmates would be placed under the old or the new systems. The randomization is consequential because among those classified during this time period, a subset of individuals were classified differently by the old and new system. Thus, Gaes and Camp (2009) were able to compare the recidivism rates of those randomly assigned to a level I security facility and those randomly assigned to a level III security facility.[23] Because the assignment to either a high or a low security prison was random, on average, the inmates that Gaes and Camp (2009) studied were identical in every other way. Any difference in recidivism can be attributed to assignment to a particular type of prison. Consistent with the criminogenic hypothesis, they found those randomly assigned to the level III facility were more likely to recidivate, and the average time to recidivism was shorter (see also Chen and Shapiro 2007, Lerman 2009, 2013). This research suggests that in addition to being an inefficient way to reduce crime, the current rate of imprisonment may actually encourage criminal behavior.

Because punishment is a complex issue, reasonable people can (and will) disagree about how to deal with lawbreakers. However, regardless of one's personal views about criminal justice policy, I hope three conclusions stand out from the foregoing discussion. First, the United States has not always been the world's incarceration leader – the expansion of the US carceral state exceeds that of all other countries. Second, mass incarceration carries real consequences and these consequences are unevenly distributed. Finally, the growth of the US carceral state has not translated into an equivalent reduction in crime. These conclusions lead to an important puzzle. If the costs are substantial and the benefits for crime reduction unclear, why did the United States become the world's most prolific imprisoner? The following section discusses two accounts for why the United States embarked on this path.

1.2   WHY DID THE UNITED STATES BECOME THE WORLD'S INCARCERATION LEADER?

Scholars have long debated the reasons for the United States' punitive turn. The crime rate offers one potential explanation. A rising crime rate, after all, would be expected to correspond with more arrests and incarcerations. An over-time analysis of the ratio of the number of people incarcerated relative to the number

---

[23]   Level I prisons are open dormitory facilities with low security perimeters. Level III prisons, by contrast, have cells adjacent to exterior walls and a secure perimeter with armed coverage (Grattet et al. 2011, p. 16).

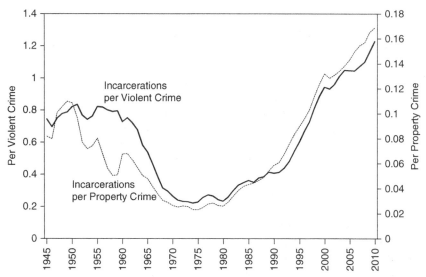

FIGURE 1.3. The rate of prisoners per violent crime (left axis) and per property crime (right axis) from 1945 to 2010.

Source: Crime Rate: Social Indicators, 1973 and Sourcebook of Criminal Justice Statistics, Table 3.106.2011; Incarceration Rate: Sourcebook of Criminal Justice Statistics Online, Table 6.28.10.

of crimes committed offers a way to evaluate the rising crime rate hypothesis.[24] A constant over-time relationship between the number incarcerated and the number of crimes committed would be consistent with crime as a fundamental determinant of the incarceration rate. By contrast, if the number incarcerated relative to the number of crimes committed increases, a shifting crime rate is unlikely to be the whole story. More incarcerations per crime committed implies a change in how criminals are dealt with, not simply how much crime is committed.

Figure 1.3 examines these patterns. The figure plots the ratio of incarcerations to violent crimes and to property crimes committed from 1945 to 2010.[25] The crime data come from the Federal Bureau of Investigation Uniform Crime Reporting (UCR) Program.[26] Although concerns exist with all crime data, the UCR data offer the best available over-time indication of violent and

[24] See, for example, Raphael and Stoll (2009) and Useem and Piehl (2008).
[25] Specifically, the series report the annual incarceration rate divided by the annual violent crime rate and annual property crime rate. The rate can exceed one because individuals are often sentenced to prison for multiple years, meaning the number of prisoners in a given year can exceed the number of reported crimes for that particular year.
[26] The data were accessed from Social Indicators, 1973 and the *Sourcebook of Criminal Justice Statistics*.

property crime in the United States. Furthermore, although some changes in data collection have occurred through time, the data are particularly well suited for evaluating long-term patterns, which would not be affected by a change in coding in a particular year.

Several patterns emerge in Figure 1.3. First, we see that the ratio of incarcerations per violent and property crime declined throughout the 1960s. Previous research emphasizes the relatively consistent incarceration rate during the 1950s, 1960s, and early 1970s (as evidenced in Figure 1.1). Yet, despite the relatively constant incarceration rate, these patterns suggest that *how* crime was dealt with varied substantially during this period, with the fewest incarcerations per crime committed in the early 1970s. Second, throughout the rise of mass incarceration, we see a substantial increase in the number incarcerated relative to the number of crimes committed. This pattern offers initial evidence that rising crime rates alone cannot account for the growth of the US carceral state. Finally, we see that by this measure, the late 1990s and 2000s reflect the most punitive period in the United States since the end of World War II. These patterns indicate that in order to understand the rise of mass incarceration we need to understand why the number of incarcerations per crime committed increased so drastically.

Scholars increasingly cite political decisions as the reason for this increase. Specifically, throughout this time period, political actors imposed prison sentences for crimes that previously carried less punitive sanctions and imposed mandatory minimum sentences for crimes that previously carried less time in prison. As Raphael and Stoll (2009, p. 65) explain, "so many Americans are in prison because through our collective public choices regarding sentencing and punishment, we have decided to place so many Americans in prison....[C]hanges in who goes to prison ... and for how long ... explain 80 to 85 percent of prison expansion over the last twenty-five years." Emphasizing the role of policy makers in this process, Spelman (2000, p. 97) refers to mass incarceration as "one of the great policy experiments of modern times." Of course, if the rise in incarcerations reflects political choices, another question emerges. Given the immense economic, social, and political costs outlined earlier, why have politicians advanced some of the most punitive policies in the world? The next section details why we should look to the public as a potential cause.

1.2.1 The importance of public opinion

The central claim of this book is that the rise of mass incarceration in the United States reflects, in large part, a political response to the public's rising punitiveness. Although some research argues that the public's preferences have influenced criminal justice outcomes (Enns 2014a, Jacobs and Carmichael 2001, Nicholson-Crotty, Peterson, and Ramirez 2009), this view is by no means conventional wisdom. In fact, much of the research on state and federal incarceration rates questions the role of public opinion. Matthews (2005) goes as far as referring to the "myth of punitiveness" and Brown (2006) describes the public as "impotent" in its ability to influence criminal justice policy. Renowned criminal justice and legal scholars Franklin Zimring and Gordon Hawkins make the point as follows:

> The ad hoc reference to punitive public attitudes when prison population increases is analogous to the attribution of rainfall to the performance of a rain dance while conveniently overlooking all occasions when the ceremony was not followed by rain but by prolonged periods of dry weather or drought. (Zimring and Hawkins 1991, p. 130)

A related view holds that the public's level of punitiveness has held relatively constant and thus cannot explain the *change* in incarceration rate (Roberts et al. 2003, pp. 27–28; Zimring and Johnson 2006, p. 266). Others suggest that a greater public influence would actually mitigate rising incarceration rates. In her analysis of state-level incarceration, Barker (2006, p. 25) concludes, "Increased citizen participation can actually set limits on state reliance on confinement." A final perspective concludes that politicians overestimate the public's punitiveness. In her pathbreaking book *The Prison and the Gallows*, Marie Gottschalk (2006, p. 27) explains, "policymaking elites also appear to misperceive public opinion on crime, viewing the public as more punitive and obsessed with its own safety than is in fact the case."[27]

In sum, current explanations of the incarceration rate range from assigning some influence to public opinion to arguing that public opinion has no effect or would actually lead to lower levels of incarceration if policy makers were more attentive to the public's wishes. As noted earlier, however, the extant literature does not ignore the role of politics in rising incarceration. In fact, while largely de-emphasizing the role of public opinion, political explanations, such as the party in power or the influence of interest groups, are increasingly cited as important determinants of mass incarceration.[28] This simultaneous emphasis on political forces and de-emphasis on public opinion produces an interesting puzzle. Scholars have long argued that electorally motivated politicians must consider their constituents' interests (Downs 1957, Fenno 1978, Mayhew 1974) and a large literature shows that policy makers respond to the public's policy preferences (e.g., Erikson, MacKuen, and Stimson 2002, Page and Shapiro 1983, Soroka and Wlezien 2010). Additionally, potential constituents are the most fundamental determinant of the origin and survival of

---

[27] Also see Cullen, Clark, and Wozniak (1985, p. 22) and Roberts and Stalans (2000, p. 294).

[28] Yates and Fording (2005, p. 1118), for example, conclude, "state punitiveness does not appear to be driven by governmental response to mass ideology ... Instead, our findings suggest that states' use of imprisonment is tied to the ideological tenor of the elite political environment and politicians' electoral incentives." Smith (2004, p. 935) reaches a similar conclusion, explaining that the increase in state incarceration rates "is not a response to citizen attitudes ... what does explain the increase: partisan control of state governments, gubernatorial election cycles, selected policy decisions, and race."

member-based interest groups (Gray and Lowery 1996, Olson 1965, Truman 1951). Why would politicians and interest group leaders, who depend on the public for their political survival, help produce the highest incarceration rate in the world if the public was unsupportive or uninterested in this outcome?

One answer to this question is that public attitudes toward crime and punishment are so "mushy" (Cullen, Fisher, and Applegate 2000, p. 58; Durham 1993, p. 8) that political actors feel they can safely ignore them. This conclusion implies that political elites have influenced the incarceration rate independent of the public's will, and the public has remained aloof to nearly forty years of prison expansion. I propose, however, that political actors have not ignored the public, but rather have been encouraged by the rising punitiveness of public opinion. This argument is consistent with the previously mentioned research on politicians, representation, and interest groups. The argument also supports the increasing evidence that political considerations influence the incarceration rate. That is, to claim that public opinion matters does not imply that politics and policy do not matter. Instead, the focus on public opinion offers a theoretical framework for understanding why we have seen such a sustained political push toward more punitive criminal justice policies. Politically motivated elites have been marching in step with the mass public.

An important aspect of this argument is the focus on opinion *change*. As I detail in Chapter 2, opinion change offers the most meaningful signal for those attentive to the public's preferences. There are several mechanisms by which these shifts in the public's punitiveness can influence the incarceration rate. First, through budgetary appropriations, state and federal legislators influence the capacity to investigate, prosecute, and incarcerate. Additionally, state and federal laws have a major influence on incarceration rates by defining what is a crime and imposing sentencing requirements. Thus, politicians' electoral incentives suggest an important avenue for public opinion to influence criminal justice outcomes. Additionally, in twenty-four states the ballot initiative offers a direct pathway for citizen influence. In numerous states, for example, citizens have enacted "Three Strikes laws," which – as we saw in the opening pages with the cases of Leandro Andrade and Gary Ewing – impose mandatory minimum sentences on repeat offenders. Furthermore, because states are more likely to adopt the policies of their neighbors (Berry and Berry 1990), the influence of the initiative may extend beyond initiative states.

Public opinion can also influence those directly involved in the criminal justice system, such as police, prosecutors, and judges. Research shows, for example, that both the police and the Federal Bureau of Investigation pay attention to their public image (Gallagher et al. 2001, Gibson 1997, Tooley et al. 2009). Prosecutors must also consider their political and organizational environment (Gordon and Huber 2009), especially in the forty-seven states that elect their district attorneys or prosecuting attorneys (Perry 2006). Additionally, Brace and Boyea (2008) find that in the thirty-eight states that elect their

Supreme Court justices, public attitudes toward the death penalty influence both the composition of the state Supreme Court and the votes of these justices. Related, Baumgartner, De Boef, and Boydstun (2008) show that shifts in public support for the death penalty influence the annual number of death sentences. At the federal level, Cook (1977) found that from 1967 to 1975, the sentences handed out by federal district judges also reflected shifts in public opinion. Furthermore, those looking at the US Supreme Court have found that despite enjoying life tenure, a strong relationship exists between the public's policy preferences and Supreme Court decisions (e.g., Casillas, Enns, and Wohlfarth 2011, Epstein and Martin 2011, McGuire and Stimson 2004).

In sum, citizen preferences can directly influence the incarceration rate through ballot initiatives and indirectly through the behavior of legislators. Furthermore, through elections as well as the broader political environment, public opinion can influence those directly involved in the criminal justice system. Of course, for public opinion to influence the incarceration rate, not all of these mechanisms need to work. The point is that despite extensive research suggesting the public exerts a minimal influence on the incarceration rate, multiple pathways exist that might produce a powerful public opinion effect.

Evidence that the public's preferences have influenced the incarceration rate would carry important implications. First, as suggested earlier, this claim offers an important addition to much of the current literature on mass incarceration. In particular, the focus on public opinion offers a theoretical framework for understanding why the country's political actors have pursued the most punitive sentencing policies in the world. Second, the focus on public opinion raises normative questions about the US criminal justice system. For example, does the responsiveness to the public reflect a model of democracy or the tyranny of the majority? Finally, this research holds implications for how we understand the future of mass incarceration in the United States. For those who would like to reduce the economic, social, or political costs of mass imprisonment, knowing why the United States became the world's incarceration leader is an important starting point. In fact, in the chapters that follow, we will see that recent decreases in the public's punitiveness can help us understand recent changes in criminal justice policy, the bipartisan shift in criminal justice rhetoric, and even public demonstrations in response to killings by police officers.

1.3 PLAN OF THIS BOOK

In order to evaluate the relationship between the public's punitiveness and the incarceration rate, we need an over-time measure of the public's punitiveness. Chapter 2 takes on this task. The chapter identifies thirty-three different survey questions that have been asked repeatedly (almost 400 times) during the past sixty years. After validating that these questions measure punitive attitudes, I combine responses to the questions into a single dynamic measure of public punitiveness. This measure allows us to see how the public's punitiveness has shifted over time. In contrast to the prominent views that public attitudes toward criminal justice are "mushy" (Cullen, Fisher, and Applegate 2000, p. 58; Durham 1993, p. 8) or stable (Roberts et al. 2003, pp. 27–28; Zimring and Johnson 2006), we see that for much of the past four decades, the public has become increasingly punitive. We also learn, however, that more recently punitive attitudes have receded some. In addition to constructing an over-time measure of the public's punitiveness, this chapter further develops the theoretical argument for why political actors, such as politicians, judges, and prosecutors, should be responsive to changes in the public's criminal justice attitudes and why this relationship should be particularly strong in the United States.

Despite my theoretical expectations that politicians and other political actors have followed the public, it is possible that causality runs the other way. In fact, a sizeable literature suggests this is the case. Thus, Chapter 3 examines whether prominent politicians were more likely to lead or follow the public on criminal justice issues. To do this, I analyze public attitudes during Barry Goldwater's 1964 presidential campaign, President Johnson's punitive shift on crime following his decisive victory over Goldwater, and polling data recorded in internal memos from Richard Nixon's 1968 presidential campaign. In all cases, the evidence runs counter to the conventional wisdom that Goldwater and Nixon pushed crime onto the national agenda. In fact, the public did not connect Goldwater to crime policy and Nixon's campaign closely followed and reacted to the public's attitudes. The chapter ends by analyzing a unique set of political surveys that asked identical questions of political elites and the mass public in 1974, 1978, and 1982. These surveys again support the expectation that public concern with crime preceded political elites' concern. Although the relationship between the public's preferences and political actors can be complicated and self-reinforcing, the evidence strongly supports the prediction that the public's punitiveness typically led those in government.

Since the public was not reacting to the most prominent politicians of the time, something else must explain the rise in the public's punitiveness, which began in the 1960s. Chapter 4 investigates why public attitudes toward crime and punishment vary over time. The analysis considers the potential influence of television crime dramas, political rhetoric, and news coverage of crime. We learn that the primary factor driving the public's punitiveness was news coverage of actual criminal activity. In particular, as crime rates rose in the 1960s and 1970s, news coverage of crime increased, and public punitiveness followed. In addition to this result, the chapter offers several important empirical contributions. For example, I document how crime rates shift in strikingly similar ways over time. Whether we examine violent or property crime rates, state crime rates, or urban crime rates, crime tends to increase and decrease largely in tandem. These similar trajectories hold important implications for news coverage of crime. Despite known biases in how news covers crime, *changes* in the amount of news coverage devoted to crime should look the same, regardless of whether the news follows violent or property crime or local or national crime. Indeed, an analysis of six different newspapers from 1950 to the present shows that all papers covered crime in very similar ways, increasing and decreasing their crime coverage in unison. Furthermore, this crime coverage closely paralleled the actual crime rate. After demonstrating these patterns, the chapter shows that shifts in news coverage of crime predict shifts in the public's punitiveness.

Together, Chapters 2, 3, and 4 establish that the public's punitiveness moves in important ways, that politicians notice when it does, and that news coverage of shifting crime rates is the primary determinant of the public's changing criminal justice attitudes. Chapter 5 goes on to analyze the relationship between the public's punitiveness and the incarceration rate. Consistent with the book's central argument, a statistical analysis of sixty years of data shows that even when controlling for the crime rate, the rate of illegal drug use, economic inequality, and the composition of government, the public's punitiveness is the most important predictor of changes in the incarceration rate. In fact, the analysis suggests that if the public's punitiveness had stopped rising in the mid 1970s, there would have been approximately 20 percent fewer incarcerations, which amounts to about 185,000 fewer individuals behind bars *each year*. We also see that more recent decreases in the public's punitiveness have slowed the rise of mass incarceration and even led to a decline in the incarceration rate. These findings offer a fundamental addition to the criminal justice literature, which has typically maintained that public attitudes have not influenced the US incarceration rate.

Chapter 6 takes the analysis to the states. Examining the relationship between public opinion and state incarceration rates is crucial because state incarcerations comprise the lion's share of sentences in the United States. To test the relationship between public opinion and state incarceration rates it is necessary to generate state-level measures of the public's punitiveness. To do this, I follow the measurement strategy developed in my previous research with Julianna Koch (Enns and Koch 2013, 2015). The result is the first over-time measures of punitiveness at the state level. I conduct two statistical analyses. The dependent variable in the first analysis is the incarceration rate in each state from the 1950s to the present. The dependent variable in the second analysis is the percent spent by each state each year on corrections. Both analyses show that even after controlling for economic conditions in the state, the composition of the state government, state demographic characteristics, and the state crime rate, the public's attitudes influence state incarceration rates and state spending on corrections. Crime rates also turn out to be an important predictor of spending and incarcerations in the states. The results further illustrate the important influence of the actual crime rate, the public's reaction to the crime rate (as mediated by news coverage), and the public's direct influence on criminal justice policy and outcomes.

Chapter 7 concludes. This chapter reminds readers that the evidence in this book cuts against nearly two centuries of thinking about the US legal system. In contrast to the standard view, we must consider public opinion if we want to understand the judicial system and the rise of mass incarceration in the United States. I then discuss what the relationship between the public's punitiveness and the legal system implies for the future of the US carceral state. The concluding chapter also aims to remind readers that the carceral state is comprised of individuals. At the end of the day, mass incarceration matters because of the profound effect it has on all involved – including police officers, prison guards, and prisoners, as well as their friends, families, and communities.

2

A forgiving or a punitive public?

The networks are in business to give people exactly what they want.

Steve Jobs (1996)[1]

Even casual television viewers know that the networks devote an impressive amount of programming to criminals and law enforcement. In fact, one might reasonably conclude that the US public has an almost insatiable appetite for stories about crime and punishment. In 2010, seven of the twenty most watched television shows were crime dramas.[2] Viewers can also choose among a host of other popular crime shows that failed to crack the top twenty, including *Blue Bloods, Bones, The Closer, Cold Case, Without a Trace,* and the various *Law & Order* series. The "if it bleeds, it leads" nature of most news reporting on crime (e.g., Pollak and Kubrin 2007) and reality series like *Cops, America's Hardest Prisons,* and *Inside American Jail* add to the criminal justice viewing options.

Many scholars have drawn a link between media depictions of crime and public opinion.[3] Yet, despite these media portrayals and television viewers' apparent interest in crime and punishment, the public's attitudes toward criminal justice policy are *not* well understood. In fact, scholars have reached disparate conclusions regarding the public's punitiveness. One view maintains that the American public has consistently held punitive attitudes. As Zimring

Sections 2.4 and 5.2 include material previously published in Enns, Peter K. 2014. "The Public's Increasing Punitiveness and Its Influence on Mass Incarceration in the United States." *American Journal of Political Science* 58(4): 857–872. Reprinted with permission.

[1] This quote is from an interview by Gary Wolf in *Wired* magazine, February 1996.
[2] Data from Nielsen. The shows were: *NCIS, The Mentalist, NCIS: Los Angeles, CSI, Criminal Minds, CSI: Miami,* and *CSI: NY.*
[3] See, for example, Beale (2006), Gilliam and Iyengar (2000), Holbrook and Hill (2005), Mutz and Nir (2010).

and Johnson (2006, p. 266) conclude, "Public hostility toward criminals has been a consistent theme in this country for a long time." At the other extreme, scholars have referred to the "myth" of punitiveness (e.g., Matthews 2005; Roberts 1997, p. 250).

This chapter makes several contributions to our understanding of the public's attitudes toward crime and punishment. First, I demonstrate how different measurement strategies have led to these vastly different conclusions about the public's punitiveness (or lack thereof). I then build on classic research by V. O. Key (1961) to argue that if we want to understand the relationship between the public's policy preferences and government outputs, we must measure over-time *change* in the public's preferences. While this is a general argument, it holds particularly large implications for the study of the public's criminal justice attitudes. By focusing on opinion change, we see that it is not only possible to generate and validate a measure of the public's punitiveness, but this punitiveness has moved in systematic and meaningful ways during the past sixty years. This chapter ends with an empirical and theoretical discussion of why we should expect the relationship between the public's preferences and criminal justice policy to be particularly strong in the United States.

2.1 PAST MEASURES OF CRIMINAL JUSTICE ATTITUDES

For more than sixty years, the Gallup Organization has asked the American public, "What do you think is the most important problem facing the country today?" Numerous scholars have turned to this "most important problem" question to measure public concern about crime.[4] Figure 2.1 reports the percent identifying crime as the most important problem from 1947 to 2012.[5] Notice that public concern for crime does *not* appear to correspond with the rise of mass incarceration through the 1970s, 1980s, and 1990s that we observed in Chapter 1 (Figure 1.1). In fact, concern for crime appears to drop substantially between 1968 and 1983, which is precisely when the prison boom began. Furthermore, concern for crime reaches its zenith around 2000, well after the major rise in mass incarceration. Given these incongruent trajectories, it is not surprising that past research has failed to find a relationship between the percentage citing crime as the most important problem and the incarceration rate (Nicholson-Crotty and Meier 2003, Schneider 2006).

---

4   See, for example, Beckett (1997), Gottschalk (2006), Nicholson-Crotty and Meier (2003), and Schneider (2006).

5   The data come from the Policy Agendas Project (www.policyagendas.org). Because multiple responses could be given to the "most important problem" question, responses have been normalized across polls to calculate the proportion of all responses that fell within the Crime topic. The data used here were originally collected by Frank R. Baumgartner and Bryan D. Jones, with the support of National Science Foundation grant numbers SBR 9320922 and 0111611, and were distributed through the Department of Government at the University of Texas at Austin. Neither NSF nor the original collectors of the data bear any responsibility for the analysis reported here.

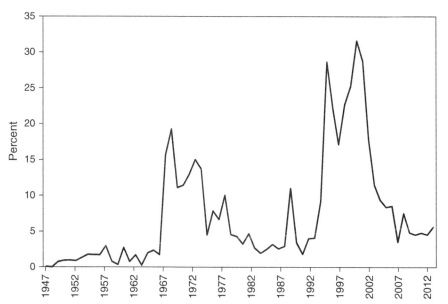

FIGURE 2.1. The percent of survey respondents indicating that crime is the most important problem facing the country from 1947 to 2012.

Source: The Policy Agendas Project.

We should not, however, view this lack of relationship as evidence against the influence of public opinion. Following King and Maruna (2009) and Hogan, Chiricos, and Getz (2005), I conceptualize the public's punitiveness as the level of public support for harsher sanctions, punishment, and crime policies.[6] Many factors suggest that we should *not* expect the "most important problem" question to be a reliable over-time measure of the public's punitiveness. Variation in the percentage identifying crime as the most important problem not only depends on concern about crime but also on perceptions of other problems facing the country, such as the economy, national defense, or the environment. Thus, the public's punitiveness is not necessarily contingent on ranking crime as the most important problem facing the country. During a recession, for example, we would expect more individuals to identify the economy as the most important problem. In this scenario, even if public attitudes were becoming more punitive, the percentage of individuals ranking crime as the most important problem would decrease as individuals shifted toward identifying the economy as the most important problem.[7] The "most important problem" question may provide information regarding the salience

[6] Also see Maruna, Matravers, and King (2004) and Maruna and King (2009).
[7] See Useem and Piehl (2008, pp. 27–28) for additional reasons why the "most important problem" question may not be a valid measure of the public's punitiveness.

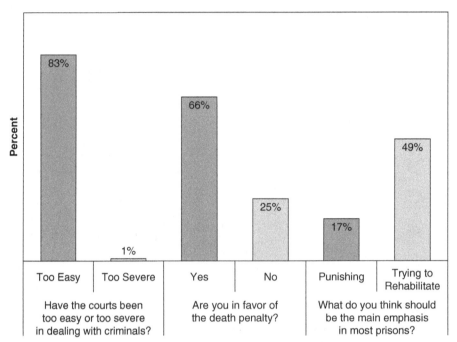

FIGURE 2.2. The percent of survey respondents offering the punitive and nonpunitive response to three criminal justice questions in 1981.

Source: Survey data from Gallup (AIPO) and Harris; obtained from the Roper Center for Public Opinion Research.

of specific policy domains (Iyengar and Kinder 1987, cf. Wlezien 2005), but it does not offer a clear indication whether the public is getting more or less punitive.

Because of concerns with the "most important problem" question, scholars have also examined survey questions that ask more directly about the criminal justice system. Figure 2.2 reports the percentage of people offering the punitive (dark gray) and nonpunitive (light gray) response to three such questions in 1981.[8] Recall from the previous chapter that in 1981 the incarceration rate had been rising for almost a decade and would continue to increase unabated for more than two more decades. Thus, 1981 offers a glimpse of the public's attitudes in the midst of the rise of mass incarceration. The responses to the three questions reported in Figure 2.2 do not, however, offer a clear indication of whether or not the public was punitive at this time.

---

[8]   The data were obtained from the Roper Center for Public Opinion Research (www.ropercenter
     .org). See Appendix A-2 for complete question wording.

The fact that 83 percent of respondents reported that the courts had been too easy on criminals – and only 1 percent indicated that the courts had been too harsh – offers evidence of a punitive public.[9] Support for the death penalty also leans punitive. Sixty-six percent of respondents favored the death penalty for those convicted of murder. The final question reported in Figure 2.2, however, offers a very different picture of the public. When given the opportunity to express support for rehabilitation in prison instead of punishment, the percent of nonpunitive responses is more than double the percent of punitive responses. Based on this question, rehabilitation appears to be a much greater priority for the public than punishment.

Figure 2.2 highlights the fact that different survey questions can offer a radically different picture of public attitudes toward punishment. Given these results, it is not surprising that scholars have reached divergent conclusions about the public's punitiveness. Since certain survey questions elicit evidence of public support for punishment while other questions suggest a far more forgiving public, some scholars have concluded that "support for get-tough policies is 'mushy' " (Cullen, Fisher, and Applegate 2000, p. 1). Because of this "mushiness," Durham (1993, pp. 8–9) goes as far as questioning the validity of public opinion data on attitudes toward punishment. I propose, however, that a focus on the different *levels* of support expressed in different survey questions can be misleading. Instead, we must consider how the public's punitiveness changes *over time*.

Since a key objective of this book is to test the over-time relationship between the public's punitiveness and changes in the incarceration rate since the 1950s, the proposal to use an over-time measure of the public's punitiveness should be uncontroversial. We must analyze change to explain change. However, beyond the fact that the research question requires an over-time analysis, there are also important theoretical reasons to focus on opinion change. As I explain in the following sections, when we consider the perspectives of politicians and other political actors, such as judges and prosecutors, it is opinion *change* that matters.

2.2 THE IMPORTANCE OF MEASURING OPINION CHANGE

It can be tempting to focus on the results of a single question from a single public opinion survey. Headlines confidently proclaim findings such as, "Death Penalty Support Is Weaker than It Seems," "Poll Finds Dissatisfaction over Iraq," and "Americans Want to Pull Back from World Stage, Poll Finds."[10] Yet political actors (as well as scholars and pundits) should focus on how

---

9   The percentages do not add to 100 because neutral categories and "don't know" responses are not shown.
10   These headlines are from the *New York Times* (1987), *New York Times* (2014), and *Wall Street Journal* (2014), respectively.

the public's attitudes *change*, not opinions at a single point in time. When considering the public's support for being tough on crime, the key question is whether the public has become *more* or *less* punitive, not what percent of Americans support a particular response. There are several reasons why opinion change offers the most informative view of the public's attitudes.

The first reason to consider opinion change is that an over-time perspective can offer a clear indication of the public's preferences, even when focusing on a single time point does not. Recall Figure 2.2, which implied that in 1981, the public overwhelmingly supported tougher court sentences and simultaneously wanted more emphasis placed on rehabilitating prisoners. By focusing on a single point in time, political actors (as well as researchers) would get a drastically different picture of the public's attitudes depending on which question they considered. Focusing on all questions would be equally problematic, possibly leading to the conclusion that no information could be gained by considering the public's preferences. Given the fact that slight variations in survey question wording can produce very divergent results, the public's seemingly incongruent responses are not entirely surprising.[11] However, if shifts in question wording can alter the percent of respondents who indicate they support or oppose a particular policy (as we saw in Figure 2.2), the *level* of support does not necessarily offer a clear indication of the public's preferences.

Focusing on opinion change, by contrast, can help clarify the public's preferences. To illustrate this point, I reconsider the three questions reported in Figure 2.2 (the courts' treatment of criminals, support for the death penalty, and punishment or rehabilitation in prisons), this time examining responses to these questions from 1970 to 1985. Figure 2.3 plots the responses during this time period.[12] When we evaluate the percentage of punitive responses to these questions *over time*, an important pattern emerges. Throughout this period, support for the punitive response increased for all three questions. Although the changes may not look dramatic, these shifts are quite substantial. Between 1970 and 1982, the percentage of people responding that the main emphasis of prisons should be punishment more than doubled from 8 percent to 19 percent. Although not shown, the decline in the belief that the main emphasis of prisons should be rehabilitation was even greater, dropping by almost thirty percentage points (from 73 percent to just 44 percent) in twelve years. Similar patterns emerge for support for the death penalty, which saw a 23 percent increase in support, and the view that courts are too lenient, which witnessed a 17 percent increase. In contrast to the image of "mushy" public attitudes that resulted when we examined a single time point, the over-time analysis produces a clear

---

[11] See, for example, Rasinski (1989), Smith (1987), Soroka and Wlezien (2010, pp. 70–71), Weaver, Shapiro, and Jacobs (1995), Wlezien and Soroka (2011, pp. 287–288).

[12] If a question was asked twice in the same year, the figure reports the average for the two questions.

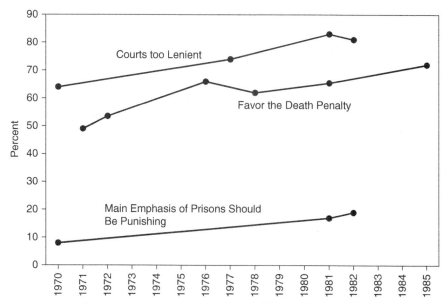

FIGURE 2.3. The percent of survey respondents offering the punitive response to three criminal justice questions from 1970 to 1985.

Source: Survey data from Gallup (AIPO) and Harris; obtained from the Roper Center for Public Opinion Research.

pattern. No matter how we ask about the criminal justice system, the public was becoming more punitive.

An over-time focus on public opinion can also clarify the preferences of different subgroups of the population. African Americans, for example, tend to express less punitive preferences than white Americans (Peffley and Hurwitz 2010, Soss, Langbein, and Metelko 2003). Democrats also tend to express less punitive preferences than Republicans. These differences could imply that policy would look different depending on whether politicians or other political actors placed more weight on the preferences of one group or another. Page and Shapiro (1992), however, have documented that different groups nearly always update their preferences in parallel.[13] When this happens, it does not matter which group political actors represent. Parallel opinion change means policy will shift in the same direction regardless of which group's preferences are considered.

Figure 2.4 illustrates this point. The figure takes the death penalty question analyzed in Figure 2.3 and plots the percent favoring the death penalty by

[13] Also see Davis (1980), Ellis, Ura, and Robinson (2006), Enns and Wlezien (2011), Kelly and Enns (2010), and Soroka and Wlezien (2010, ch.8). As partisans have become increasingly sorted (e.g., Levendusky 2009), they have become the main exception to this pattern.

race, region, and partisanship from 1971 to 1985. Since these group estimates are based on a subset of the survey respondents, we must remember that the sampling margin of error is larger than when we examine all survey respondents. Thus, in Figure 2.4, we are most interested in the overall trajectory of each group's death penalty preferences, not in whether deviations exist in any particular year (because these deviations could be the result of sampling error).

Figure 2.4(a) reports the percent of respondents favoring the death penalty for whites and African Americans. Consistent with past research, white

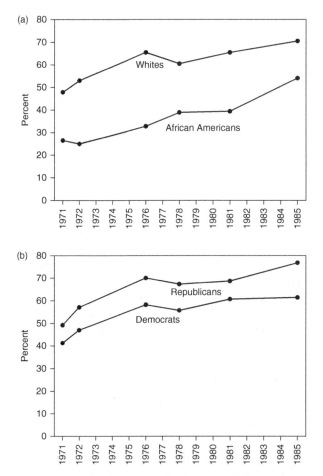

FIGURE 2.4. Support for the death penalty by race, partisanship, and region from 1971 to 1985 (a) Race (b) Partisanship (c) Region.

Source: Survey data from Gallup (AIPO); obtained from the Roper Center for Public Opinion Research.

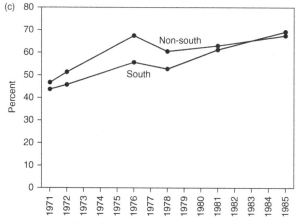

FIGURE 2.4. (*cont.*)

respondents indicate more punitive preferences at each time point. What may come as a surprise is the fact that African Americans became more punitive in parallel with whites during this period. The same pattern emerges with partisans in Figure 2.4(b). Republicans favor the death penalty more than Democrats, but Democrats became more supportive of the death penalty along with Republicans. Figure 2.4(c) considers support for the death penalty among Southerners and non-Southerners. We again see the familiar pattern of parallel opinion change that emerged for racial and partisan groups. Somewhat surprisingly, the level of support for the death penalty is also similar for Southerners and non-Southerners, with non-Southerners showing slightly more support for the death penalty than Southerners in the 1970s.[14]

Figure 2.4 suggests that all groups were becoming more punitive in tandem during the late 1970s and early 1980s. These results are consistent with the work of Page and Shapiro (1992) as well as the work of Ramirez (2013), who have also found evidence that different groups become more or less punitive together. Although some groups are reliably more punitive than others, when we consider opinion change, all groups look about the same. The next section explains why it is these changes in opinion that matter most.

[14] Southern states include AL, AR, GA, FL, KY, LA, MS, OK, NC, SC, TN, TX, VA. In an analysis of death penalty support in the General Social Survey during the 1970s, I have also found that a slightly higher proportion of non-Southerners indicated support for the death penalty than Southerners.

2.3   HOW DO POLITICAL ACTORS THINK ABOUT PUBLIC OPINION?

In addition to offering a coherent signal of the public's preferences, for political actors opinion change is the relevant concept of interest. Theoretically, opinion change relates most closely to the decision making of government. Rarely do we observe a completely new policy that has never been on the political agenda. Instead, government outputs (e.g., legislation, court decisions, executive orders) typically adjust policy in a liberal or conservative direction. As Stimson, MacKuen, and Erikson (1995, p. 543) explain,

> Most political decisions are about change or the prevention of change. Governments decide to change health care systems, to reduce environmental regulations, to develop new weapons systems, or to increase subsidies for long staple cotton growers. Or not. Thus, political decisions have a directional force to them, and their incremental character is inherently dynamic.

Criminal justice policy also reflects this dynamic process. Legislators decide whether to increase, decrease, or maintain spending on law enforcement and prisons. The Supreme Court decides whether standards of evidence should be more or less rigorous. Police departments decide whether to adjust the frequency of neighborhood patrols. Although the magnitude of proposed change may vary, decisions can be understood as shifting policy in a more punitive direction, shifting policy in a less punitive direction, or maintaining the status quo.

The dynamic characteristic of criminal justice policy (and government more generally) means that political actors face a direct incentive to consider opinion change. When public opinion changes – that is, when the public becomes more (or less) punitive – political actors should adjust policy in that direction to keep in line with the public's preferences. Stimson, MacKuen, and Erikson (1995, p. 545) make the point as follows: "When politicians perceive public opinion change, they adapt their behavior to please their constituency and, accordingly, enhance their chances of reelection." Shifting policy in the direction of the public's preferences helps ensure that the voters who elected the candidate are not alienated. This argument dovetails with Tonry's (2004) notion of changing "sensibilities."[15] Although I use the term *punitiveness*, Tonry explains, "policy changes, and their putative effects, are both often the consequences of previous broad-based changes in social norms and attitudes" (2004, p. 129).

Of course, politicians are not always singularly focused on the public's preferences. Furthermore, even judges and prosecutors who face reelection might prioritize other considerations (such as the law and the facts of the case) much more than the public's preferences. For the judges and prosecutors who are not elected, as well as for the police, we might expect the public's preferences to matter even less. However, even when public opinion is just a

---

[15]   Also see Garland (2001).

tertiary consideration, opinion change can offer a meaningful signal to these political actors.

To understand why, V. O. Key's (1961) concept of latent (or anticipated) opinion offers a useful starting point. As Zaller (2003, p. 311) explains, "latent opinion is opinion that might exist at some point in the future in response to the decision makers' actions and may perhaps result in political damage or even defeat at the polls."

From this perspective, political actors should *not* make decisions based on current levels of public support. Instead, they should decide based on how popular they expect the decision to be once enacted.[16] Importantly, this logic applies to *any* decision maker who places *some* value on the public's preferences. Consider a local judge. Although we should expect the law and the case facts to weigh heavily on a judge's rulings, it is plausible that judges sometimes also consider the public. Thirty-nine states elect their trial judges, so these judges face a direct incentive to avoid unpopular rulings. Additionally, even judges who do not face elections may seek to avoid unpopular rulings based on a desire to maintain their personal reputations or their courts' reputations, or because they believe courts should not ignore the public will. Indeed, based on survey interviews with judges in the Iowa district court system, Gibson (1980) finds that some judges report that public opinion is an appropriate criterion of judicial decision making (see also Becker 1966).

Of course, even if some judges consider public opinion some of the time, most people probably do not have strong views about their local judge or the cases at hand. If a judge valued public support, *current* opinion would likely offer no guide. Most individuals are probably not even aware of the cases under consideration. However, the public's inattentiveness does not imply that a judge's decision could never induce a negative (or positive) reaction from the public. The absence of public attention to local judicial behavior makes latent opinion especially important in this context.

Suppose a judge issued a string of rulings that contradicted public sentiment, perhaps handing down sentences that repeatedly appeared too lenient (or too harsh) to the public. This pattern of rulings might become newsworthy and the public might react to the news depiction. If so, latent opinion would be activated. This line of reasoning led Casillas, Enns, and Wohlfarth (2011) to posit that even when ruling on cases that are *not* salient to the public, the Supreme Court faces incentives to avoid decisions that deviate from the public's preferences. They argue that repeated decisions that deviate from the public's preferences may, in fact, lead to media scrutiny of previously unknown cases.

---

[16] In the words of Easton (1965, p. 433), "all we need to consider is whether the [policy] outputs have positive or negative supportive results." Although he did not use the language of latent opinion, Bentley (2008 [1908], pp. 226–227) expressed a similar concept when discussing "indifferent taxpayers." He wrote, "There is a tendency to action among them. If sufficiently goaded they will certainly come to 'know' their own interest."

This argument also parallels Stimson's (1999) "zone of acquiescence." Stimson (1991) argues that as long as policy makers do not stray too far from public opinion – that is, they remain within the public's "zone of acquiescence" – the public would rather pay attention to things other than politics. If political actors stray outside of this zone, however, the media may bring the deviation to light, igniting the public's ire. Thus, the anticipation of the public's reaction can constrain political actors even when the public is not well informed about the issue or when public opinion is not the decision maker's primary consideration.

For those who do not want to stray outside the public's zone of acquiescence, opinion change offers the best indication of the public's potential response (i.e., of latent opinion). To understand the connection between opinion change and latent opinion, consider the following scenario. Suppose a political actor has a sense that the public's mood has shifted in a punitive direction. Making a decision that appears less punitive than in the past – opposite the shift in the public's preferences – would be most likely to elicit negative latent opinion. Thus, the two safest options are to maintain the status quo or shift the status quo in a more punitive direction. The magnitude of opinion change offers information to decide between these two options. The larger the perceived opinion shift, the more likely the decision should move in the punitive direction. Future opinion change also offers a guide. For example, if a decision was made to maintain the status quo and opinion continued to shift in a punitive direction, moving in a more punitive direction becomes the safer choice. By contrast, if a more punitive option was chosen and opinion moves in the opposite direction, reversion to the status quo is the optimal approach.

The key insight is that whether a political actor strategically makes decisions based on the public's preferences or whether the public's preferences are tertiary and the individual's goal is simply to avoid decisions that might ignite the public's ire, opinion change offers the best information about latent public opinion. For legislators, these decisions might be whether or not to support proposed policies, like more (or less) money for prisons or stricter (or less strict) sentencing laws. For legal practitioners, relevant decisions include whether or not to prosecute, grant parole, or hand down a particular sentence. For any of these decisions, opinion change offers the best indication of the public's reaction.[17]

To summarize, when analyzed at a single time point, seemingly related survey questions can provide conflicting views of the public's preferences. We have seen, however, that attention to the over-time patterns of these questions reveals a coherent indication of the public's preferences. Furthermore, when political actors consider the public (or even segments of the public), they should pay attention to this opinion change. This focus on opinion change is not

---

[17]   Thus, even though citizen groups are not typically well represented in the criminal justice system (Miller 2008), increases and decreases in the public's punitiveness should be expected to influence both politicians and those directly involved in criminal justice.

meant to imply that the public's preferences are the only factor that influences criminal justice outcomes. Nor do I wish to imply that the public's preferences influence all political actors. Rather, I contend that if some political actors consider the public's preferences, their decisions (and resulting policy outcomes) should reflect *changes* in public opinion. Importantly, even if a political actor is minimally attentive to the public's preferences – only considering the public enough to avoid unpopular decisions that could activate negative latent opinion – this person should consider opinion change. Of course, some political actors may actively anticipate shifts in the public's preferences to keep policy in line with the public's shifting preferences (Stimson, MacKuen, and Erikson 1995). In either case, we should expect criminal justice policy to reflect shifts in the public's punitiveness.

Political actors can gauge opinion change in many ways. We have seen that knowledge of the public's shifting preferences can come from opinion surveys. Political actors can also turn to a variety of other sources of information, such as constituent letters and phone calls, letters to the editor of the local newspaper, or even conversations at the coffee shop. Indeed, as a member of Congress explained to Richard Fenno (1977, p. 889), "You have no idea how invaluable these [breakfast] meetings are for me. They keep me in touch with my home base. If you don't keep your home base, you don't have anything." Most likely, political actors use a variety of methods to sense opinion shifts. As Kingdon (1984, p. 146) explains, "People in and around government sense a national mood. They are comfortable discussing its content, and believe that they know when the mood shifts."

2.4 MEASURING THE PUBLIC'S PUNITIVENESS

I have argued that if political actors care about public support, it is opinion change that matters most. Thus, the current task is to construct an over-time measure of the public's punitiveness. As noted earlier, the public's punitiveness refers to the level of the public's support for harsher penalties and crime policies. Given this focus on harsh penalties and policies, I use public support for being tough on crime interchangeably with the public's punitiveness.[18] Thus, increases (decreases) in the public's punitiveness (or public support for being tough on crime) reflect increases (decreases) in the percent of the public that supports harsher penalties and policies.

Figure 2.3 offers an important lesson for measuring over-time preferences. We saw that despite different levels of punitiveness across three survey questions, support for the punitive option shifted in tandem, indicating that the public was moving in a punitive direction. The common trajectories across

---

[18] Although it is possible that an individual could support less harsh policies but still support being tough on crime, for ease of presentation, I treat the two interchangeably.

the three questions provide an indication of how public support for being tough on crime was moving.

Consistent with the patterns in Figure 2.3, my earlier research shows (Enns 2010, 2014a) that multiple survey questions can be combined to generate a measure of the public's punitiveness.[19] The logic of using multiple survey questions to measure a single dimension of public opinion is as follows. If responses to different survey questions reflect opinions about the same underlying issue, the percentage responding in support of (or opposition to) each question should change in tandem (Stimson 1999). When the public's preferences for being tough on crime ebb and flow, we can think of public opinion as an unobserved variable and any survey question that relates to the treatment or punishment of criminals that has been asked at multiple time points can be considered an indicator of the change in the underlying variable.[20] With a sufficient number of questions asked at repeated time points, we can estimate the underlying dimension of the public's punitiveness.

An analysis of public opinion data and the extant literature suggests four relevant categories of questions that relate to the public's punitiveness (see, e.g., Shaw et al. 1998, Warr 1995).The first category includes questions about criminals' rights and the punishment of criminals.[21] It seems uncontroversial to suggest that increases (or decreases) in support for punishing or using force on criminals correspond with shifts in punitiveness. The second category includes questions about the death penalty. Responses in support for the death penalty and the belief that the death penalty deters crime are coded as indicators of support for being tough on crime. Again, it seems reasonable to assume that those who support death as a form of punishment are generally in favor of being tough on crime and criminals (Baumer, Messner, and Rosenfeld 2003, Silver and Shapiro 1984). The third category includes questions about support for spending on fighting crime and on the criminal justice system. Following past research, I code support for spending on crime as an indicator of support for harsher penalties and policies (Barkan and Cohn 2005, Shaw et al. 1998). The final category includes questions that relate to confidence and trust in the police and the criminal justice system. A wide range of literature finds that individuals who are concerned with crime and residents of high crime neighborhoods tend

---

[19] Weaver (2007) was the first to generate an over-time measure of the public's punitiveness in this manner. She generated a measure of the public's punitiveness from 1953 to 1980 that was based on eleven different survey questions. (The subsequent analysis relies on thirty-three survey questions asked a total of 381 times to generate a measure of public support for being tough on crime from 1953 to 2012.) Importantly, prior to 1980, when these two measures overlap, they show very similar patterns, with decreasing levels of punitiveness in the 1950s and rising punitiveness beginning in the mid 1960s. Ramirez (2013) has also shown that multiple items can be combined in this way to generate a measure of punitive sentiment.

[20] In statistics, we typically refer to unobserved variables as latent variables. In order to avoid confusion with Key's notion of latent opinion described earlier, I do not use this term here.

[21] See Appendix A-2 for all question wording.

to have less confidence in the police (e.g., Baker et al. 1983, Jang, Joo, and Zhao 2010, Maxson, Hennigan, and Sloane 2003).[22] Based on this research, I propose that *less* confidence in the police or the justice system will correspond with more concern with crime and thus greater support for being tough on crime.[23]

I do not include any measures of racial bias in the measure of the public's punitiveness. At first, this decision may come as a surprise. As the Introduction documented, the rise of mass incarceration has had a disproportionate influence on Latinos and African Americans. Furthermore, racial attitudes and biases have consistently been linked to punitiveness and attitudes toward the criminal justice system (e.g., Barkan and Cohn 1994, Hurwitz and Peffley 1997, Pickett and Chiricos 2012, Soss, Langbein, and Metelko 2003, Unnever and Cullen 2010).[24] This research implies, however, that the questions I have included to measure the public's punitiveness *already* incorporate any racial considerations reflected in punitive attitudes. In fact, my focus on survey questions that relate directly to the criminal justice system is the most appropriate way to account for racial bias in punitive attitudes over time. Asking directly about criminal justice policies, like support for the death penalty or increased spending on police, allows respondents to express punitive responses without revealing potentially socially unacceptable reasons (like racial prejudice) for holding these preferences. Thus, my measurement strategy does not imply that racial attitudes do not matter. Instead, to the extent that racial attitudes influence punitiveness, my measure of the public's support for being tough on crime already incorporates these considerations.

As a next step, I used the Roper Center Public Opinion Archives, the American National Election Study (ANES), and the General Social Survey (GSS) to identify all opinion questions that relate to attitudes toward the treatment of criminals, the death penalty, spending to prevent crime, and lack of confidence in the police and the criminal justice system. Since the goal is to measure

[22] Others have argued that causality runs the other way (e.g., Skogan 2009) or that a reciprocal relationship exists (e.g., Ho and McKean 2004). Importantly, all three perspectives support the current coding strategy; that is, lower levels of confidence in the police and criminal justice system correspond with higher levels of concern for crime and support for being tough on crime.

[23] In Enns (2014b) I provide additional individual-level evidence to support including survey questions about lack of confidence in the criminal justice system in the punitive opinion index. It is worth noting, however, that recent highly publicized police killings like those of Eric Garner in Staten Island, NY, Michael Brown in Ferguson, MO, and Walter Scott in North Charleston, SC may have changed the relationship between lack of confidence in the police and punitive attitudes. This possibility is an important avenue for future research, but does not affect the current period of analysis, which ends prior to these events.

[24] For other important work on the relationship between racial attitudes, perceptions about race and crime, and criminal justice attitudes, see Chiricos, Welch, and Gertz (2004), Chiricos et al. (2012), Hetey and Eberhardt (2014), Hurwitz and Peffley (2005), Metcalfe, Pickett, and Mancini (2015), and Pickett et al. (2012).

over-time opinion change, I retained each question that was asked three or more times. This strategy left thirty-three questions that all relate to attitudes toward crime and punishment that were asked repeatedly (a total of 381 times) between 1953 and 2012.[25] Figure 2.5 offers an indication of whether opinion on these various questions changes together or distinctly.

Figure 2.5(a) plots the percentage offering the punitive response (and a two-period moving average) for seven survey questions.[26] I report these seven questions because they reflect the question or questions that were asked during the longest time span for each of the four indicators of tough-on-crime attitudes identified earlier. Because we are interested in opinion change, Figure 2.5(b) reports the same data with the series shifted to a common intercept.[27] The over-time patterns are identical to Figure 2.5(a). However, with the level of support set to a common point on the y-axis, the over-time movements – which is what we are interested in – are easier to evaluate. The commonalities are striking. In fact, it is difficult to identify which series corresponds with which question. This is exactly what we would expect if the four types of questions (support for the harsh treatment of criminals, the death penalty, spending to prevent crime, and lack of confidence in the police and the criminal justice system) all reflect common underlying attitudes toward being tough on crime. The similarities also illustrate that the measure does not depend on any single question category. All indicators tell roughly the same story about the public's punitiveness.

Having established that different survey questions that relate to public support for being tough on crime all move in tandem, the next step is to combine them into a single measure of the public's punitiveness. Recall that in addition to the seven question series plotted in Figure 2.5, I was able to identify twenty-six survey questions that relate to the public's punitiveness. One option would be to simply calculate the average of the percent offering the punitive response to each survey question in each year. This would give a reasonable approximation of the public's punitiveness. James Stimson (1999), however, has developed an even more nuanced approach. Stimson has developed an algorithm that first scales each series to a common metric, so they are aligned as in Figure 2.5(b) (as opposed to the different levels in Figure 2.5(a)). The algorithm then uses a factor analytic approach to estimate the common

---

[25] As an additional robustness check, I also estimated a measure of the public's punitiveness that includes three questions about perceptions of criminal activity. These crime perception questions correlate strongly with the measure of public punitiveness and all subsequent analyses are robust to using this alternate opinion measure, based on 450 questions.

[26] Following Stimson (1999), the percent offering the punitive response was divided by the percent offering the punitive response plus the percent offering the nonpunitive response.

[27] The sensitivity of survey marginals to shifts in question wording make the differences in levels in Figure 2.5(a) virtually meaningless (e.g., Soroka and Wlezien 2010, p. 70; Stimson 1999, p. 48). Furthermore, the differences in levels are not relevant to understanding *changes* in public opinion or how these changes influence the incarceration rate.

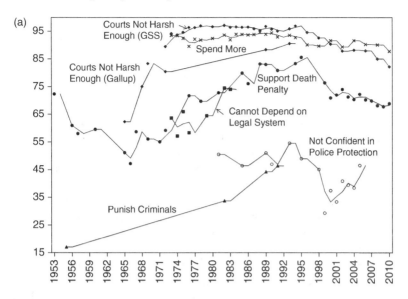

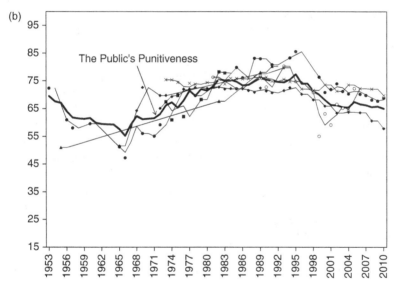

FIGURE 2.5. Seven indicators of the public's punitiveness from 1953 to 2010: (a) natural metric and (b) set to a common intercept.

Source: Survey data obtained from the Roper Center for Public Opinion Research, the General Social Survey, and the American National Election Study.

over-time variance of the question series. Identifying the common over-time variance between series ensures that any variance in opinion responses that reflects measurement error or preferences that are not related to punitiveness are not incorporated into the analysis. Thus, if any of the items did not adequately measure the public's punitiveness, it would not contribute to the overall measure.

The result of Stimson's algorithm is a measure of the public's punitiveness.[28] The thick black line in Figure 2.5(b) plots this measure, which combines all relevant information from the thirty-three question series that ask about support for being tough on crime. The similarities between the final estimate of the public's punitiveness and the seven series reported in Figure 2.5 indicate the additional question items used to generate the index (that are not shown in the figure) also reflect common underlying preferences for being tough on crime.

The common over-time movements of the individual series and the overall measure of punitiveness in Figure 2.5(b) offer compelling evidence in support of the measurement strategy. However, as an additional validation check, I examine the correlation between the overall measure of the public's punitiveness and each of the thirty-three question series used to generate the measure. This is the standard approach used to evaluate time series opinion indices (Enns and Kellstedt 2008, Kellstedt 2003, Stimson 1999). Table 2.1 reports these correlations. A positive correlation indicates that the individual series moves in common with, and thus contributes to, the overall series. Correlations near zero or negative correlations suggest that the individual series do not share common movement with the overall index. The table also reports the range of years when the question was asked, the number of times the question was asked, and the number of different years the question was asked (if the same question was asked more than once in a single year, these last two values will be different). The questions in the table are organized into the four categories described in the text: support for the death penalty, support for harsher punishment, support for more spending on the judicial system, and lack of confidence in the judicial system. Across all question types, we see a pattern of strong positive correlations with the overall index, which suggests that these questions reflect preferences for being tough on crime.[29]

---

[28] The thirty-three indicators explain 56 percent of the variance in the resulting series. This is an impressive result considering that Stimson has consistently found values around 40 percent in his measures of policy mood. Although Stimson (1999) developed this methodology in order to estimate the public's overall policy mood, the method is well suited to measure opinion about specific policy domains (Baumgartner, De Boef, and Boydstun 2008, Kellstedt 2003, McAvoy and Enns 2010). For full details, see Stimson (1999) as well as www.unc.edu/~jstimson/Software.html.

[29] Only three questions have negative correlations. Not only is it common for a few questions to have negative correlations in this type of measurement exercise (e.g., Enns and Kellstedt 2008, Kellstedt 2003, Stimson 1999), but two of the questions were not asked very often, suggesting that the negative correlations could simply reflect measurement error. For a variety of additional validation checks, see Enns (2014*a,b*).

TABLE 2.1. *Correlations between each question series and the overall measure of the public's punitiveness*

Question	Correlation	Date range	Times asked	Years asked
Death penalty questions				
Favor death penalty (Gallup)	0.951	1953–2012	49	34
Favor death penalty (GSS)	0.941	1974–2010	26	26
Prefer death penalty (Gallup)	0.806	1985–2010	19	16
Favor death penalty (ABC)	0.951	1981–2007	14	11
Death penalty right amount (Gallup)	0.782	2002–2011	10	10
Death penalty fair (Gallup)	0.313	2000–2011	10	9
Believe in death penalty (Harris)	0.328	1973–2003	8	8
Death penalty deters (Gallup)	0.923	1985–2011	6	6
Prefer death penalty (ABC)	0.580	2000–2006	6	6
Favor death penalty (Time)	0.971	1989–2003	6	6
Death penalty deters (Harris)	0.983	1973–1983	3	3
Harsher punishment questions				
Courts not harsh enough (GSS)	0.739	1972–2010	28	28
Use force (ANES)	−0.535	1968–1992	6	6
Courts not harsh enough (Gallup)	0.826	1965–1993	7	6
Stop criminal activity (ANES)	0.210	1970–1978	5	5
Prisons, police, and judges (Gallup)	0.616	1989–2000	7	5
Courts too lenient (Harris)	0.946	1970–1982	4	4
More important to punish (Gallup)	0.898	1955–1991	4	4
Prisons should punish (Harris)	0.952	1971–1980	3	3
Harsher sentences (Harris)	0.491	1978–1984	3	3
Spending on judicial system questions				
Spend more halting crime (GSS)	0.621	1973–2010	27	27
Spend more on law enforcement (GSS)	0.899	1984–2010	18	18
Spend more (Roper)	0.473	1984–2010	15	15
Spend more (ANES)	−0.133	1984–2008	8	8
Spend more on police (GSS)	0.944	1985–2006	4	4
Lack of confidence in judicial system questions				
Police not honest (Gallup)	0.761	1977–2009	25	24
Lack confidence in police (Gallup)	−0.101	1993–2012	20	20
Lack confidence in police protection (Gallup)	0.697	1981–2005	14	14
Lack respect for police (Gallup)	0.765	1965–2005	8	7
Lack confidence in legal system (Roper)	0.766	1973–1983	7	7
Police don't adequately protect (Time/CNN)	0.874	1989–1997	5	4
Lack confidence in legal system (GSS)	0.336	1991–2008	3	3
Lack confidence in courts (Gallup)	0.887	1985–1990	3	3

Note: Eigen estimate 3.3 out of possible 5.88. Percent of variance explained = 56.08.

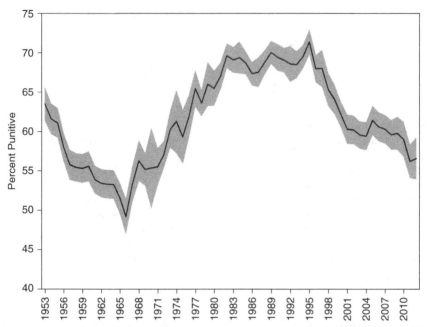

FIGURE 2.6. The public's punitiveness from 1953 to 2012 (with 95 percent confidence intervals in gray).

Source: Survey data obtained from the Roper Center for Public Opinion Research, the General Social Survey, and the American National Election Study.

Having validated the measurement strategy, Figure 2.6 plots the over-time measure of the public's punitiveness with 95 percent uncertainty estimates. This punitive opinion index suggests that the public's preferences for being tough on crime are not "mushy" (Cullen, Fisher, and Applegate 2000, Durham 1993) or stable (Roberts et al. 2003, pp. 27–28; Zimring and Johnson 2006). Instead, we see important over-time variation, with rising levels of punitiveness from the mid 1960s into the 1990s. This is an important result. Although some have suggested that the public has become more punitive (e.g., Ditton and Wilson 1999, Frost 2010, Garland 2001, Useem and Piehl 2008), this measurement strategy offers strong empirical support for these claims (see also Ramirez 2013). We also see that public support for being tough on crime appears to have declined since the mid 1990s, matching the descriptive picture provided by Clear and Frost (2014, p. 4), who write, "the waning of the punitive ethic has been going on for a while." We will see throughout this book that these increases and decreases in the public's punitiveness are crucial to understanding the US carceral state.

It is perhaps worth emphasizing that the ups and downs evident in Figure 2.6 are more important than the level at any particular time. This point is consistent with the previous discussion of why politicians (and scholars) should focus on opinion change. But this point also highlights the fact that the level of support for a particular survey question may mean something different at different time points. To illustrate this point, consider survey questions about support for the death penalty, which are an important component of the overall measure of punitiveness. Between 1972 and 1976, capital punishment was not allowed in the United States following the US Supreme Court decision *Furman v. Georgia*. By contrast, between 2006 and 2010, there were 230 executions. Furthermore, these executions occurred within a media climate that highlighted the innocence of many inmates on death row (e.g., Baumgartner, De Boef, and Boydstun 2008). Given these two very different contexts, it would not be surprising if a survey response in support of (or in opposition to) the death penalty meant something different in the early 1970s and the late 2000s. Because levels of support are not necessarily comparable across time, we should be cautious about making comparisons in the level of punitiveness at two different time points. For example, despite relatively similar percentages in the percent punitive in 1974 and 2008, we cannot say for sure that the public was equally punitive in these two years. Thus, we should not expect an equivalent criminal justice system at these time points. Instead, we should focus on the year-to-year changes in punitiveness and the magnitude of these changes. The fact that public punitiveness was increasing around 1974 and decreasing around 2008 is what we expect the criminal justice system to reflect. It is opinion change that matters.

The measure in Figure 2.6 will play a fundamental role in this book. The subsequent chapters explain why the public's punitiveness has shifted as it has and they document how these shifting public attitudes have influenced criminal justice policies and the incarceration rate. Before turning to these analyses, however, the following pages explain why the connection between the public's attitudes and the incarceration rate should be particularly pronounced in the United States.

2.5 PUBLIC OPINION AND AMERICAN EXCEPTIONALISM

A central argument of this book is that the increases in the public's punitiveness observed in Figure 2.6 were a fundamental cause of the rise in mass incarceration in the United States. As the Introduction explained, this argument offers an important addition to standard accounts in the literature. I propose that one reason previous research has failed to uncover a relationship between the public's support for being tough on crime and criminal justice outcomes is the absence of an over-time measure of the public's punitiveness. The measure developed in the previous section circumvents this problem. However, prior to testing the relationship between the public's punitiveness and criminal justice outcomes, another consideration warrants discussion.

Some skeptics of a public opinion effect point to the abolition of the death penalty in Europe and Canada to argue that political elites in these countries have ignored their citizens' attitudes toward crime and punishment. Gottschalk (2006, p. 227), for example, explains that after World War II, "Leading European countries abolished the death penalty in the face of strong, sometimes overwhelming, public support for its retention."[30] The following section examines how the argument that political leaders in other democracies have ignored their constituents influences our predictions for the United States. The discussion proceeds with two points. First, I suggest that it is too early to conclude that criminal justice policy in other countries ignores public opinion. Second, I argue that institutional features of the United States make this country a particularly likely case for observing a strong public opinion effect.

2.5.1 A brief consideration of cross-national data

Canada abolished the death penalty in 1976. According to Key's notion of latent opinion described earlier, before eliminating capital punishment, political leaders should have anticipated the public's reaction to this decision. Unfortunately, surveys on support for the death penalty in Canada do not exist prior to 1976. However, a 1977 survey indicates that 72 percent of Canadians supported capital punishment in the case of murder. The high level of support for the death penalty at this time would be consistent with the view that political elites in Canada ignored the public's attitudes. However, since we do not have a measure of public support for the death penalty prior to 1976, we cannot know if public support was declining. The lack of over-time data during this period limits our ability to draw firm conclusions about how political actors might have perceived latent opinion.

Reliable over-time opinion data does, however, exist from 1979 to 2009. During this period, the Environics Focus Canada Surveys asked about Canadians' support for the death penalty in exactly the same way thirteen times.[31] Although other questions that measure the public's punitiveness have not consistently been asked in Canada, Table 2.1 indicates that (at least in the US context) support for the death penalty corresponds with other measures of support for being tough on crime. Thus, it seems reasonable to view increases and decreases in support for the death penalty in Canada as a proxy for public punitiveness.

Figure 2.7 plots the percent who favor capital punishment for certain crimes and the incarceration rate.[32] Two important patterns stand out. First, notice that support for the death penalty was highest in the late 1970s and early

---

30 Also see Marshall (2000) and Moravcsik (2001).

31 The survey question from 1977 referenced earlier was worded differently so it is not directly comparable to these questions.

32 The incarceration data reflect the annual rate of adult offenders in provincial and federal custody (www.statcan.gc.ca/pub/85-002-x/2012001/article/11715/c-g/desc/desc01-eng.htm).

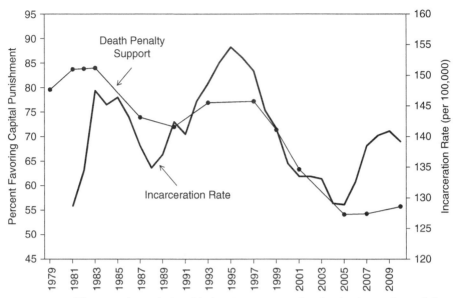

FIGURE 2.7. The over-time relationship between support for the death penalty and the incarceration rate in Canada from 1979 to 2010.

Source: Survey data from Environics Focus Canada. Incarceration data from Statistics Canada, Canadian Centre for Justice Statistics, Corrections Key Indicator Report for Adults.

1980s, following the abolishment of the death penalty. Since this time, support has declined by almost thirty percentage points. Given the absence of opinion data prior to 1976, we cannot observe the public's immediate reaction to the abolition of the death penalty in Canada, but in the long run, latent opinion did not offer a forceful backlash to the end of capital punishment. To the contrary, support for the death penalty declined. Second, we see an over-time relationship between support for the death penalty and the incarceration rate. The relationship is not perfect, but the two series rise and fall together. Although this pattern cannot establish a link between the public's preferences and criminal justice outcomes in a causal sense, this is the pattern we would expect if such a link existed.

As noted earlier, European countries have also received attention for abolishing the death penalty against the public's preferences. Survey questions about criminal justice attitudes are relatively sparse in the European context. However, in 2001, the Eurobarometer asked respondents in fifteen countries

The survey data come from the Environics Focus Canada Survey (www.queensu.ca/cora/). Responses reflect the percent who support the death penalty divided by the percent who support the death penalty plus the percent who oppose the death penalty.

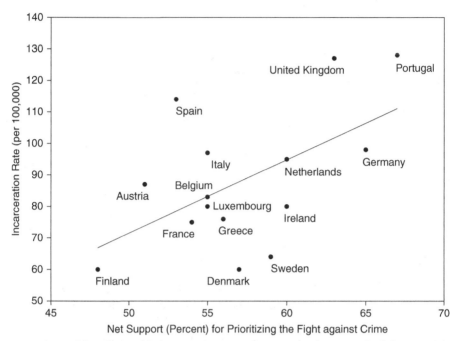

FIGURE 2.8. The relationship between incarceration rates and support for fighting crime in European countries in 2001.

Source: Survey data from the 2001 Eurobarometer. Incarceration data from the International Centre for Prison Studies (www.prisonstudies.org).

whether they supported a stronger effort fighting crime in the European Union. Ideally, we would be able to look at changes in the public's preferences. However, when comparing across countries, a single point in time can be informative. If political leaders consider the public's preferences, and thus expand and limit the scope of the criminal justice system as the public becomes more or less punitive, at any moment in time we would expect a cross-sectional relationship between public opinion and criminal justice outcomes. That is, the most punitive countries should correspond with the highest incarceration rates and the least punitive countries should have the lowest incarceration rates. Figure 2.8 uses the Eurobarometer data from 2001 to offer such a snapshot. A reasonably strong relationship emerges. The correlation between support for fighting crime and incarceration rates is $r = 0.55$.[33]

---

33 To calculate support for fighting crime across countries, in each country the percent responding "should not take action" was subtracted from the percent responding "should give priority ... to the fight against crime."

2.5.2 The political landscape in the United States

The patterns in Figures 2.7 and 2.8 are not meant to be definitive. But they do suggest that we should not rush to dismiss the possibility that criminal justice policy reflects the public's preferences in other countries. Equally important, however, the institutional structure of the United States makes this country a particularly likely place to observe a strong relationship between over-time changes in the public's punitiveness and the incarceration rate. Thus, even if a limited (or no) relationship exists between public opinion and criminal justice outcomes in other countries, the characteristics of the US political environment support the prediction that we will observe such a relationship with the US incarceration rate.

This expectation builds on the work of Stuart Soroka and Christopher Wlezien, who have conducted the most extensive research to date on the over-time relationship between public preferences and policy outcomes across countries (Soroka and Wlezien 2010, Wlezien and Soroka 2011, 2012). Soroka and Wlezien show that the political system of the United States is more responsive to the public's shifting preferences than the parliamentary systems in most of Europe and Canada.[34] They suggest several explanations for why we observe more responsiveness in the United States. Presidential systems, for example, are more likely to be responsive than parliamentary systems because of the direct connection to the public and because presidents typically have more influence over policy than executives in parliamentary systems. Additionally, in contrast to multiparty systems, which depend on coalitions across disparate parties, it is easier for a single party to respond to the public's preferences.[35] The winner-take-all aspect of majoritarian government may also produce a greater incentive to respond to the public because a failure to respond to shifting public sentiments has bigger consequences on election day. Furthermore, as mentioned in Chapter 1, most states elect certain prosecutors and judges, and in twenty-four states citizens can directly influence policy through the ballot initiative. Thus, even if we ignore the evidence presented in Figures 2.7

---

34 Federalism can dampen the over-time relationship between public opinion and policy because the different actors at different levels of government make it harder to identify who is responsible (Wlezien and Soroka 2011). However, in the US context, this dampening effect is greatly decreased because of "layer cake" federalism (Soroka and Wlezien 2010, p. 50), which leads citizens to have a surprisingly strong sense of what level of government is responsible for various issues, particularly among salient policy areas (Arceneaux 2005, 2006, Schneider and Jacoby 2012). In Canada, by contrast, the division of powers is much more ambiguous across the federalist system.

35 Some have argued that the fact that a presidential system like the United States has more veto points in the policy-making process than parliamentary systems will lead to less policy change in the US context (e.g., Tsebelis 2002). The amount of policy change does not, however, speak to whether the policy change that does occur corresponds with the public's preferences (Soroka and Wlezien 2010, p. 58). Thus, we should not conflate the amount of policy change with how much policy change reflects the public's shifting preferences.

and 2.8, the institutional framework of the US political system suggests that the purported absence of a public opinion effect in other countries should not keep us from testing the public's influence on the incarceration rate in the United States.

2.6 CONCLUSION

Despite television viewers' apparent enthusiasm for crime shows, there has been little scholarly agreement about the public's attitudes toward crime and punishment. This chapter has made four important points about public opinion and the public's punitiveness. Perhaps the most important point is the theoretical argument about how we should measure public opinion when testing theories of representation. I argued that if we want to understand how political actors consider public opinion, we must focus on opinion *change*. Whether political actors strategically follow the public's preferences or simply aim to avoid decisions that ignite negative latent opinion, change in the public's preferences offers the most meaningful information.

A second point demonstrated that when we analyze opinion change, survey data offer a coherent message about the public's attitudes. In contrast to decades of research that offers conflicting portrayals of the public's attitudes toward crime and punishment, the over-time analysis produced a clear picture of the public's punitiveness and how punitive attitudes have changed. The third point relates to the punitiveness of different segments of the population. Consistent with research by Page and Shapiro (1992) and Ramirez (2013), we saw that different racial, regional, and partisan groups all became more supportive of the death penalty roughly in tandem during the 1970s and 1980s. This "parallel" opinion change means that regardless of whose preferences political actors consider, they would get the same messages about whether the criminal justice system should become more or less punitive.

Finally, I provided suggestive evidence that public opinion corresponds with criminal justice policy in other countries and I explained why any such effect should be even stronger in the United States. Now that we have seen how the public's punitiveness changes over time, Chapter 3 asks whether prominent politicians who advocated for tough-on-crime positions in the 1960s, 1970s, and 1980s led or followed the mass public.

A-2   APPENDICES TO CHAPTER 2: QUESTION WORDING

A-2.1 Questions used in Figures 2.2 and 2.3

Retrieved May 2, 2013 from the iPOLL Databank, The Roper Center for Public Opinion Research.

1. Harris Survey. Generally, do you feel the courts have been too easy in dealing with criminals, too severe, or do you think they have treated criminals fairly? (Oct 1970; Mar 1977; Jan 1982; May 1982)
2. Gallup Poll (AIPO). Are you in favor of the death penalty for persons convicted of murder? (Oct 1971; Mar 1972; Nov 1972; Apr 1976; Mar 1978; Jan 1981; Feb 1981; Jan 1985)
3. Harris Survey. Now what do you think should be the main emphasis in most prisons–punishing the individual convicted of a crime, trying to rehabilitate the individual so that he might return to society as a productive citizen, or protecting society from future crimes he might commit? (Oct 1970; Jan 1981; May 1982)

A-2.2 Questions used in footnote 14

General Social Survey Cumulative Data File

1. GSS (CAPPUN). Do you favor or oppose the death penalty for persons convicted of murder? (1974, 1975, 1976, 1977, 1978)
2. GSS (REGION). South = South Atlantic, East South Central, and West South Central

A-2.3 Questions used in Table 2.1

These questions are listed in the order they appear on Table 2.1. The questions come from the General Social Survey, the American National Election Study, and the iPOLL Databank [Retrieved May 2, 2013], The Roper Center for Public Opinion Research.

1. Favor Death Penalty (Gallup): Are you in favor of the death penalty for persons (a person) convicted of murder?
2. Favor Death Penalty (GSS): Do you favor or oppose the death penalty for persons convicted of murder?
3. Prefer Death Penalty (Gallup): If you could choose between the following two approaches, which do you think is the better penalty for murder – the death penalty or life imprisonment, with absolutely no possibility of parole?
4. Favor Death Penalty (ABC): Turning to another subject, the death penalty: are you in favor of the death penalty for persons convicted of murder?
5. Death Penalty Right Amount (Gallup): In your opinion, is the death penalty imposed – too often, about the right amount, or not often enough?
6. Death Penalty Fair (Gallup): Generally speaking, do you believe the death penalty is applied fairly or unfairly in this country today?

7. Believe in Death Penalty (Harris): Do you believe in capital punishment (death penalty) or are you opposed to it?

8. Death Penalty Deters (Gallup): Do you feel that the death penalty acts as a deterrent to the commitment of murder – that it lowers the murder rate, or not?

9. Prefer Death Penalty (ABC): Which punishment do you prefer for people convicted of murder: the death penalty or life in prison with no chance of parole?

10. Favor Death Penalty (Time): Do you favor or oppose the death penalty for individuals convicted of serious crimes such as murder?

11. Death Penalty Deters (Harris): Suppose it could be proved to your satisfaction that the death penalty was not more effective than long prison sentences in keeping other people from committing crimes such as murder, would you be in favor of the death penalty or would you be opposed to it?

12. Courts Not Harsh Enough (GSS): In general, do you think the courts in this area deal too harshly or not harshly enough with criminals?

13. Use Force (ANES): There is much discussion about the best way to deal with the problem of urban unrest and rioting. Some say it is more important to use all available force to maintain law and order – no matter what results. Others say it is more important to correct the problems of poverty and unemployment that give rise to the disturbances. Where would you place yourself on this scale, or haven't you thought much about this? (7-point scale shown to R)

14. Courts Not Harsh Enough (Gallup): In general, do you think the courts in this area deal too harshly or not harshly enough with criminals?

15. Stop Criminal Activity (ANES): Some people are primarily concerned with doing everything possible to protect the legal rights of those accused of committing crimes. Others feel that it is more important to stop criminal activity even at the risk of reducing the rights of the accused. Where would you place yourself on this scale, or haven't you thought much about this? (7-point scale shown to R)

16. More Prisons, Police, and Judges (Gallup): Which of the following approaches to lowering the crime rate in the United States comes closer to your own view – do you think more money and effort should go to attacking the social and economic problems that lead to crime through better education and job training or more money and effort should go to deterring crime by improving law enforcement with more prisons, police, and judges?

17. Courts too Lenient (Harris): Generally, do you feel the courts have been too lenient (too easy) in dealing with criminals, too severe, or do you feel they have been treated fairly?

18. More Important to Punish (Gallup): In dealing with men who are in prison, do you think it is more important to punish them for their crimes, or more important to get them started "on the right road"?

19. Prisons Should Punish (Harris): There are different opinions about the main purpose of prisons. Which one of the statements on this card comes closest to expressing your point of view on prisons? Punish criminals and keep them away from the rest of society or keep criminals separate from the rest of society until they can be rehabilitated and returned to society?

20. Harsher Sentences (Harris): (Frequently on any controversial issue there is no clear-cut side that people take, and also frequently solutions on controversial issues are worked out by compromise. But I'm going to name some different things, and for each one would you tell me whether on balance you would be more in favor of it, or more opposed to it?) ... Harsher prison sentences for those convicted of crimes

21. Spend More Halting Crime (GSS): We are faced with many problems in this country, none of which can be solved easily or inexpensively. I'm going to name some of these problems, and for each one I'd like you to tell me whether you think we're spending too much money on it, too little money, or about the right amount. First (Halting the rising crime rate) ... are we spending too much, too little, or about the right amount on (Halting the rising crime rate)?

22. Spend More on Law Enforcement (GSS): (Law enforcement) ... are we spending too much, too little, or about the right amount on (Law enforcement)?

23. Spend More (Roper): (We are faced with many problems in this country, none of which can be solved easily or inexpensively. I'm going to name some of these problems, and for each one I'd like you to tell me whether you think we're spending too much money on it, too little money, or about the right amount.) ... Halting the rising crime rate

24. Spend More (ANES): If you had a say in making up the federal budget this year, for which (1986 AND LATER: of the following) programs would you like to see spending increased and for which would you like to see spending decreased: Should federal spending on [dealing with crime] be increased, decreased, or kept about the same?

25. Spend More on Police (GSS): Listed below are various areas of government spending. Please indicate whether you would like to see more or less government spending in each area. Remember that if you say "much more," it might require a tax increase to pay for it. The police and law enforcement

26. Police Not Honest (Gallup): How would you rate the honesty and ethical standards of people in this field – very high, high, average, low, or very low? Policemen

27. Lack Confidence in Police (Gallup): (Now I am going to read you a list of institutions in American society. Please tell me how much confidence you, yourself, have in each one – a great deal, quite a lot, some, or very little?) the police

28. Lack Confidence in Police Protection (Gallup): How much confidence do you have in the ability of the police to protect you from violent crime – a great deal, quite a lot, not very much, or none at all?

29. Lack Respect for Police (Gallup): How much respect do you have for the police in your area – a great deal, some, or hardly any?

30. Lack Confidence in Legal System (Roper): (Now, taking some specific aspects of our life, we'd like to know how confident you feel about them.) Do you feel very confident, only fairly confident, or not at all confident … We can on the whole depend on the justice of our legal system?

31. Police Don't Adequately Protect (Time/CNN): Do you feel adequately protected by the police from being a victim of crime?

32. Lack Confidence in Legal System (GSS): How much confidence do you have in … courts and the legal system? … Complete confidence, a great deal of confidence, some confidence, very little confidence, no confidence at all

33. Lack Confidence in Courts (Gallup): How much confidence do you have in the ability of the courts to convict and properly sentence criminals?

A-2.4 Questions used in Figures 2.7 and 2.8

1. Are you for, or against … capital punishment in cases of murder? (Environics Focus Canada [Obtained from the Canadian Opinion Research Archive (www.queensu.ca/cora/)]: 1977)

2. Now I would like to talk about capital punishment, that is the death penalty. Would you say you are in favour of capital punishment for certain crimes or are you against capital punishment under any circumstances? (Environics Focus Canada [Obtained from the Canadian Opinion Research Archive (www.queensu.ca/cora/)]: May 1979; Apr 1981; Feb 1982; Feb 1983; Mar 1987; Jun 1990; Sep 1993; Oct 1997; Apr 1999; Apr 2001; 2005 (#4); Dec 2007; Sep 2010)

3. Some people expect the European Union to become (even) more active than now in certain areas. For each of the following, please tell me if you consider it a key priority or not. The fight against crime (2001 Eurobarometer (http://ec.europa.eu/public_opinion/cf/index_en.cfm))

3

Who led whom?

Public opinion was well ahead of political opinion in calling attention to the rising problem of crime.

James Q. Wilson (1975, p. xvi)

Public opinion matters. At least that is the central argument of this book. Many scholars, however, have argued that on the issue of criminal justice, the public has *followed*, not led, politicians.[1] The argument that politicians have led the mass public offers a potential challenge to this book's thesis. After all, if public opinion simply follows political elites, we cannot think of the public as influencing criminal justice outcomes. Thus, this chapter examines the onset of tough-on-crime political rhetoric and whether this rhetoric typically followed or led public opinion. This chapter proceeds as follows. First, I explain why we might expect political elites to follow the public's preferences. I then use survey data, campaign speeches, and archival memos to evaluate these claims. The analysis pays special attention to Barry Goldwater and Richard Nixon, two of the politicians most associated with the onset of tough-on-crime rhetoric.

Before proceeding, I should clarify how I use the terms *political elites* and *politicians*. The term *political elites* can refer to a broad group that includes politicians as well as others in government who are not elected (such as cabinet appointees and judical appointees) and those directly connected to politicians and government (such as campaign advisers). Throughout this chapter, however, I use *political elites* and *politicians* interchangeably. I use this more narrow conception of political elite because the visibility of

---

[1] In her important book *Making Crime Pay*, Katherine Beckett (1997, p. 25) writes, "there is no evidence that political elites' initial involvement in the wars on crime and drugs was a response to popular sentiments." Emphasizing the role of Barry Goldwater's presidential campaign, Vesla Weaver similarly concludes, "Several other scholars echo the finding that public concern with crime is *the tail to the kite of elite initiative*" (2007, p. 264, italics mine).

politicians – especially politicians of national prominence – means they are best positioned to influence public opinion. Thus, the discussion of political elites primarily focuses on presidents and presidential candidates in order to consider the political elites *most* likely to influence the public. The media represent another important source of elite information. Although media convey political information, because they are outside of the political system, I do not consider media as "political" elites. I explore the relationship between media and punitive attitudes in Chapter 4.

3.1 POLITICAL AND PUBLIC CONCERN FOR CRIME

To some extent, the public and politicians influence each other. For example, public opinion may influence what politicians say or the policies they enact. However, these political speeches and policies, which were designed to reflect public opinion, may, in turn, influence the public. Although the relationship between the public's preferences and political elites can be complicated and self-reinforcing, this chapter aims to identify whether the public has *typically* led or followed political elites. That is, acknowledging that the public and political elites can and do influence each other, was one more likely to lead the other through the rise of mass incarceration?

As noted earlier, many scholars argue that political elites have led the public. For example, in *The Politics of Injustice*, Beckett and Sasson (2004, p. 46) state, "we show that conservative politicians have worked for decades to alter popular perceptions of crime, delinquency, addiction, and poverty, and to promote policies that involve 'getting tough' and 'cracking down.'" In contrast with this view – but consistent with this chapter's opening quote from James Q. Wilson – I argue that the public has generally *led* political elites. Two considerations support this contention.

First, as noted in Chapter 2, politicians face an electoral incentive to consider the public. Stimson, MacKuen, and Erikson (1995, p. 559) explain, "politicians are keen to pick up the faintest signals in their political environment. Like antelope in an open field, they cock their ears and focus their full attention on the slightest sign of danger." The logic of this behavior is straightforward. Politicians jeopardize their electoral advantage if they deviate from the public's shifting policy preferences. Druckman and Jacobs' (2011) in-depth analysis of the opinion polls conducted by Ronald Reagan's administration and Reagan's political speeches illustrate this finding. They show that throughout his presidency, Reagan carefully calibrated his public statements to reflect the preferences expressed in the opinion polls.

Second, the duration and scope of the expanding carceral state make this a particularly unlikely case for politicians to have led the public. Especially over long periods, politicians' ability to manipulate public opinion is limited (Canes-Wrone 2006, Edwards 2003). It is hard to imagine politicians successfully shifting public opinion in an increasingly punitive direction throughout more than three decades of rising incarceration rates. The fact that both Republicans and Democrats (particularly at the federal level) have supported more punitive criminal justice policies (Beckett 1997; Garland 2001; pp. 13–14; Mauer 2006, ch.4; Weaver 2007) makes this scenario even less likely. In the most polarized political environment in generations (McCarty, Poole, and Rosenthal 2006), we would not expect both parties to unite behind more punitive criminal justice policies if they did not feel their constituents supported this action.

To reiterate, this argument does *not* imply that political elites never influence the public's criminal justice attitudes. Beckett (1997), for example, has shown that political attention to crime influences the percent of the public indicating that crime is the most important problem facing the country and Ramirez (2013) finds that presidential speeches can influence punitive attitudes. Additionally, Weaver (2007) shows that political elites can influence how the public thinks about crime, and that following the civil rights movement, politicians helped bring race and crime together in the public's mind. Acknowledging the importance of these arguments, the key claim here is that political elites face strong incentives to follow the public and are unlikely to be able to lead the public for extended periods of time (see also Garland 2001, pp. 145–146).[2]

In order to test the expectation that politicians typically followed shifts in the public's punitiveness, I focus on national political figures. The focus on national political figures reflects two considerations. First, existing evidence that the public followed political elite rhetoric has focused on national politicians. As Beckett and Sasson (2004, p. 71, italics mine) explain, "Beginning in the 1960s, conservative politicians at the *national level* began to focus an unusual degree of attention on the problem of street crime" (see also Beckett 1997, Weaver 2007). Thus, the subsequent analyses are designed to speak as closely as possible to this extant literature. Second, the high profile of national politics makes this a most likely case for observing elite leadership. The public is typically uninformed about politics and political discourse, and this is especially true for state and local politics (Delli Carpini and Keeter 1996, Lyons, Jaeger, and Wolak 2013). Since the public is most likely to notice national-level political discourse, the focus on prominent national politicians offers a best case scenario for observing elite influence. I begin by focusing on the 1964 and 1968 presidential campaigns. These campaigns are crucial because they correspond with an increase in the public's punitiveness (as indicated in Figure 2.6) and with the onset of punitive rhetoric at the national level that Beckett and Sasson identified.

---

[2] As noted earlier, it is also possible that the public's preferences and political rhetoric reinforce each other, as politicians initially respond to an increase in public punitiveness and then further encourage punitive attitudes through speeches and campaign ads. The analysis in Chapter 4 allows for this type of endogeneity.

3.2 BARRY GOLDWATER'S 1964 PRESIDENTIAL CAMPAIGN

Barry Goldwater has come to embody the image of political elite influence on the public's criminal justice attitudes. Citing Goldwater's acceptance speech at the Republican National Convention, historian Michael Flamm (2005, p. 31, italics mine) explains, "*At that moment*, law and order became an important part of national political discourse." In her influential article on race and the development of crime policy, Vesla Weaver (2007, p. 242) similarly concludes, "the person to succeed in raising the public's awareness of crime and its connection to a wide variety of other social malaise was Barry Goldwater." Writing shortly after the 1964 presidential campaign, Richard Hofstadter (2008, p. 120) made the point as follows:

> crime, juvenile delinquency, divorce, illegitimacy, mental illness, school dropouts, drug addiction, pornography, riots, and hoodlumism. These were terrifying things with which he [Goldwater] proposed to deal, and one could infer from this that his campaign on the moral realities was even more significant than anything he had to say about economic policy.

Despite the scholarly emphasis on Goldwater's tough-on-crime rhetoric, several factors suggest that Goldwater's presidential campaign may *not* have influenced the public as previously thought.[3] First, evidence of his influence has been largely anecdotal. Scholars have accurately pointed to Goldwater's tough-on-crime statements during the campaign and to evidence of public concern with crime at the time, but these scholars have not shown that Goldwater was the source of public concern.

Second, not only did Goldwater lose the election, he lost by a landslide. Johnson's 61.1 percent of the popular vote was (and remains) the largest popular vote share in any US presidential election. Additionally – and perhaps not surprising given the election outcome – Goldwater is credited with having run a terrible campaign. J. William Middendorf, an early member of Goldwater's campaign, explained, "he was often an inept campaigner, irritable and impatient" (2006).[4] It would be surprising if an unpopular candidate who is thought to have run a poor campaign influenced the public in a substantial way. This is particularly true because even in the best circumstances, the influence of presidential campaigns is limited. Presidential campaigns primarily serve to help voters connect existing "fundamentals," such as the state of the economy,

---

3 For additional scholarly accounts highlighting the importance of Goldwater's tough-on-crime political rhetoric, see Alexander (2010, p. 41), Beckett (1997, p. 31), Beckett and Sasson (2004, p. 49), Christianson (1998, p. 276), Gordon (1994, p. ix), and Loo and Grimes (2004).

4 Reaching a similar conclusion shortly after the campaign, political scientist Donald Stokes (1966, pp. 25–26) wrote, "It is not hard to believe that some of the disarray of Goldwater's popular image was due to his extraordinarily bad press ... If the newspapers gave Mr. Goldwater extraordinarily rough treatment for a Republican candidate, Goldwater's own posture toward the press was part of the reason."

demographic considerations, and presidential approval to voters' electoral choice (e.g., Campbell 2008, Gelman and King 1993). Furthermore, recent research even questions how much campaigns influence these fundamental considerations (Enns and Richman 2013). To the extent that campaigns shift voter attitudes, this shift occurs among partisans who align their policy preferences to match the policy positions of the candidate they plan to support (Lenz 2009, 2012). In other words, had Goldwater run an effective campaign, we would expect a shift in criminal justice attitudes only among his supporters who did not already hold tough-on-crime opinions. We would certainly not expect Goldwater's campaign to change "national political discourse."

It is, of course, true that Goldwater took a tough stance on crime during his presidential campaign. In his acceptance of the Republican nomination for president, he declared, "We Republicans seek a government that attends to its inherent responsibilities of maintaining a stable monetary and fiscal climate, encouraging a free and a competitive economy and enforcing law and order." It is also correct that the public was concerned with crime at this time. Figure 3.1

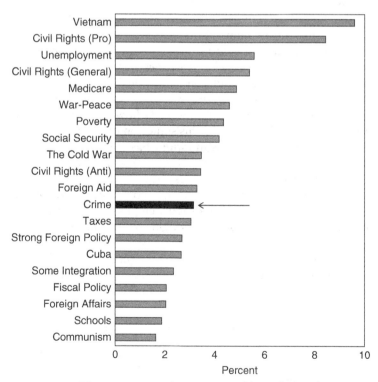

FIGURE 3.1. The twenty most important problems facing the country – according to the US public – during the 1964 presidential campaign.

Source: 1964 American National Election Study.

illustrates how the public's concern for crime related to other political issues in 1964. The figure reports the top twenty responses the public gave to an American National Election Study (ANES) survey question that asked about "the most important problems the government should try to take care of when the new President and Congress take office in January."[5]

In Chapter 2, I explained why this type of "most important problem" question is *not* well suited to evaluate over-time changes in the public's punitiveness. However, this question does offer information about the relative importance of or concern with crime at this particular point in time. We see that crime was the twelfth most likely mentioned issue. In terms of domestic policies, concern for crime ranked behind civil rights, poverty, and Social Security/Medicare, but ahead of taxes, fiscal policy, and education. Crime was not the most pressing issue at this time, but it did register with the public. The question, then, is whether this public concern reflects a *reaction* to Goldwater's tough-on-crime rhetoric or whether, as I have suggested, the public's concern was largely independent of Goldwater.

As a first step toward evaluating Goldwater's potential influence, I rely on another question asked by the ANES. I look at responses to an open-ended question, which asked, "Is there anything in particular about Goldwater that might make you want to vote for him? What is that?" Surveyors coded all responses to this open-ended question and these responses were subsequently grouped into ninety-four categories.[6] The categories include highly specific policy areas, such as "farm policy," "stand on education," "stand on medical care," and "fiscal policy, e.g., taxes, interest rates, money policy, budgets." The specificity of these categories allows us to examine how many respondents indicated that they supported Goldwater for his stance on crime. Respondents were allowed up to five responses to this question. Based on Figure 3.1, we know that crime registered as a concern with some of these respondents. Thus, if Goldwater was "raising the public's awareness of crime," we might expect a large proportion of respondents to indicate that crime was a reason for supporting Goldwater. By contrast, if Goldwater's emphasis on crime had a weaker effect on the public than previously thought, we would expect fewer mentions of crime.

It turns out that *none* of the ninety-four reasons for supporting Goldwater refer to crime. ANES survey respondents simply did not connect crime with their support for Goldwater.[7] The ANES also asked respondents who

---

5   The ANES interviewed 1,834 adults about politics and the upcoming election during the final two months of the presidential campaign. The data were made available by the Inter-university Consortium for Political and Social Research (ICPSR). The data were originally collected by the Survey Research Center Political Behavior Program. Neither the original collectors of the data nor ICPSR bear any responsibility for the analyses or interpretations presented here.

6   These categories are listed in Appendix A-3.1.

7   The only response that could even remotely be considered linked to crime was "like stand on immorality in country." Out of the 1,322 positive comments about Goldwater (recall that

opposed Goldwater for reasons for their opposition. Again, despite the open-ended nature of the question and the opportunity to list five different concerns, crime did *not* emerge as a reason for opposing Goldwater. Although scholars remember Goldwater's campaign for his references to crime, not a single respondent in the ANES indicated crime or Goldwater's positions on crime as a reason for supporting or opposing his candidacy.[8]

As a second test of the potential influence of Goldwater's campaign, I return to the ANES questions about the most important problems the government should try to take care of. If Goldwater's campaign rhetoric was increasing awareness about crime, we would expect that those who were more attentive to the campaign should be more likely to express concern with crime. To measure attention to the campaign, I rely on three questions about how much attention respondents paid to the presidential campaign and four factual questions about Goldwater and Johnson. I then combine all of the questions into a single index of campaign knowledge and attention. Respondents with the minimum value on this index reported paying no attention to the campaign on the radio, on television, or in newspapers, and they did not correctly answer any of the factual candidate questions. Respondents with the maximum value reported following the campaign on the radio, on television, and in the newspapers a good deal, and they correctly answered all four factual candidate questions.[9] Using this summary measure of factual knowledge about the candidates and attention to the campaign, I grouped respondents according to whether they were the most, middle, or least attentive to the campaign. Figure 3.2 reports the percent of respondents who indicated crime was an important problem for these three categories. To the extent that differences emerge across groups, it is the *least* informed about the election who express the most concern about crime. If Goldwater's campaign rhetoric produced public concern about crime, we would not expect this pattern of results.

---

respondents could list up to five attributes), only five comments (0.38%) mentioned his stand on immorality.

8 A similar result emerges in the work of Epstein and Ranney (1966). Immediately following Goldwater's loss, Epstein and Ranney surveyed a representative sample of Wisconsin adults in order to determine why individuals in Wisconsin supported or opposed Goldwater. Epstein and Ranney's survey asked about seventeen issues and the degree of importance respondents attached to each issue in influencing their presidential preference. Again, *none* of the issues referred to crime. Immediately following the 1964 presidential campaign, two of the most prominent political scientists at the time did not consider the issue of crime or law and order sufficiently important to include in their study of why voters supported or opposed Goldwater.

9 The campaign attention questions asked whether and (if so) how often respondents heard about the campaign through the newspaper, radio, and television. The factual questions asked what state the candidate was from and the religion of the candidate. Appendix A-3.2 provides the exact question wording. To generate the summary measure, each variable was scaled to range from 0 to 1 and then I took the average across the seven variables.

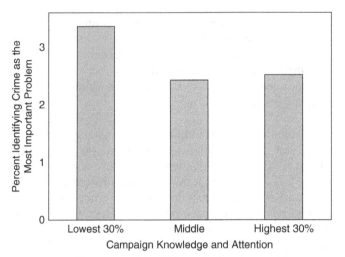

FIGURE 3.2. The percent identifying crime as the most important problem, by campaign awareness.

Source: 1964 American National Election Study.

A survey conducted by the Gallup Organization in October 1964 offers a final look at Goldwater's potential influence. This survey asked, "How much trust and confidence would you have in the way Lyndon Johnson [Barry Goldwater] and his administration would handle each of these problems ... Maintaining law and order?" The emphasis previous research placed on Goldwater's tough-on-crime stance suggests that respondents should express more confidence in Goldwater's ability to maintain law and order than in Johnson's ability. The results do not support this prediction. The dark gray bar on the left in Figure 3.3 reports the percentage of respondents indicating that they have trust and confidence in Goldwater's handling of law and order minus the corresponding percent for Johnson. The negative value for this bar demonstrates that more respondents expressed confidence and trust in Johnson's ability to maintain law and order than in Goldwater's ability. Specifically, the percent of respondents indicating that they had a "very great deal of" or "considerable" trust and confidence in Johnson's ability to maintain law and order was fourteen percentage points greater than that of Goldwater.

The left bar in Figure 3.3 suggests that the public had more confidence that *Johnson* would maintain law and order than Goldwater. This result is at odds with the view that Goldwater was drawing the public's attention to the issue of crime. It is possible, however, that this trust and confidence in Johnson reflects overall support for Johnson, not specific support for his ability to maintain law and order. The light gray bar in the right of Figure 3.3 helps

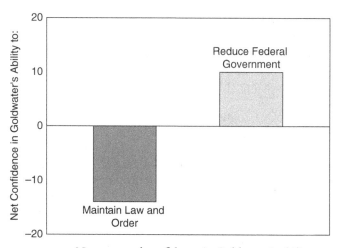

FIGURE 3.3. Net trust and confidence in Goldwater's ability to maintain law and order and to reduce the power of the federal government (relative to Johnson) in October 1964. (Negative values indicate less confidence in Goldwater than in Johnson.)

Source: Hopes and Fears, Oct 1964. Retrieved Oct 12, 2013 from the iPOLL Databank, The Roper Center for Public Opinion Research.

evaluate this possibility. The same survey that asked about maintaining law and order also asked which candidate respondents trusted to stop the trend toward a more powerful federal government. The light gray bar again reflects the percent indicating confidence and trust in Goldwater minus the corresponding percent for Johnson. In contrast to the law and order result, the positive value indicates that more respondents expressed confidence that Goldwater would curb the federal government's power relative to Johnson. Together, the results in Figure 3.3 suggest that the American public associated Goldwater more with limiting the federal government than they did Johnson, but this was not the case for maintaining law and order.

Vesla Weaver (2007, p. 243) accurately summarizes the literature when she explains, "Goldwater is credited in almost folklore like ways with the first intimations of 'law and order.'" The foregoing analysis, however, demystifies Goldwater's legendary status. Of course, we cannot conclude that Goldwater's speeches had no effect on the public. It may be, for example, that Goldwater's stance on civil rights and his emphasis on urban riots encouraged the public to link racial considerations with punitive attitudes (e.g., Alexander 2010, Lerman and Weaver 2014*b*, Weaver 2007). Goldwater may have also helped alert media and other politicians to the public's shifting punitiveness. But the evidence overwhelmingly suggests that Goldwater's influence was less than previously thought. Not a single respondent in the 1964 ANES survey mentioned Goldwater's position on crime as a reason to support or oppose his candidacy, and respondents expressed more confidence in Johnson's ability to maintain law and order. Importantly, Goldwater *did* emphasize law and order during his campaign. Furthermore, the opinion data indicate a reasonably high level of public concern with crime. Yet I was unable to uncover evidence that this concern stemmed from Goldwater's campaign.

As discussed earlier, the lack of connection between Goldwater's campaign and the public's attitudes toward crime and punishment is consistent with the political science literature, which finds limited effects of presidential campaigns – even when they are successful. This result is also consistent with Flamm's (2005) archival research. Although Flamm argues that Goldwater brought law and order into "national political discourse," based on internal memos from Goldwater's campaign, he also concludes that "polls showed [Johnson] was vulnerable in only one area: law and order" and that Goldwater's subsequent emphasis on law and order was a "calculated political tactic" (p. 41). These quotes suggest that instead of leading, Goldwater may have strategically followed the public on this issue.

3.3 JOHNSON'S SHIFT ON CRIME

Lyndon Johnson's commanding win over Barry Goldwater offers another opportunity to consider the elite leadership and the public opinion hypotheses. After assuming the presidency on November 22, 1963 (following President John F. Kennedy's assassination), Johnson mentioned crime twelve times before the 1964 presidential election.[10] In each case, Johnson took a very liberal stance, emphasizing the social roots of crime and the need to address crime through social programs. For example, in his annual message to Congress on the District of Columbia budget in January 1964, Johnson explained, "A substantial proportion of serious crimes, in the District as elsewhere, is committed by juveniles ... Law enforcement has its necessary role, but the significant efforts must come in the fields of education, recreation, health, employment, and welfare."[11]

In May 1964, Johnson placed a similar emphasis on deterring crime through social programs when describing a grant designed to "fight juvenile delinquency." Johnson explained, "This money will help bring about needed improvements in schools, vocational training, employment services, [and]

---

[10]   These twelve instances are based on a search of The American Presidency Project (including election campaign documents and documents from the Office of the Press Secretary) for "crime" and "Johnson."

[11]   January 21, 1964, Lyndon B. Johnson: Annual Message to the Congress, the District of Columbia Budget. www.presidency.ucsb.edu/ws/index.php?pid=26014&st=johnson&st1=crime#ixzz2jWJMwbhp

crime prevention."[12] During the presidential campaign, Johnson also directly contrasted his approach to crime with Goldwater's punitive tone:

> let those take note who preach against crime on the one hand, and on the other deny our children the right to have an education: It doesn't do you any good to just go around the country talking against crime. You have to vote against crime, and when the roll is called on measures in the Congress that will control crime, that will drive away the ancient enemies of mankind – disease, illiteracy, poverty, and ignorance – you must answer those roll calls.[13]

The contrast between Goldwater's tough-on-crime rhetoric and Johnson's emphasis on addressing crime by its root causes offers a clear prediction for the elite leadership and public opinion hypotheses. Given Johnson's decisive win over Goldwater and the fact that he made the war on poverty a key aspect of his presidency, if presidents have the capacity to lead the public, we would expect Johnson to continue his focus on dealing with crime through social programs. Given his overwhelming victory and subsequent popularity – Johnson's approval ratings hovered around 70 percent through March 1965 – this would seem like a best case scenario for elite leadership.[14] By contrast, if Johnson perceived that he was out of step with public attitudes because the public was becoming more punitive, the argument developed in the previous chapter predicts that Johnson should shift his policy statements in a more punitive direction to align with the public (or at least to avoid prompting negative latent opinion).

Consistent with the public opinion hypothesis, almost immediately after his inauguration, Johnson's rhetoric shifted in a more punitive direction. On January 21, 1965, in his annual message to Congress on the District of Columbia Budget, Johnson shifted away from his focus one year earlier on the social causes of crime. In this speech, he mentioned the "punishment of criminal acts" and he explicitly stated that "more must be done."[15] In February, Johnson went even farther, explicitly stating that addressing the causes of crime was not sufficient. Johnson proclaimed:

> Crime will not wait while we pull it up by the roots. We must have a fair and effective system of law enforcement to deal with those who break our

---

[12] May 9, 1964, Lyndon B. Johnson: Remarks in New York City before the 50th Anniversary Convention of the Amalgamated Clothing Workers. www.presidency.ucsb.edu/ws/index.php?pid=26237&st=johnson&st1=crime#ixzz2jWM1qwMs

[13] October 12, 1964, Lyndon B. Johnson: Remarks at the Coliseum in Denver. www.presidency.ucsb.edu/ws/index.php?pid=26596&st=johnson&st1=crime#ixzz2jWMlGqJJ

[14] Between late November 1964 and late March 1965, Johnson's lowest approval rating was 69 percent and his highest approval rating was 71 percent. Specific question details appear in Appendix A-3.4.

[15] Lyndon B. Johnson: Annual Message to the Congress on the District of Columbia Budget. www.presidency.ucsb.edu/ws/index.php?pid=27007&st=johnson&st1=crime#ixzz2jWR96CER

laws. We have given too low a priority to our methods and institutions of law enforcement–our police, our criminal courts and our correctional agencies ... The police are our front line, both offensive and defensive, in the fight against crime.[16]

Johnson was moving from a focus on addressing the roots of crime to also emphasizing an offensive fight against crime. One month later, Johnson's punitive rhetoric evolved further. In a "Special Message to the Congress on Law Enforcement and the Administration of Justice," Johnson began by stating, "Crime has become a malignant enemy in America's midst." He went on to proclaim, "We must arrest and reverse the trend toward lawlessness ... I believe the way to do so is to give new recognition to the fact that crime is a national problem – and to intensify our crime prevention and crime-fighting at all levels of government."[17]

Johnson's abrupt punitive turn seems like a clear attempt to shift his rhetoric in the direction of public opinion. Given the short time frame of his rhetorical shift, it would be surprising if a change in objective conditions accounted entirely for his punitive turn. Indeed, Weaver (2007) explains that Johnson administration officials argued for a tougher stance on crime based on "The obvious *public concern* over this matter during the [1964 presidential] campaign" (Weaver 2007, p. 243, italics mine).[18] Consistent with this interpretation, Ramsey Clark, who served as attorney general under Johnson, explained in a 1969 interview that "It was pretty obviously clear to President Johnson, and I think unquestionably his crime message in February or March of '65 stemmed directly from his anticipation of this as a growing issue."[19] It appears that public support for being tough on crime was the driving force behind Johnson's punitive shift.

3.4 OPINION POLLS AND NIXON'S PRESIDENTIAL CAMPAIGNS

Richard Nixon's successful 1968 presidential campaign provides another prominent example of tough-on-crime political rhetoric. Beckett (1997, p. 38) explains, "As a result of its prominence in the election campaign, the crime issue received an unprecedented level of political and media attention in 1968. And the conservative initiative bore fruit." Nixon's campaign has also received substantial attention for successfully employing the "Southern Strategy," which

---

16 Lyndon B. Johnson: Special Message to the Congress on the Needs of the Nation's Capital. www.presidency.ucsb.edu/ws/index.php?pid=27427&st=johnson&st1=crime#ixzz2jWRqAjN7

17 Lyndon B. Johnson: Special Message to the Congress on Law Enforcement and the Administration of Justice. www.presidency.ucsb.edu/ws/index.php?pid=26800&st=johnson&st1=crime#ixzz2jWPYftub.

18 Weaver's (2007) work has typically been interpreted as offering support for the argument that political elites have led the public, but I interpret these quotes as supporting the important influence of public opinion.

19 Ramsey Clark Oral History Interview V, June 3, 1969.

used racial conservatism to appeal to white Southerners (Boyd 1970, Newell 2013, Phillips 2015 [1969], Tonry 2011, Weaver 2007).[20] The question remains, however: How much was Nixon leading the public as opposed to following the public? Consistent with the cases discussed earlier, an in-depth analysis of Nixon's internal campaign memos suggests that his focus on crime was a political calculation based on his campaign's perceptions of public opinion at the time.

To understand the potential political calculus, it is important to realize that Nixon's tough-on-crime rhetoric was a relatively recent development. During his 1960 run for the presidency, Nixon gave 282 speeches or public remarks. Surprisingly, Nixon mentioned crime only three times, and in each case it was to illustrate a point about international relations, not domestic crime policy.[21] For example, speaking from a train platform in Centralia, IL, Nixon explained:

> when you're dealing with dictators, the way to war is to give in to their blackmail. Let me put it in terms all of us will understand. You go here today and ask the chief of police – I think he's standing right down here in front of me. You ask the chief of police how he keeps crime under control. You know what he'll tell you? He'll tell you that you've got to make it so that crime doesn't pay. If crime doesn't pay, people don't engage in it. Now that's true with nations too.[22]

Particularly noteworthy is the seemingly cavalier reference to crime. Nixon implies that domestically crime is under control because "crime doesn't pay." By 1968, however, crime was a central theme of Nixon's speeches. In fact, his August 8, 1968 acceptance speech for the Republican nomination placed more emphasis on crime than his entire 1960 campaign. Nixon referred to "the crime that plagues the land" and he promised, "a war against organized crime in this

---

[20] As Tonry (2011, pp. 2–3) points out, the phrase "Southern Strategy" dates from the late 1960s, but the roots of the Republican strategy to "appeal to the fears and biases of Southern and working-class whites," can be traced to the 1940s. Interestingly, Kevin Phillips, who was a strategist in Nixon's 1968 presidential campaign and who is viewed as the architect of the "Southern Strategy," has maintained that this was not a strategy, but a "portrait of American *presidential* voting behavior from the Civil War days to 1968" (Phillips 2015 [1969], p. xxii; also see p. xv).

[21] These speeches and remarks, which occurred between August 1 and November 7, 1960, were accessed from the University of Santa Barbara's The American Presidency Project, (www.presidency.ucsb.edu/1960_election_speeches.php?candidate=37#axzz2ixIRGDdX). I also searched for other words related to crime. "Law and order" was never mentioned and "juvenile delinquency" was mentioned once by Nixon (August 2, 1960).

[22] October 28, 1960. American Presidency Project: Richard Nixon: Remarks of the Vice President of the United States, Rear Train Platform, Centralia, IL (www.presidency.ucsb.edu/ws/index .php?pid=25496&st=nixon&st1=crime#ixzz2j18bVqzC). The second speech that referenced crime was also made on this day (in Tolono, IL) and the third speech on crime was made on October 14.

country" and that "The wave of crime is not going to be the wave of the future in the United States of America."[23]

Why did Nixon's public stance on crime shift dramatically between his 1960 and 1968 presidential campaigns? To answer this question, I pored through the White House Special Files Collection, which is housed at the Richard Nixon Presidential Library.[24] These files contain thousands of memos from Nixon's 1968 presidential campaign, and these memos indicate a persistent focus on public opinion polls and, in particular, public concern with crime. An early example comes from a July 9 memo – almost two months before the Republican nominating convention. Robert Ellsworth, the campaign's national political director, sent the memo to other prominent members of the campaign, such as John Mitchell, the national campaign manager, and H. R. Haldeman, Nixon's chief of staff. The memo, titled "Notes on Strategy and Tactics through November 5," stated:

> An ORC poll conducted for the Nixon organization in February 1968 showed that in California, Illinois, New Hampshire, New Jersey, Ohio, Pennsylvania and Wisconsin, Vietnam was regarded by over 70% of all voters as the one single problem the President should concentrate on solving. Similarly, race relations, *crime and lawlessness* and the high cost of living/taxes, generally in that order, rated with nearly equal intensity all across the nation [italics mine].[25]

The memo then went on to discuss "recent Gallup polls" and develop specific strategies based on this public opinion data.

> The implication is clear for these key states: strong get-out-the-vote efforts should be organized among the business and professional classes; Nixon should campaign to manual workers on themes (such as law and order) that appeal to them and stay away from economic themes that alienate them, and he should avoid talking about farm problems.

The Nixon campaign was developing a law and order strategy based on its perceptions of public opinion. A week later, a memo to Patrick Buchanan, one of Nixon's principal speech writers, called for more polls, stating "we should ask open-ended questions to find out what is bothering people, ask them who they think would do something about the problems they indicate bother them,

23   The American Presidency Project: Richard Nixon: Address Accepting the Presidential Nomination at the Republican National Convention in Miami Beach, FL (www.presidency .ucsb.edu/ws/?pid=25968#ixzz2jEsddPv4).
24   The Nixon Presidential Returned Materials Collection: White House Special Files consists of materials designated by archivists of the National Archives and Records Administration's Nixon Presidential Materials Project as political or personal. These materials – seventy-two boxes in total – were returned to the Nixon estate beginning in April 1994 and were first made available for research in 2007.
25   The memo was archived in the Richard Nixon Presidential Library White House Special Files Collection, Box 33, Folder 13.

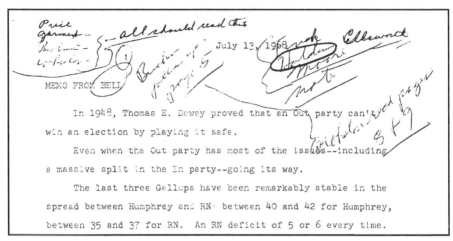

FIGURE 3.4. The top of an internal memo from Richard Nixon's 1968 presidential campaign.

Source: Richard Nixon Presidential Library White House Special Files Collection, Box 33, Folder 13.

and ask them whether they believe RN could solve the problems." The memo apparently resonated. Handwritten and underlined at the bottom of the memo, it reads, "Haldeman – good idea."[26]

A mid-July memo placed further emphasis on the public's crime attitudes. As Figure 3.4 shows, the memo was from Jeffrey Bell, a Nixon campaign aide. At the top of the memo, the last names of prominent members of the campaign have been handwritten, along with the note, "all should read this."[27] As is evident in Figure 3.4, the memo began by emphasizing that "The last three Gallups have been remarkably stable in the spread between Humphrey and RN – between 40 and 42 for Humphrey, between 35 and 37 for RN." On the second page, an underlined section reads, "The Gut vote, then, is leaning toward Humphrey. But this group is not happy. It is concerned, in particular, about the following things: 1. Crime. They are worried about the safety of their families. They are sick of permissiveness in the courts, the city halls, and the Administration."[28] The poll data suggested that Nixon was trailing Humphrey and that crime was on the public's mind. Nixon's campaign strategists saw focusing on crime as an important way to appeal to voters and thus gain in the polls.

[26] Richard Nixon Presidential Library White House Special Files Collection, Box 35, Folder 7.
[27] Price refers to Raymond Price, who was Nixon's chief speech writer. Garment, refers to Leonard Garment, who assisted the campaign and became White House Counsel. Other legible names include Buchanan, Ellsworth, and Haldeman. Memo from July 13, 1968.
[28] Richard Nixon Presidential Library White House Special Files Collection, Box 33, Folder 13.

The internal memos indicate that throughout the campaign, Nixon's team continued to study poll data and continued to highlight evidence of the public's concern with crime. Another example comes from an early October memo, which reported:

> The findings following are based on telephone interviews with a random sampling of 1,469 voters in California, Illinois, Michigan, Missouri, Ohio, Pennsylvania, New Jersey, New York, and Wisconsin ... Vietnam (68%) remains the overriding issue of most importance in the minds of voters. Next most frequently mentioned are civil rights (29%), crime and violence (22%), riots/civil disorder (18%), taxes and economic problems (18%).[29]

The campaign's persistent use of poll data and the consistent emphasis on crime attitudes suggests that Nixon's focus on law and order was a strategic attempt to appeal to voters by aligning his policy statements with voter preferences. Furthermore, the reference to these states indicates that the campaign understood the public concern for crime to be a national issue.[30] Between 1960 and 1968, the Nixon campaign noticed shifting public attitudes about crime and punishment and adjusted its political strategy accordingly.

Interestingly, archival records suggest that Democrats' positions on crime were also responsive to public preferences during the 1968 election. In a 1972 interview, Milton S. Gwirtzman (a top aide to Robert Kennedy's presidential campaign) reflected on Kennedy's position on crime during the primary (prior to Kennedy's assassination). He explained, "Some of the younger staff were concerned when he [Robert Kennedy] shifted emphasis in Indiana to more of a law and order stance. But he didn't change. He made a basic political judgment of what he had to do" (Milton S. Gwirtzman, March 16, 1972). Similar statements were made about Hubert Humphrey, who was the Democratic presidential candidate in 1968. Lawrence O'Brien (Humphrey's campaign director) recalled, "Humphrey took a strong position on law and order. We had controversy regarding this position. That's reflected in the material. I firmly believed that, regardless of the Nixon posture, the climate in America was such that the average American would look carefully at a candidate in this area and would expect him to take a strong and, indeed, tough position" (Lawrence O'Brien, Oral History Interview XXVI, August 26, 1987). Although perhaps to a lesser extent, it appears that in 1968, like Nixon, Kennedy and Humphrey also noticed the public's shifting attitudes, leading the Democratic candidates to shift their positions in a more punitive direction.

---

[29] Richard Nixon Presidential Library White House Special Files Collection, Box 36, Folder 14.
[30] The breadth of the polling focus is also evident elsewhere. For example, a memo to Haldeman on November 4, 1964, stated, "Latest South Dakota poll, interviewing done October 25–27 and published on October 30, shows the following: ... "Agriculture. War in Vietnam and law and order are the principal issues affecting South Dakota voters." (Richard Nixon Presidential Library White House Special Files Collection, Box 36, Folder 12.)

3.5 MASS AND ELITE OPINION IN THE 1970S AND 1980S

A close inspection of Goldwater's 1964 presidential campaign, Johnson's public positions on law and order, and Nixon's internal memos from 1968 suggests that these political figures followed the public's increasing support for being tough on crime. This is a striking pattern of results. Previous research has argued that these presidential campaigns set the law and order agenda for the public. It appears that the opposite was true.

As a final test of whether the public typically led or followed politicians on crime, I turn to data from the Chicago Council on Global Affairs. These data offer a unique opportunity to compare the public's attitudes toward crime with the attitudes of a variety of elites. In December 1974, the Chicago Council on Global Affairs (which was then known as the Chicago Council on Foreign Relations) commissioned a survey of 1,593 American adults and 328 individuals in leadership positions. About a fifth of the respondents in leadership positions were political leaders, such as US senators, US representatives, and officials in executive agencies like the Department of State. Other leaders surveyed were from the business community, media outlets, higher education, and groups such as unions, churches, and volunteer organizations.[31]

Although most questions in the survey focus on global affairs, a few questions relate to domestic politics. Of particular interest is a question on the most important problem facing the country. We have seen that this type of "most important problem" question is not well suited for measuring over-time changes in punitive attitudes. However, because this survey interviewed both political elites and the mass public, the "most important problem" question offers an ideal indicator of which group was more concerned with crime at particular points in time.

I begin by focusing on political elites' responses to the "most important problem" question in 1974, the first year the survey was conducted. Figure 3.5 reports these responses.[32] Given the fact that the United States was experiencing an economic recession and the oil embargo by Arab members of the Organization of Petroleum Exporting Countries (OPEC) had only recently ended, not surprisingly, inflation, the economy, the energy crisis, and recession top the list of the most important problems facing the country.

What is surprising is that crime is tied for the bottom of the list. Political elites' concern for crime was below a host of other domestic issues, such as poverty and hunger, housing, health care, taxes, and food shortages. It appears

---

[31] Chicago Council on Foreign Relations. American Public Opinion and US Foreign Policy, 1975. Conducted by Louis Harris & Associates and the Chicago Council on Foreign Relations. ICPSR edn. Ann Arbor, MI: Inter-university Consortium for Political and Social Research [producer and distributor], 1999. http://doi.org/10.3886/ICPSR05808.v1

[32] Because respondents could offer more than one answer, I calculate the percent of responses offered for each category out of the total number of responses.

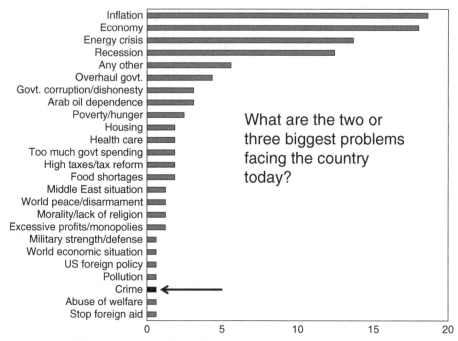

FIGURE 3.5. The percent of political elites citing crime as one of the biggest problems facing the country, December 1974.

Source: Chicago Council on Foreign Relations. American Public Opinion and US Foreign Policy, 1975.

that in 1974, these political leaders did *not* consider crime one of the most important problems. Of course, we are most interested in how concern with crime among elites compares to public concern with crime. The elite leadership hypothesis predicts that elites will be more concerned with crime than the public. The public opinion hypothesis, which I have developed, predicts that public concern with crime would be greater than and would precede elite concern. To examine these predictions, Figure 3.6 reports the responses of the public, political elites, and all elites for the 1974 survey and the next two Chicago Council surveys, which were conducted in 1978 and 1982.[33]

A striking pattern emerges. At every time period, the mass public was more concerned with crime than political elites or elites in general. In fact, in 1978, not a single political elite mentioned crime as a most important problem. By contrast, 4 percent of the public's responses mentioned crime. Examining percentages actually understates the differences across these groups.

33 The "All Elites" category includes political elites, but also includes elites who did not hold government positions, such as interest group leaders and business leaders.

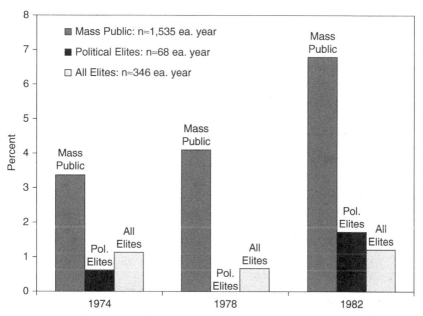

FIGURE 3.6. The percent of the mass public, political elites, and all elites citing crime as one of the biggest problems facing the country in 1974, 1978, and 1982.

Source: Chicago Council on Foreign Relations. American Public Opinion and US Foreign Policy.

For example, in 1978, out of thirty-two topics mentioned by the public, crime was the sixth most important concern. Again, crime did not even make the list for political elites. These data support the previous conclusions based on Goldwater, Johnson, and Nixon. Public concern with crime appears to have led concern among political elites.

3.6 CONCLUSION

This chapter has focused on public and political elite attitudes toward crime and punishment during the 1960s, 1970s, and early 1980s. This is a critical period in the development of the US carceral state. As we saw in Chapter 1, after decades of a roughly constant incarceration rate, in the early 1970s the proportion of those incarcerated began to steadily rise. Additionally, Goldwater's campaign in 1964 and Nixon's campaign in 1968 have been credited with drawing public attention to crime and being tough on crime. Although the public's preferences and politicians' rhetoric can reinforce each other, the evidence in this chapter suggests that political elites during the period typically responded to the public.

Of course, one could argue that political elites were not, themselves, concerned with crime but they emphasized the issue in public during this period because they felt that their constituents were concerned with crime. This scenario reinforces the current argument. If politicians made punitive statements in public that they did not express in private (i.e., in the anonymous surveys reported in Figures 3.5 and 3.6), this would suggest that their public sentiments were designed to reflect the public's preferences.

Another consideration is whether an analysis of state political elites (as opposed to federal political elites) would produce different results. In their analysis of gubernatorial state of the state addresses between 2001 and 2004, Unah and Coggins (2013) find that during these years, governors' rhetorical focus on law and order correlates with state incarceration rates. At times, state political leaders may indeed influence their constituents' policy preferences. The previous analysis, however, focused on national-level political leaders in order to offer a most likely test of the elite leadership hypothesis. Attention to politics is notoriously low in the United States (e.g., Delli Carpini and Keeter 1996), and this is especially true for local politics (Lyons, Jaeger, and Wolak 2013). In fact, in a 2007 Pew Survey, 34 percent of respondents did not correctly identify their state governors.[34] The lack of public attention to state politics makes the previous focus on nation-level politics a most likely case for observing elite leadership. The focus on national politicians was also designed to speak to previous literature that attributes these political figures with having an overwhelming influence on the public's attitudes toward crime and punishment. As Marc Mauer (2006, p. 45) explains, "Barry Goldwater's presidential campaign in 1964, followed by Richard Nixon's campaign in 1968, heralded the theme of 'law and order' for the first time in a national political context."

Thus, the results in this chapter revise conventional wisdom in several ways. First, while Goldwater did take a tough-on-crime stance in his campaign, no evidence emerged to support the claim that the public was influenced by his positions. Second, the political focus on crime and punishment in the 1960s, 1970s, and 1980s appears to have been a targeted response to the public's rising support for being tough on crime. Third, evidence suggests that prominent Democrats, such as Lyndon Johnson, Robert Kennedy, and Hubert Humphrey, also followed the public's lead on crime. The potential role of Democrats in the rise of mass incarceration, and their response to public opinion, has been largely ignored in previous research (though see Murakawa (2014)).

Although the evidence overwhelmingly suggests that political elites responded to the public's shifting support for being tough on crime, we should not conclude that political elite rhetoric never matters. However, the lack of

---

34 Pew Research Center for the People & the Press News Savvy Poll, Febuary 2007. Retrieved June 18, 2014 from the iPOLL Databank, The Roper Center for Public Opinion Research.

evidence of political elite leadership does raise an important question. Why did the public's attitude become more punitive during this period? The next chapter aims to answer this question.

A-3 APPENDICES TO CHAPTER 3

A-3.1 Pro-Goldwater comments

These categories come from the 1964 ANES and correspond with questions V640027a, V640027b, V640027c, V640027d, V640027e. Anti-Goldwater comments correspond with questions V640028a, V640028b, V640028c, V640028d, and V640028e.

Experience and abilities

1. Good man. Well-qualified for the job. Capable. R has heard good things (unspecified). Experienced (na what kind).
2. War experience. War hero. Military experience.
3. Successful record. Is a good senator.
4. Government or political experience. Has experience in civil government.
5. Good administrator. Good executive ability. Good organizer.
6. Will cut spending. Run government economically.
7. Other experience and ability.

Character and background

1. Has dignity.
2. A leader. Great natural-born leader (no other specification).
3. Strong man. Decisive. Self-confident. Aggressive.
4. Will save America. America needs a man like him. A man you can follow. People have confidence in him. Inspiring.
5. "Politician" (positive reference).
6. Independent. No one runs him. He's his own boss.
7. R talks of Goldwater as protector – will take care of things. Knows what to do.
8. Man of humility. Knows his own limitations. Doesn't pretend to know all the answers.
9. Man of integrity, principle. Man of high ideals, high moral purpose. Honest, doesn't make deals.
10. Public servant. Man of duty. Conscientious.
11. Patriotic. For Americans. Will be good for the country.
12. Understands the problems. Well-informed. Understands the people. Realistic, down-to-earth.
13. Educated. Scholarly. Intelligent, smart.
14. Like his religion. He's religious.

15. Wealthy. Made own money. Worked his way up. Knows what it is to be poor. Personally wealthy – won't be tempted, influenced by money.
16. Good family life. Like his family, wife, children, relatives.
17. Hard-working. Would be a full-time president. Would stay on the job. Ambitious.
18. Stable. Balanced.
19. Like stand on corruption in government. Baker, Jenkins scandals.

Personal attraction

1. Like him as a person. Like his face. Nice personality. Pleasant. Good sense of humor.
2. Kind. Warm. Likeable. Gets along with people. Has people's interests at heart.
3. Sincere.
4. Democratic (nonpartisan meaning).
5. Good speaker. Makes a good appearance.
6. He's in good health. Not too old.
7. He's well known.
8. Other personal characteristics.
9. He's from the West, Arizona.

Issues – not available whether domestic or foreign

1. Agree with Goldwater. Agree with (like) his policies.
2. Position on issues is clear. Know where he stands. Talks straight to the point.
3. Will support and continue Republican policies (na whether domestic or foreign).
4. Stand on communism (na whether domestic or foreign).

Stand on domestic policies

1. Would handle domestic affairs well. Has the experience to handle domestic affairs.
2. Would cut down government activity. Stop this socialism.
3. Fiscal policy, e.g., taxes, interest rates, money policy. Budgets.
4. Will bring better times. Lower cost of living. Employment. Jobs, increase minimum wage.
5. For states' rights, free enterprise, individual initiative. Against big government.
6. Liberal. More liberal than most Republicans. More for social welfare and/or government economic activity. Will listen to, bring in, liberals.
7. Conservative. Middle of the road. Not too radical. Represents conservative wing of Republican Party. Will listen to, bring in, conservatives.

8. Stand on antipoverty program. Manpower retraining.
9. Stand on civil rights (na direction of stand on race problem).
10. For civil rights, e.g., for desegregation, school integration, civil rights law.
11. Against civil rights, e.g., against desegregation. Willing to go easy on desegregation and school integration.
12. Farm policy.
13. Stand on labor. On union corruption, right-to-work laws, Taft-Hartley, Hoffa.
14. Stands on conservation, on public power (TVA, REA, etc.) On "giveaway programs" – natural resources, on public works, on highways.
15. Other domestic policy reference.
16. Stand on Social Security. Unemployment compensation.
17. Stand on education.
18. Stand on medical care, e.g., Medicare, care for the aged.

Stand on foreign affairs

1. Will handle foreign policy well. Familiar with world situation. Experience abroad, travel. Foreign countries respect him.
2. Likes, agrees with Goldwater foreign policy (unspecified).
3. Internationalist. Favors aid to, cooperation with, other countries.
4. Isolationist. Keeps out of other countries' affairs. Will reduce spending abroad, foreign aid. Will put UN, allies in their place.
5. Will stop communism abroad. Can handle Russia.
6. Defense and preparedness. Will raise defense spending. Firm foreign policy.
7. Can handle specific trouble spots, e.g., Middle East, Cuba, Congo, Berlin, Vietnam, Cyprus.
8. Will win prestige race with Russia. Will raise America's prestige in world.
9. Will keep peace. Better chance for peace under Goldwater. Working for disarmament. Will keep us out of war. Worked for test ban. Will control nuclear weapons.
10. Other foreign policy reference.
11. Like stand on the draft.

Like Goldwater because good for, will help –

1. All the people, good for everyone, no special privileges. Equitable policies, "the people."
2. Common people, poor people, working-class people, the laboring man.
3. Labor, labor unions.
4. Business, big business, industry.
5. Small business or businessman (specific reference to size).

6. Farmers.
7. Negroes.
8. Like Goldwater because he will keep some groups in check, e.g., labor, business, Negroes.
9. Other groups whom Goldwater will help. Include references to middle-class or white collar workers, or to sectional interests, veterans, etc.
10. Old people, the aged.

Candidate as party representative

1. He's a Republican, the Republican nominee. A good Republican.
2. Not controlled by party. Not a machine man.
3. Like him because he's not like most Republicans.
4. Like the men around him, his associates.
5. Like his speeches, campaign tactics.
6. Goldwater's relationship to vice-presidential candidate.
7. Other references tying Goldwater and Republican party.

Other

1. "I just like him"; would vote for him. Prefer him (no specific content).
2. Goldwater will bring change. Time for a change.
3. Any indication that R being influenced by others.
4. Like stand on extremism. Connection with extremists.
5. Other miscellaneous (positive).
6. Like stand on immorality in country.
7. INAP., nothing, no mention. DK. NA. No additional mentions.
8. Don't know much about him (neutral, not positive).
9. Refuses to say.

A-3.2 ANES questions (Figure 3.2)

Most important problem: What would you personally feel are the most important problems the government should take care of when the new president and Congress take office in January?

Campaign attention: The following questions were combined to generate a measure of how much attention respondents paid to the campaign.

1. We're interested in this interview in finding out whether people paid much attention to the election campaign this year. Take newspapers, for instance – Did you read about the campaign in any newspaper? (If yes) How much did you read newspaper articles about the

election – regularly, often, from time to time, or just once in a great while?

2. How about radio – Did you listen to any speeches or discussions about the campaign on the radio? (If yes) How many programs about the campaign did you listen to on the radio – a good many, several, or just one or two?

3. How about television – Did you watch any programs about the campaign on television? (If yes) How many television programs about the campaign would you say you watched – a good many, several, or just one or two?

4. Speaking of candidates and voting, we're interested in what sorts of things people notice about the candidates. Take Senator Goldwater, for instance: Have you heard what part of the country he comes from? (Where is that?) (What state?)

5. Do you happen to know what his [Senator Goldwater's] religion is? (Which is that?)

6. Now take President Johnson: Have you heard what part of the country he comes from? (Where is that?) (What state?)

7. Do you happen to know what his [President Johnson's] religion is? (Which is that?)

A-3.3 Trust and confidence in Goldwater and Johnson questions (Figure 3.3)

Let's look at some specific problems. How much trust and confidence would you have in the way Lyndon Johnson [Barry Goldwater] and his administration would handle each of these problems – a very great deal, considerable, not very much, or none at all? …

1. Maintaining law and order.
2. Stopping the trend toward a more powerful federal government.

A-3.4 Johnson's approval ratings

Approval: Do you approve or disapprove of the way Johnson is handling his job as president?

Data provided by the Roper Center for Public Opinion Research (Downloaded November 5, 2013). Conducted by Gallup Organization: November 20–25, 1964; January 7–12, 1965; January 28–February 2, 1965; February 19–24, 1965; March 18–23, 1965.

4

Explaining the public's punitiveness

"Crime up 15% Here Last Year," *Washington Post* headline, January 11, 1964

"Crime Rate Rises 10% Here in Year, Increase Equal to Nation's," *New York Times* headline, January 29, 1964

In early 1964, news of rising crime rates echoed throughout the nation. In addition to the articles cited above, the *Washington Post* and the *New York Times* announced rising crime rates with headlines like "Serious Crime in January up 34% over Same Month Last Year," "Serious Crime up 29% in Montgomery County," "New Patrol to Fight Rising Crime Rate," and "F.B.I. Reports a 10% Rise in Serious Crime in 1963." Similar stories played out in sunny California and the unusually temperate Chicago. Headlines in the *Los Angeles Times* informed readers that "Glendale Police Report Crimes in City Exceeded 2,000 during 1963" and "Juvenile Crime up 12%." The *Chicago Tribune* proclaimed, "Major Crime Rises Sharply in Milwaukee" and "Crime Soars; Blame Weather: Wilson Cites Lack of Snow during Balmy January." Regardless of where one lived, news was highlighting increasing criminal activity.

This chapter shows that throughout the past sixty years, news reports like these have drawn attention to shifting crime rates and have shaped the public's punitiveness in fundamental ways. The argument that the news media follow the crime rate and that these news reports influence the public's support for being tough on crime may sound intuitive. Indeed, some evidence suggests the public became more punitive as crime increased during the 1960s and 1970s (Mayer 1992, Niemi, Mueller, and Smith 1989). Yet this argument does not represent the prevailing scholarly view. Summarizing the dominant perspective on the topic, Michelle Alexander (2010, p. 54) explains, "The level of public concern about crime and drugs was only weakly correlated with actual crime rates, but highly correlated with political initiatives, campaigns, and partisan appeals."[1] Thus, the connection this chapter draws between crime, news, and public opinion offers a crucial new understanding of the development of punitive attitudes in the United States. This chapter also builds on the findings in Chapter 3, offering further evidence that political elites were more likely to follow, not lead, the public's shifting preferences.

In order to identify the relationships between crime, news coverage of crime, and the public's punitiveness, this chapter begins by documenting how crime rates have increased and decreased across the country since the 1950s. Of particular note is that regardless of whether we examine violent, property, national, or local crime rates, criminal activity appears to increase and decrease in uniform and systematic ways. This chapter then examines how the news has covered these shifting crime rates, focusing in particular on the rising crime rates of the 1960s and 1970s. Even though the news media consistently over-report violent crime and the proportion of criminal activity committed by racial minorities, *changes* in the amount of crime in the news correspond closely with changes in the actual crime rate. This chapter ends with a statistical analysis of sixty years of data. We see that since the middle of the past century, shifts in news coverage of crime have had a profound influence on the public's punitiveness.

4.1 CRIME RATES OVER TIME

Before we can understand how news covers crime, we need a sense of how criminal activity has changed during the rise of mass incarceration. I use the FBI's Uniform Crime Reports (UCR) to measure the crime rate over time. The UCR data offer several advantages. Scholars have shown that these data offer a valid indication of over-time shifts in the amount of criminal activity (e.g., Gove, Hughes, and Geerken 1985, McDowall and Loftin 2007), and the data are available for the entire period of interest.[2] Furthermore, Donohue and Wolfers (2005) compare the UCR homicide rate and the homicide rate compiled from Vital Statistics sources, based on death certificates. Since 1950, the two homicide rates correlate at $r = 0.98$, indicating that the UCR homicide rate

---

[1] See also Beckett (1997, pp. 14–27) and Beckett and Sasson (2004, pp. 8, 116).

[2] Of course, concerns exist with all crime data because criminal activity is a difficult concept to measure. Importantly, comparisons of the UCR with the National Crime Victimization Survey (NCVS) offer strong evidence of the over-time validity and reliability of the Uniform Crime Reports. The NCVS, which began in 1973, is a twice-a-year survey of approximately ninety thousand US households that is conducted by the Bureau of Justice Statistics. The survey measures the frequency, characteristics, and consequences of criminal victimization. Although the NCVS and UCR do not define crime in identical ways, once these differences are accounted for, the over-time crime estimates from the NCVS correspond very closely with the estimates from the UCR (Biderman and Lynch 1991, Blumstein, Cohen, and Rosenfeld 1991, 1992, McDowall and Loftin 2007, Rand and Rennison 2002). The close over-time correspondence between the two measures supports the conclusion that the UCR captures actual changes in criminal activity (also see Tonry 2004, pp. 117–118).

is indeed a valid and reliable measure. The UCR data are also advantageous because they represent crimes *reported* to the police. Unreported crimes are important and often of scholarly interest, but we would not expect the news media to be aware of unreported crimes. Additionally, even if errors entered the UCR data, as the opening quotes indicate, news sources relied on these statistics.[3] In order to understand the sources of news reporting on crime, we must focus on the crime and crime statistics that have been reported.

Figure 4.1(a) shows the rate of the four types of violent crime reported in the UCR. Figure 4.1(b) depicts the three types of property crime in the UCR. In order to highlight the over-time trajectories of these crime rates, all series have been scaled to have a common minimum and maximum value. Figures 4.1(a) and 4.1(b) also include an *overall* measure of the violent and property crime rate (thick black line).[4] Whether we look at specific violent crimes, property crimes, or the overall measure of criminal activity, crime rates appear to move largely in tandem (see also McDowall and Loftin 2005, Tonry 2004). Statistical analysis confirms this visual impression.[5] Of course, some differences do exist (i.e., the murder rate and the burglary rate have declined more quickly than the other series), but overall, violent and property crimes tend to follow similar trajectories. This is an important result. Despite the fact that media tend to over-report violent crime (Marsh 1991), this tendency does not necessarily bias *over-time* patterns of crime coverage. Whether the news focused on violent crimes, property crimes, or all criminal activity, the over-time patterns would be roughly the same.

Of course, the amount of criminal activity and the amount of news coverage of crime is not equivalent across all regions of the country. This geographic heterogeneity could have important implications for news coverage and the public's response to this coverage. For example, if crime went up in the

3 Weaver (2007, p. 245), for example, expresses some concern for the UCR data by quoting Wilson (1975, p. 14), who writes, "it is doubtful that any large city has continuously participated in the Uniform Crime Reporting program since 1930 without there having been some purposeful, major defection from UCR standards at some time during that period." Important for the current analysis, Wilson (1975, p. 27) also explains, "most authorities will agree that the magnitude of the crime problem is reasonably well represented by graphs based on UCR data – that index crime began a gradual upward trend in the mid 1950s and that the upward trend was sharply accelerated after the mid 1960s." The validity of the over-time patterns in the UCR crime data that Wilson highlights is especially reassuring because these over-time patterns are the focus of my analysis.

4 The overall measure is based on a principal components analysis, based on the common over-time variance of the individual violent and property crime rates. This measure does not include the larceny rate because a change in how larceny data were coded in 1960 produces a spike in the series at that time point. This decision does not influence the results. If larceny is included in the crime index, the resulting index correlates with the index reported in Figure 4.1 at $r = 0.999$.

5 Cronbach's alpha $= 0.72$ and principal components analysis shows that the various crime rates load onto a single factor (eigenvalue $= 5.20$), which explains 87 percent of the variation in the series. The next largest factor has an eigenvalue of 0.65.

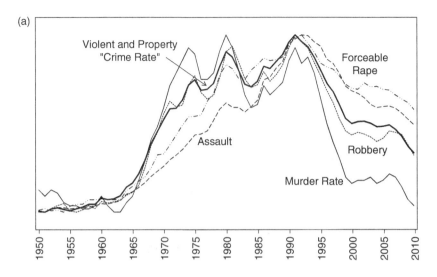

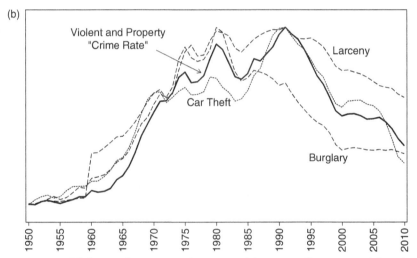

FIGURE 4.1. Violent and property crime rates with an overall measure of the crime rate from 1950 to 2010: (a) violent crime rates and (b) property crime rates.

Source: The 1960–2010 data come from the *Sourcebook of Criminal Justice Statistics Online* (www.albany.edu/sourcebook/csv/t31062010.csv). The data prior to 1960 come from Tables 2/1 and 2/15 in the 1973 Office of Management and Budget Social Indicators.

Northeast and down in the South, we would expect divergent patterns of news coverage and distinct shifts in punitiveness in the two regions. It turns out, however, that from an over-time perspective, this type of heterogeneity is largely absent in the data. Figure 4.2 reports the over-time correlation

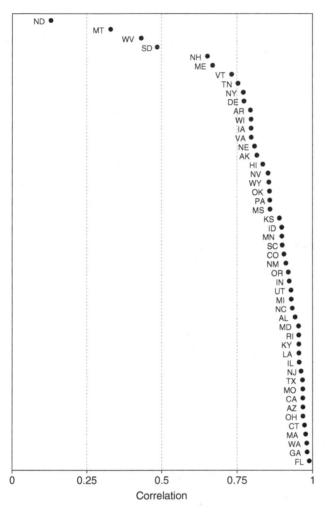

FIGURE 4.2. The correlation between the national violent crime rate and state violent crime rates from 1960 to 2010.

Source: Uniform Crime Reporting Statistics – UCR Data Online www.ucrdatatool.gov/.

between the national violent crime rate and the violent crime rate in each state from 1960 to 2010.[6] Although the previous analysis shows that violent and property crimes move in similar ways, I focus on the violent crime rate because, as noted earlier, these crimes generate the most media attention. The pattern of strong correlations indicates that increases and decreases in violent crime move roughly in tandem across the states. For thirty-six states, the

---

[6] Prior to 1960, the UCR data are not available at the state or local levels.

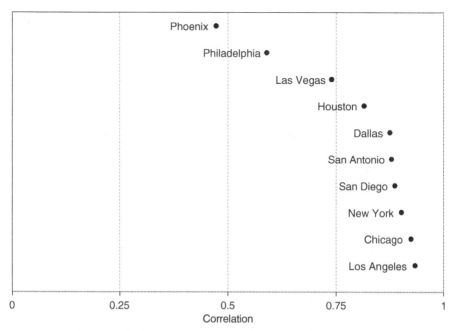

FIGURE 4.3. The correlation between the murder rate in the ten largest metropolitan police departments and the national violent crime rate from 1985 to 2012.

Source: Uniform Crime Reporting Statistics – UCR Data Online www.ucrdatatool.gov

correlation is greater than $r = 0.80$ and only four states have a correlation of less than $r = 0.65$. These patterns suggest that regardless of whether a news story focused on state crime or national crime, reporting would change in very similar ways.

Figure 4.3 shifts the focus to the nation's ten largest metropolitan police departments. The figure compares the murder rate in these cities with the national violent crime rate between 1985 (the first year the metropolitan crime data are available) and 2012. Since local news disproportionately focuses on murders (Gilliam et al. 1996), comparing the murder rate in urban areas with the national violent crime rate allows us to determine if this news media bias holds implications for over-time patterns of crime coverage. Similar over-time trajectories are again the norm, suggesting that the focus of local news on murders does not necessarily lead to incorrect inferences about increases and decreases in the crime rate. For each of the nation's ten largest police districts, we observe a positive correlation between the city's murder rate and the nation's violent crime rate. The correlation for seven of the cities is greater than $r = 0.80$ and the lowest correlation is $r = 0.47$. These results reinforce McDowall and Loftin's (2009, p. 307) conclusion that there is "a clear single [crime] pattern that operates across the nation's major urban areas" (also see, Tonry 2004, p. 122).

4.1.1 Implications of similar crime trajectories

Whether we examine violent crime, property crime, state crime, or crime in the nation's largest cities, we have seen that crime rates appear to rise and fall in tandem. These similar over-time trajectories hold important implications for news reporting on crime.[7]

As noted earlier, a sizeable literature has documented that news media have consistently over-reported violent crime incidences.[8] As Reiner (2002, p. 383) explains, "From the earliest studies (e.g., Harris 1932) onwards, analyses of news reports have found that crimes of violence are featured disproportionately compared to their incidence in official crime statistics or victim surveys." This over-reporting means that at any particular point in time, the proportion of news coverage devoted to violent crime will be greater than the actual proportion of crimes that are violent. This consistent pattern leads to an important prediction. The news media's habitual bias toward focusing on violent crime means that crime reporting should accurately reflect *over-time* change in the violent crime rate. Additionally, since shifts in the property crime rates roughly parallel shifts in violent crime rates, consistently overemphasizing violent crime will translate to an accurate *over-time* reflection of the overall crime rate. Furthermore, because crime shifts in similar ways across geographic regions, regardless of the news source (local or national), we should expect similar over-time patterns of crime coverage. In sum, despite misrepresenting the amount and type of crime, increases and decreases in news coverage of crime should follow changes in the actual crime rate.

In an impressive study of crime in Bloomington, IL, Soroka (2014) finds results that offer initial support for this argument. Soroka focused on Bloomington because he was able to obtain *weekly* data on all crimes reported to the Bloomington police department and all stories dealing with crime in the local newspaper, the *Bloomington Pantagraph*. Not surprisingly, Soroka finds that the *Pantagraph* over-reports violent crimes and underreports nonviolent

---

7   These similar trajectories also hold crucial implications for understanding the causes of crime and the best ways to prevent crime. Researchers and policy makers often focus on specific geographic areas, looking for local explanations for increases or decreases in criminal activity. For example, a recent issue of *Justice Quarterly* was devoted to "New York's Crime Drop Puzzle" (Rosenfeld, Terry, and Chauhan 2014). The similar over-time crime trajectories documented here suggest that national-level factors must also be considered when studying the causes of local crime shifts (see also Baumer and Wolff 2014, McDowall and Loftins 2009, and Tonry 2004).

8   Also as noted earlier, news coverage of crime over-reports the proportion of criminals who are nonwhite (Barlow 1998, Gilliam et al. 1996, Pollak and Kubrin 2007). I discuss the implications of this reporting bias later.

crimes. However, consistent with the expectations mentioned earlier, he finds a positive and significant relationship between the number of news stories about crime and the number of violent crimes reported to the police in the previous week. This relationship is important because, as we saw in Figure 4.3, the murder rate in urban areas corresponds with the violent crime rate at the national level. Regardless of whether the news focuses on local or national crime, we have reason to believe that news coverage will shift in similar ways. To test this prediction, the following section develops a measure of news coverage of crime that extends from 1950 to 2010.

4.2 MEASURING NEWS ABOUT CRIME

In order to know if news coverage tracks the crime rate and if this news coverage influences the public's attitudes, we need a measure of news coverage of crime. Given the long period of interest (the 1950s to the present), I focus on crime reporting in newspapers. The radical changes in television viewing during this period (i.e., the explosion of television viewership in the 1950s and 1960s and the rapid expansion of cable television beginning in the 1970s) make over-time comparisons of television news impossible.[9] Although newspapers have changed some, the format and circulation of major newspapers have been relatively constant through this period. For these reasons, newspapers offer the best measure of news coverage over long periods of time (Baumgartner, De Boef, and Boydstun 2008, Dardis et al. 2008).

Measuring the amount of newspaper coverage of crime over a sixty-year period is a potentially daunting task. Fortunately, specific aspects of the issue of crime suggest a relatively straightforward approach. I propose that knowing whether or not an article includes the word "crime" offers an efficient and accurate way to identify if the news story was about or related to crime. Put simply, it is hard to write about crime without mentioning "crime." The word "crime" creeps into articles about crime in a variety of different ways, such as "after the crime," "the crime was," "committed the crime," "increase in crime," "charged with the crime," "the crime rate," "a federal crime," "alleged crime," "organized crime," "a heinous crime," "combat crime," "committee on crime," or "serious crime." Not every article about crime will include the word "crime," but most will. Equally as important, when the word "crime" does appear in an article, it is unlikely that the article does not relate to crime or criminal activity in some way. Thus, counting the number of newspaper articles that mention the word "crime" each year offers a way to measure the amount of news coverage of crime. Furthermore, knowing how many articles were written about crime each year offers a clear indication of whether news coverage of crime was increasing or decreasing.

---

9 See Prior (2007, p. 13) for an overview of shifts in the media environment.

Can ignoring the details of the articles and simply counting the number of articles that mention the word "crime" really produce a valid measure of news coverage? On one hand, the assertion that more articles with the word "crime" should correspond with more news coverage of crime seems intuitive. On the other hand, one might reasonably wonder how much information is lost by ignoring the details of articles and instead focusing on the presence (or absence) of a single word. It is thus necessary to evaluate my proposed word count approach. News coverage of economic conditions offers an ideal context to test this measurement strategy. Just like the word "crime" is likely to appear in stories about crime and unlikely to appear otherwise, the words "unemployment" and "inflation" should appear in articles about these two topics and they should be unlikely to appear in articles that do not relate to unemployment or inflation. It is also reasonable to expect that, like the crime rate, when the unemployment rate or the inflation rate increases (decreases), the number of articles about unemployment or inflation also increases (decreases). Because the Bureau of Labor Statistics regularly measures the unemployment and inflation rates, we can test these predictions. If the number of newspaper articles containing the word "unemployment" or the word "inflation" match the actual unemployment or inflation rates, we will have evidence that counting the number of articles with these words offers a valid and reliable measure of objective conditions. Failure to find a strong over-time relationship will suggest otherwise.

Figure 4.4 tests these expectations by reporting the annual unemployment rate and annual percent change in the inflation rate from 1950 to 2010 along with the number of articles in the *New York Times* that included the word "unemployment" and the number of articles with the word "inflation."[10] To make over-time comparisons easier, all series have been standardized to a common minimum and maximum value. The close correspondence between the series is extraordinary. From 1950 to the 1980s, the number of articles mentioning "unemployment" or "inflation" moves almost perfectly in sync with the actual unemployment and inflation rates. Some divergence emerges later in the series, but the increases and decreases continue to move virtually in tandem. Simply knowing how many news articles mentioned these words provides an accurate indication of objective economic conditions. If news follows the actual crime rate, the same types of patterns should emerge when we count the number of articles with the word "crime."

4.2.1 The rise of crime and news coverage of crime

The previous analysis of the unemployment and inflation rates focused just on the *New York Times*. For the analysis of crime coverage, I rely on six

---

[10] The *New York Times* articles were accessed through ProQuest historical newspapers, which is a database of newspapers that (for most titles) includes digital reproductions of every page from every issue, cover to cover.

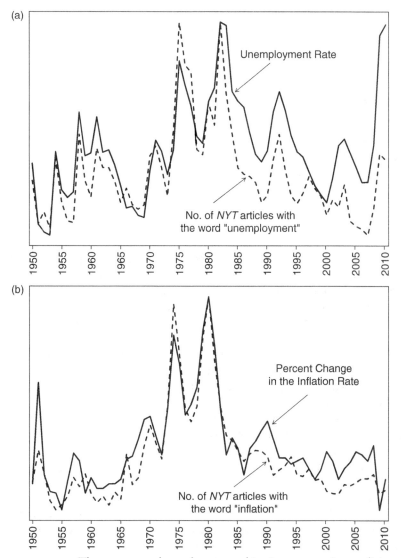

FIGURE 4.4. The correspondence between objective economic conditions and the number of articles mentioning (a) "Unemployment" and (b) "Inflation."

Source: The unemployment rate data come from the US Department of Labor Bureau of Labor Statistics (http://data.bls.gov/timescrics/LNS14000000). The inflation rate data come from Table 24 of the January 24 CPI Detailed Report (www.bls.gov/cpi/cpid1401.pdf). The *New York Times* articles were accessed through ProQuest Historical Newspapers.

TABLE 4.1. *The correlation between the number of "crime" articles in each newspaper and the overall index based on all newspapers*

Newspaper	Correlation	Date Range
New York Times	0.968	1950–2010
Washington Post	0.893	1950–1997
Wall Street Journal	0.964	1950–1996
Los Angeles Times	0.922	1950–1990
Chicago Tribune	0.826	1950–1990
Boston Globe	0.952	1950–1982
Percent of Variance Explained	85.56	

prominent newspapers: the *New York Times, Washington Post, Wall Street Journal, Los Angeles Times, Chicago Tribune*, and *Boston Globe*. These six newspapers offer two important advantages. First, since the goal is to generate a national-level measure of media attention to crime, incorporating stories from prominent newspapers from across the country ensures that one paper or one region does not drive the results. Second, the use of these six papers allows a test of the prediction that across different regions, news coverage of crime will change in similar ways over time. The digital availability of these newspapers varies in recent years, but all papers are available between 1950 and 1982 – the key period of interest.

To combine the frequency of articles mentioning crime from the six newspapers into a single measure of news coverage of crime, I use the same approach that I used to combine public opinion series to generate the measure of punitive public opinion in Chapter 2. Recall that Stimson's (1999) Wcalc algorithm first scales each series to a common metric, so differences in the amount of coverage across newspapers at any point in time do not influence the final measure. This is an important first step because the number of crime articles in each newspaper may differ for reasons we are not interested in, such as the size of the newspaper, the amount of local crime, or even a particular editor's perceptions about how interested the newspaper's readers are in crime. Instead of these cross-sectional differences, we want to understand over-time variation in news coverage. Thus, in the second step, an overall measure of news coverage is calculated based on the common over-time variation across the six newspapers.

Table 4.1 reports the over-time correlation between the number of articles in each newspaper that mentioned the word "crime" each year and the resulting measure of crime news coverage. The strong correlations, which range from $r = 0.83$ to 0.97, indicate that, consistent with expectations, crime reporting in all six newspapers follows a common trajectory. This result is consistent with the earlier findings that crime rates tend to move in similar ways across the country. These similar over-time patterns of crime news coverage in various parts of the country are also consistent with the parallel shifts in support for the death penalty among Southerners and non-Southerners in Figure 2.4(c) and the similar shifts in punitiveness across geographic regions documented by Ramirez (2013, p. 25). After all, if news coverage of crime shifts largely in parallel across the country, we would expect punitiveness to also shift in parallel. The strong correlations in Table 4.1 also validate the measurement strategy. The next step is to evaluate how the overall measure of crime news coverage relates to the actual crime rate.

Earlier in this chapter, Figure 4.1 demonstrated that both property and violent crime rates began increasing in the 1960s and continued to increase through the 1970s. Additionally, in Chapter 3, we saw that during this time period national political leaders like Goldwater, Johnson, and Nixon noticed rising public concern with crime and adjusted their campaign strategies and public statements accordingly. I thus begin the analysis by focusing on this critical time period. I then proceed to a statistical analysis of the years 1950 to 2010.

Figure 4.5 plots the crime rate and the measure of news coverage of crime from 1950 to 1982. To aid visual comparison, both series have been scaled to a common minimum and maximum value. Consistent with expectations, newspaper coverage of crime did indeed track the rising crime rate. In fact, the two series move virtually in tandem. This is a critical finding. Conventional wisdom holds that increases in media attention to crime typically do *not* track officially reported crime (Beckett and Sasson 2004, p. 8). Here we see, however, that during this critical period, news coverage of crime did indeed follow the crime rate.[11]

4.3 CRIME REPORTING AND THE PUBLIC'S PUNITIVENESS

The patterns in Figure 4.5 suggest that news coverage of crime closely followed the rising crime rate in the 1960s and 1970s. There are several reasons to suspect that more news coverage of crime would push the public's attitudes in a punitive direction. To understand this prediction, we need to think about how news coverage of crime typically *frames* the issue. Media frames offer a central organizing idea that makes sense of relevant events and suggests what is at issue (Gamson and Modigliani 1987).[12] Several aspects of the typical crime

---

[11] Of course, a variety of factors influence how much news media cover crime and how they cover crime (e.g., Boydstun 2013, Melossi 2008, Potter and Kappeler 2006). The critical point, however, is that even with these various factors, we observe a strong over-time relationship between the crime rate and news coverage of crime.

[12] See also Druckman (2001), Gitlin (1980), Scheufele (1999), and Tuchman (1978).

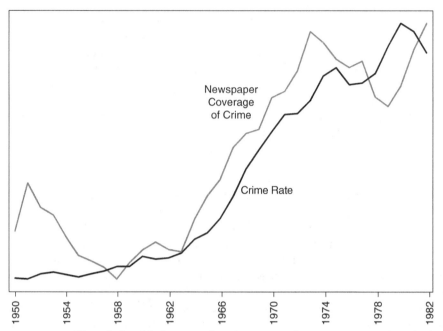

FIGURE 4.5. The relationship between the crime rate and newspaper coverage of crime from 1950 to 1982.

Source: The crime rate is based on the FBI Uniform Crime Reports. Newspapers were accessed through ProQuest Historical Newspapers.

news frames suggest that more (less) crime coverage will lead to more (less) punitive attitudes.

First, the fact that crime reporting tends to focus on violent crimes (Reiner 2002, Soroka 2014) suggests that more news coverage of crime will heighten public concern and demand for action. Second, crime reporting almost always adopts what Iyengar (1991; see also Graber 1980) calls "episodic" frames. Instead of offering "thematic" frames, which emphasize the broader context surrounding an event, such as how social conditions can influence criminal activity, episodic frames focus on the individual (perpetrator or victim) and the criminal act. Episodic framing of violent crime is likely to correspond with punitive attitudes.[13] Thus, as the frequency of crime reporting increases, and individuals are exposed to more of these episodic frames, support for being tough on crime is expected to increase. A third factor of crime reporting is that at least since the 1960s, news media consistently over-report the proportion

---

[13] As Soroka (2014, p. 82) explains, there is a "near-total absence of goodness from stories about crime (save perhaps for stories on the successful capture of criminals, or the release of the falsely accused)."

of criminals who are nonwhite (Barlow 1998, Gilliam et al. 1996, Pollak and Kubrin 2007). These reporting biases have important consequences, leading the public to associate racial minorities with criminal activity (Hurwitz and Peffley 1997). Beyond producing misconceptions about who commits crimes, these racial biases in reporting lead to more punitive attitudes among the public (Eberhardt et al. 2004, Hetey and Eberhardt 2014, Hurwitz and Peffley 2005, Johnson 2008). Thus, the consistent patterns of news reporting on crime offer a straightforward prediction for opinion change. More (less) exposure to these frames should correspond with more (less) punitive attitudes.[14]

This prediction has a strong theoretical foundation in the public opinion literature. There are two dominant models of opinion updating. On-line processing holds that updating can be relatively automatic. According to this model, as individuals receive information about a topic, they keep a mental running tally of directional signals (Hastie and Park 1986, Lodge, Steenbergen, and Brau 1995). In the current context, as an individual encounters more (less) news exposure about crime, we would expect the running tally in favor of a punitive response to increase (decrease). In contrast to on-line processing, John Zaller's (1992) Receive-Accept-Sample (RAS) model offers a memory-based account of information processing. According to the RAS model, when expressing an opinion, individuals rely on considerations that come to mind. These considerations are typically based on recently received information that is salient. Thus, if the news coverage of crime increases (decreases), the number of punitive considerations will be higher (lower), increasing the probability of a punitive survey response. Individuals probably use both processes (the more automatic on-line tally and the memory-based RAS model) to varying extents, depending on the individual and the issue.[15] Importantly, both models make the same prediction in this case. Given the episodic nature of crime frames, as well as the focus on violent crimes and crimes committed by racial minorities, more news coverage of crime should increase the number of frames that lead to punitive attitudes, increasing the public's overall support for being tough on crime.

To evaluate this argument, Figure 4.6 plots the public's punitiveness and the amount of news coverage of crime from 1950 to 1982 (to aid comparison, the series have been standardized to a common range). Consistent with expectations, a strong relationship emerges. Public attitudes appear to follow a few years behind news coverage, with declining punitiveness in the 1950s and increasing punitiveness in the 1960s. We should be careful, however,

---

[14] Although not the focus here, more news stories about crime could also have an agenda-setting effect, where the public views crime as a more important issue area, and a priming effect (Iyengar and Kinder 1987). For Iyengar and Kinder (1987), priming occurs when more news coverage of a topic leads the public to place more weight on that topic when evaluating political figures and policies.

[15] See Chaiken and Trope (1999) for an overview of dual-process models.

not to overemphasize the apparent low point in the public's punitiveness in 1966. Due to a scarcity of survey questions that relate to punitiveness in the early 1960s, the estimates during these years contain more measurement error than we would like. We can be very confident in the declining punitiveness through the 1950s and the rising punitiveness in the mid 1960s and through the 1970s. These overall patterns are based on numerous survey questions and thousands of survey responses.[16] Unfortunately, however, the data do not allow us to pinpoint the exact nadir of the public's punitiveness. Our inability to pinpoint the precise year the public's punitiveness began to rise is relevant because the evidence in the previous chapter suggested that Goldwater and Johnson noticed rising public concern and punitiveness in 1964. It appears that the lack of opinion data in the early 1960s leads us to depict the rise in the public's punitiveness as occurring slightly later than it actually did.[17] The overall pattern, however, is clear. In the 1960s, news coverage of crime went up and the public's punitiveness followed.

The 1960s were a tumultuous era. In the midst of rising crime rates, the civil rights movement, and the Vietnam War, in 1963 the public witnessed the assassination of President Kennedy. Malcolm X's assassination followed in 1965 and then in 1968 both Dr. Martin Luther King Jr. and Robert Kennedy were assassinated. During this period, the public also witnessed urban riots and the National Guard response. Certainly, the confluence of these events played a role in the public's punitive response to rising crime rates. The right portion of Figure 4.6 and the subsequent analyses show, however, that the relationship between crime, news coverage, and the public's punitiveness was not limited to the 1960s. Thus, while these historical conditions certainly mattered, the relatively consistent over-time relationship suggests that the public response to news coverage of crime was not limited to a specific historical period.

The close correspondence between the amount of news reporting on crime and the public's punitiveness also speaks to the literature on moral panics (e.g., Best 2011, Cohen 1972, Hall et al. 1978, Tonry 2004). Moral panic refers to a media- and elite-led public reaction to an event that "is out of all proportion to the actual threat offered" (Hall et al. 1978, p. 16). While moral panics can certainly reinforce or perhaps even serve as a catalyst to the relationship between crime and punitive attitudes, the relatively consistent relationship between crime news and punitive attitudes in Figure 4.6 suggests that moral panics do not fully explain shifts in the public's punitiveness.[18] If moral panics were the main factor at work, we would expect short-lived spikes

---

[16]   Specifically, the estimates from the late 1950s, mid 1960s, and early 1970s are based on 6,563, 11,751, and 13,983 survey responses, respectively.

[17]   To ensure that this possibility does not affect the conclusions of the statistical analysis, Appendix A-4.1 conducts an additional analysis, analyzing data only from 1967 to 2010. The results remain unchanged.

[18]   This perspective is consistent with Tonry's (2004, ch.4) view that the effect of moral panics depends on the presence of a "window of opportunity."

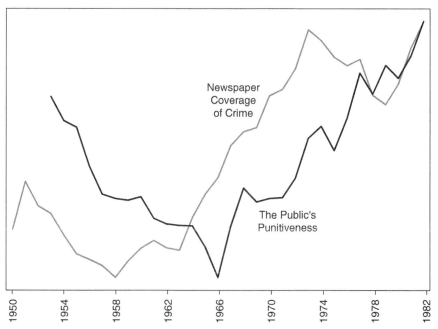

FIGURE 4.6. The relationship between newspaper coverage of crime and the public's punitiveness from 1950 to 1982.

Source: Newspapers were accessed through ProQuest Historical Newspapers. The opinion data were described in Chapter 2.

in news coverage and punitiveness. Instead, Figure 4.6 shows a roughly steady increase in news coverage of crime and the public's punitiveness that lasted more than a decade. The public may have reacted out of proportion to the actual threat, but the relationship between news coverage and punitiveness appears quite consistent over time.

4.4 THE RISE OF CRIME DRAMAS ON TV

As suggested at the start of Chapter 2, the news is not the only information source on crime. Since the 1950s, crime dramas have pulled in high ratings for the television networks (Snauffer 2006). The popularity of these shows raises the question of whether crime dramas have also influenced the public's attitudes or whether these television programs have been a response to the public's interests and concerns. The quote from Steve Jobs that opened Chapter 2 suggested that the television networks follow the public and "give people exactly what they want." Research suggests, however, that these shows can lead to more punitive attitudes among viewers (Beale 2006, Gilliam and Iyengar

2000, Holbrook and Hill 2005, Mutz and Nir 2010). Thus, we might expect the prevalence of crime dramas and the public's punitiveness to be mutually reinforcing.

In order to analyze the potential influence of crime television, I obtained the Nielsen Television Index National Ranking Report for the Top 20 Prime Time Programs from 1960 to 2010.[19] I then classified each show by the type of program (crime drama, Western, sitcom, reality-based show, sports, etc.). After identifying the crime dramas, for each year, I summed the percentage of households tuned in to a crime show during the average minute to create an annual indicator of the number of households watching crime dramas. Figure 4.7 reports this measure of the proportion of households watching crime dramas along with the crime rate and the public's punitiveness from 1960 to 1990. All series have been standardized to a common minimum and maximum value.

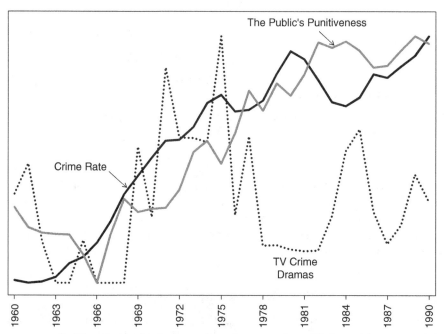

FIGURE 4.7. The relationship between the crime rate, the public's punitiveness, and the proportion of households watching crime dramas from 1960 to 1990.

Source: The crime rate is based on the FBI Uniform Crime Reports. The opinion data were described in Chapter 2. Television viewership data come from the Nielsen Television Index National Ranking Report for the Top 20 Prime Time Programs.

---

[19] Data prior to 1960 are not available.

As noted earlier, we do not know the exact year the public's punitiveness began to increase, but the data suggest that the crime rate began to increase first, followed by the public's punitiveness, and then we see a steep uptick in the popularity of crime dramas in 1969. Through the mid 1970s, all three series continued to increase. The crime rate and the public's punitiveness continued to rise through 1990, but in the late 1970s, viewership of crime dramas dropped substantially. This decline likely stems, at least in part, from the short-lived family viewership hour, which replaced popular prime-time shows with more family-oriented programming. This disconnect between the declining popularity of crime dramas and the public's rising punitiveness suggests that over-time shifts in the public's punitiveness were much more closely related to the crime rate than crime television. This does not mean that crime dramas have no effect on public opinion. By contrast, those directly exposed to crime dramas are more likely to express punitive attitudes (e.g., Mutz and Nir 2010). But it does appear that crime dramas were not a major player in the rise of punitive attitudes and the expansion of the carceral state.

4.5 CRIME, NEWS, AND THE DEVELOPMENT OF A LAW AND ORDER SOCIETY FROM 1950 TO 2010

The 1960s and 1970s set the foundation for the expansion of the US carceral state. The previous figures examined this time period in order to see how crime, news coverage of crime, crime dramas on television, and the public's punitiveness moved during these critical years. We saw that beginning in the 1960s, the crime rate rose dramatically and the news media and the public noticed. Television programming showed some overlap with these series in the 1970s, but not so much in the 1960s or 1980s.

In this section, I extend the period of inquiry to 2010 and conduct a statistical analysis of these relationships. The empirical analysis ensures that the patterns observed earlier meet statistical standards of scrutiny and that they apply to the entire period of interest. I begin with an analysis of the crime rate, news coverage of crime, the proportion of households watching crime dramas on television, and the public's punitiveness. I then add two measures of political attention to crime to control for the possibility that the public was simply following the lead of political elites.

Table 4.2 examines the relationships between the crime rate, news coverage of crime, television crime dramas, and the public's punitiveness. I use Granger causality tests to evaluate the over-time relationships between these variables. Granger causality tests assess whether past values of a variable (such as news coverage of crime) are statistically related to another variable (such as the public's punitiveness) when controlling for past values of that variable. If knowing the previous values of crime news coverage (when controlling for past values of the public's punitiveness) helps us predict current values of the public's punitiveness, we say that news coverage Granger-causes the public's punitiveness.[20]

Column 1 reports whether past values of crime news, crime dramas, and the crime rate correspond with the public's support for being tough on crime. The values in the table are *p*-values. Values below 0.05 indicate a statistically significant relationship and provide evidence of Granger causality. Thus, the results in Column 1 provide compelling evidence that past values of the crime rate and news coverage of crime Granger-cause the public's punitiveness. These findings reinforce the visual impressions in Figures 4.5 and 4.6, further supporting the claim that public attitudes reflect shifts in the actual crime rate. This relationship is unlikely to be direct, however. King and Maruna (2009) show that criminal victimization is not a good predictor of punitiveness. The evidence of a direct relationship between the crime rate and punitive attitudes in Table 4.2 likely results because the measure of crime news does not capture all of the crime-related news information that the public receives.

Although not quite statistically significant ($p = 0.08$), the evidence is suggestive that public attitudes also follow television crime dramas. Figure 4.7 intentionally focused on the 1960s, 1970s, and 1980s in order to highlight the relationship between crime television and the public's attitudes during the onset of mass incarceration. We saw that during the late 1970s, despite declining viewership of crime dramas on television, punitive attitudes continued to rise. However, when we consider the entire time period, the relationship is more complex. This full analysis offers suggestive evidence regarding the potential influence of crime dramas on the public's punitiveness.

Two other important results stand out in Table 4.2. First, consistent with expectations, in Column 2 we see evidence that crime news does indeed track the crime rate ($p = 0.056$). Second, in Column 3 television crime dramas appear to track the public's punitiveness. This could result because more crime drama programming appears during prime time as the public becomes more punitive, or because the public gravitates toward crime shows when concerned with crime. Either way, viewership of crime dramas appears to follow punitive attitudes. Not surprisingly, the variables in the statistical analysis do not predict the actual crime rate. That is, the actual crime rate does not respond to news coverage of crime, television crime dramas, or public attitudes. Although the causes of changing crime rates are multifaceted (e.g., Farrall and Jennings 2012) – and beyond the scope of this book – economic conditions are thought to be an important determinant of the crime rate (Chiricos 1987, Hale 1998, Jennings, Farrall, and Bevan 2012, Rosenfeld and Fornango 2007) and are thus controlled for in the analyses in subsequent chapters. Interestingly, the

---

[20] The first step is to estimate a Vector Autoregressive (VAR) model. The VAR model regresses each variable on lagged values of that variable and lagged values of the other variables. A Granger test is then conducted. See, for example, Granger (1969, 2004).

TABLE 4.2. *The relationship between the crime rate, news coverage of crime, television crime dramas, and public opinion from 1960 to 2010*

	The public's punitiveness	Crime news	Television crime dramas	Crime rate
The public's punitiveness	–	0.401	0.048	0.118
Crime news	0.015	–	0.311	0.606
TV crime dramas	0.080	0.097	–	0.285
Crime rate	0.000	0.056	0.758	–

Note: Table cells indicate the probability that lagged values of the predictor variable do *not* influence the dependent variable (thus, values <0.05 indicate a significant relationship). Results are based on a Granger test following a VAR model.

Great Recession in 2008 and 2009 appears to be a prominent exception to the relationship between economic conditions and crime rates (Uggen 2012).

Tables 4.3 and 4.4 introduce two measures of political elite influence to the analysis. The first measure is the percentage of congressional hearings devoted to issues of crime and punishment. I select congressional hearings as a measure of political behavior for two reasons.[21] First, congressional hearings are substantively important. Hearings signal legislative attention to an issue (Jones and Baumgartner 2005, p. 185) and they have been linked to program creation and expansion (Baumgartner and Jones 1993). Second, congressional hearings are highly visible (Iyengar 2011, pp. 217–219), and thus offer a clean test of the elite leadership hypothesis. The second measure of potential political elite influence captures all presidential statements on crime during the period of analysis. Mark Ramirez (2013) has identified every presidential statement regarding "crime" or "criminal behavior" and then coded each sentence mentioning these words as either emphasizing a punitive frame, a treatment frame (which focused on the need to deal with the roots of criminal activity), or neither frame.[22] The result is an over-time measure of how

[21] The congressional hearings data come from the Policy Agendas Project. To limit the focus to congressional hearings on criminal issues, I used the general topic "Law, Crime, and Family Issues" but excluded the subtopic "Family Issues." The data were originally collected by Frank R. Baumgartner and Bryan D. Jones, with the support of National Science Foundation grant number SBR 9320922, and were distributed through the Department of Government at the University of Texas at Austin and/or the Department of Political Science at Penn State University. Neither NSF nor the original collectors of the data bear any responsibility for the analysis reported here.

[22] These data are available through 2006. The original data are from the Public Papers of the President compiled by the Office of the Federal Register, National Archives, and Records

TABLE 4.3. *The relationship between the crime rate, news coverage of crime, public opinion, and congressional attention to crime from 1953 to 2010*

	Congressional hearings on crime	The public's punitiveness	Crime news	Crime rate
Congressional hearings	–	0.074	0.974	0.160
The public's punitiveness	0.013	–	0.624	0.335
Crime news	0.027	0.000	–	0.292
Crime rate	0.988	0.000	0.025	–

Note: Table cells indicate the probability that lagged values of the predictor variable do *not* influence the dependent variable (thus, values <0.05 indicate a significant relationship). Results are based on a Granger test following a VAR model.

TABLE 4.4. *The relationship between the crime rate, news coverage of crime, public opinion, and presidential rhetoric on crime from 1953 to 2006*

	Presidential tone on crime	The public's punitiveness	Crime news	Crime rate
Presidential tone	–	0.063	0.389	0.665
The public's punitiveness	0.026	–	0.539	0.257
Crime news	0.024	0.070	–	0.717
Crime rate	0.060	0.000	0.046	–

Note: Table cells indicate the probability that lagged values of the predictor variable do *not* influence the dependent variable (thus, values <0.05 indicate a significant relationship). Results are based on a Granger test following a VAR model.

punitive presidential statements on crime were each year. Again, this measure is advantageous because presidential statements are regularly covered in the news and are thus highly visible to the public.

Table 4.3 presents the results using congressional hearings on crime as the measure of political attention to crime. In order to analyze all available data, this model does not include crime dramas because the television ratings data go back only to 1960. Looking at Column 1, we see evidence that public support for being tough on crime Granger-causes congressional attention to crime issues ($p = 0.013$). This result is consistent with the findings in Chapter 3.

Administration. Punitive frames coincided with statements that emphasized the permissiveness of the judicial system (and thus the need to do more). Treatment frames emphasized the need to deal with the roots of criminal activity.

It appears that political attention to crime followed the public's punitiveness. We also see that congressional hearings on crime issues followed news coverage of crime ($p = 0.027$). Looking at Column 2, although the Granger test is not statistically significant, we see some evidence that congressional hearings influence the public's attitudes ($p = 0.074$). This result offers some support to previous research that argues that politicians have influenced the public's punitiveness (e.g., Beckett 1997, Beckett and Sasson 2004, Weaver 2007). Interestingly, in Column 3, we do not see evidence that congressional hearings on crime influence news coverage of crime ($p = 0.974$). Most Americans do not directly experience congressional hearings. Thus, any influence of congressional hearings would be mediated by news coverage. The fact that we do not find evidence that news coverage of crime followed congressional hearings complicates the political leadership hypothesis.[23]

Looking at Columns 2 and 3, we see evidence that both crime news and the crime rate influence the public's punitiveness and that the crime rate influences news coverage of crime. The analysis strongly reinforces the visual impressions provided by the figures earlier in this chapter. Crime rates appear to influence news coverage, which influences the public's punitiveness, which influences government action. Political activity may reinforce these relationships, but overall, the results are consistent with expectations. As in Table 4.2, in the final column we do not observe any statistically significant relationships, suggesting that the variables in the model do not help explain the crime rate.

Table 4.4 includes an alternate measure of political rhetoric, the tone of presidential speeches about crime. The presidential tone variable is advantageous because the media's attention to the president means this is a most likely case for the political elite leadership hypothesis. This analysis ends in 2006 because that is the final year for which we have data on the tone of presidential crime mentions (Ramirez 2013).

The results reinforce the findings in Table 4.3. In Column 1, the evidence suggests that whether presidents take a punitive or treatment-oriented position on crime depends on the public's preferences ($p = 0.026$), news coverage of crime ($p = 0.024$), and possibly the crime rate ($p = 0.060$). In Column 2, the evidence suggests that in addition to responding to the crime rate ($p = 0.000$) and crime news ($p = 0.070$), the public's punitiveness may also reflect presidential tone ($p = 0.063$). This result is consistent with Ramirez (2013). Again, however, the influence of presidential rhetoric is complicated by the results in Column 3, which imply that presidential rhetoric does *not* influence news coverage of crime ($p = 0.389$). Thus, the results in Column 2 are consistent with political rhetoric reinforcing the public's attitudes, but we do not find evidence of the expected mechanism. We do find evidence, however,

---

[23] Appendix A-4.1 estimates additional VAR models and Granger tests to ensure that these conclusions are robust to alternate model specifications. The evidence in support of the public opinion hypothesis is even stronger in these alternate specifications.

that news coverage reflects the actual crime rate. Not surprisingly, according to Column 4, presidential tone, the public's punitiveness, and news coverage of crime do not influence the actual crime rate.

4.6 CONCLUSION

The news consistently misses the mark on crime, drawing a disproportionate amount of attention to violent crimes and crimes committed by people of color. This leads to the well-known result that the public overestimates the amount of violent crime and disproportionately associates African Americans and other racial minorities with criminal activity. Yet we have also seen that shifts in news coverage of crime and shifts in the public's punitiveness track the actual crime rate. The analysis suggests that during the past sixty years, when news covered crime, the public noticed and adjusted its preferences accordingly. This is an important result that substantially revises conventional wisdom about the relationship between crime rates, media coverage, and public punitiveness.

Yet a systematic response to increases and decreases in media coverage of the crime rate does not necessarily imply a rational or well-informed response. If the news media relied on different crime frames, increased (decreased) crime coverage would not necessarily provoke more (less) support for being tough on crime. For example, if news coverage of crime emphasized thematic frames, perhaps focusing on the causes of crime, ways to prevent crime, or imperfections in the judicial system, we would *not* expect more news coverage of crime to automatically translate to more punitive attitudes. Baumgartner, De Boef, and Boydstun (2008) show that this is precisely what happened with media coverage and public support for the death penalty. During the mid 1990s, media coverage of the death penalty began to emphasize what they call the "innocence" frame. That is, news coverage of the death penalty increasingly emphasized imperfections in the justice system, evidence of innocence through exonerations, and humanizing portrayals of defendants. As this shift occurred, public support for the death penalty began to decline.[24] Of course, the innocence frame is not independent from the crime rate. As crime rates decreased, media were more likely to emphasize the innocence frame when reporting on the death penalty. Indeed, between 1980 and 2005, the correlation between the crime rate and the innocence frame was an impressive $r = 0.86$. This relationship reinforces the chapter's findings regarding news coverage of crime and its influence on public opinion. Just as important, however, if media portrayals of crime and the broader criminal justice system (not just the death penalty) included the innocence frame and provided more accurate and nuanced depictions of crime, more news coverage and more information could lead to *less* punitive attitudes.

---

[24] See also, Baumgartner, Linn, and Boydstun (2010) and Dardis et al. (2008).

We should also keep in mind that news coverage of crime is not the only factor influencing the public's attitudes. Although the results were less consistent, we saw some evidence that television crime dramas and political elite rhetoric might reinforce the public's punitiveness. Furthermore, these relationships may vary over time.[25] In her analysis of public perceptions of whether crime is the most important problem, Beckett (1997) finds different patterns for 1964 through 1974 and 1985 through 1992. Indeed, the changing media environment, strengthening partisan attachments, and evolving tough-on-crime rhetoric could all influence the strength of the relationships observed in this chapter. Nevertheless, the rising crime rate and corresponding news coverage appear to have substantially influenced the public's punitiveness during the rise of mass incarceration (i.e., Figures 4.5 and 4.6). Furthermore, the various statistical results reported in this chapter and the appendix to this chapter cover a range of time periods (i.e., 1953 to 2010, 1953 to 2006, 1960 to 2010, and 1967 to 2010), suggesting that crime and news coverage of crime have consistently influenced the public's punitiveness during the past sixty years.

Two other important lessons emerge from this chapter. First, crime rates move in very similar ways in the United States. This conclusion holds for analyses of violent crime rates and property crime rates, as well as crime rates in the states and urban centers. Some important differences exist, but similar trajectories are the norm. These commonalities hold implications for news coverage of crime. They also hold implications for how we understand the causes of crime. If crime moves in similar ways across regions, we cannot think of crime as a completely local issue (McDowall and Loftins 2009). This fact implies that we cannot evaluate the success (or failure) of local crime initiatives – such as rising or falling crime rates in a particular city – without considering the broader social and structural forces that influence common national trends in criminal activity (Tonry 2004, p. 98).

The second lesson is a methodological point about content analysis. We saw that knowing how many news articles mentioned a single word, like "unemployment," "inflation," and "crime," provided an impressive measure of objective conditions. These words are unique in that they relate directly to the topic of interest and that they are unlikely to appear in news stories about other issues. Nevertheless, this type of content analysis may prove fruitful for other topics. For example, immigration is another issue where a single word likely signals the topic and may correspond with a specific type of media frame. Particularly for extended periods of time and historical analyses, knowing how many articles mentioned a particular word can provide an excellent measure of news coverage of that topic.

---

[25] Research shows, for example, that the strength of the relationship between objective economic conditions and economic evaluations can vary over time (Enns and McAvoy 2012).

A-4   APPENDIX TO CHAPTER 4

A-4.1 Robustness of the Granger causality analysis

In order to evaluate the robustness of the previous findings, I replicate the VAR analyses and Granger tests in this chapter, excluding the measure of news coverage of crime. This measure has several desirable properties. First, the analysis of "unemployment" and "inflation" demonstrated that knowing how many articles mention a particular word can offer an excellent measure of objective conditions. Second, consistent with expectations, Figure 4.6 and Tables 4.3 and 4.4 showed that news coverage of crime follows the actual crime rate. Nevertheless, any measure of news coverage will contain some measurement error. Thus, an alternate strategy is to simply estimate the statistical model excluding crime news coverage, allowing the crime rate to directly influence the public's attitudes, congressional hearings, and presidential statements. We know that the public and members of Congress do not directly experience all crime. Thus, news coverage undoubtedly mediates any such relationship. However, by allowing a direct statistical relationship, we ensure that the measurement of news coverage does not drive the previous results.

The results reinforce the earlier findings and further support the public opinion hypothesis. We again see evidence that public opinion follows the crime rate and informs congressional hearings on crime. However, we no longer see evidence that congressional hearings influence the public. This result runs counter to the political elite leadership hypothesis.

Another consideration is the timing of the analysis. This chapter mentioned that we cannot precisely identify the exact change in the public's punitiveness in the early 1960s because of the sparsity of repeated questions during these years. To ensure that this period does not drive the conclusions we reach, I repeated the analysis in Table A-4.1, excluding the years prior to 1967. These results,

TABLE A-4.1. *The relationship between the crime rate, public opinion, and congressional attention to crime from 1953 to 2010*

	The public's punitiveness	Congressional hearings on crime	Crime rate
The public's punitiveness	–	0.044	0.170
Congressional hearings	0.279	–	0.447
Crime rate	0.000	0.169	–

Note: Table cells indicate the probability that lagged values of the predictor variable do *not* influence the dependent variable (thus, values <0.05 indicate a significant relationship). Results are based on a Granger test following a VAR model.

TABLE A-4.2. *The relationship between the crime rate, public opinion, and congressional attention to crime from 1967 to 2010*

	The public's punitiveness	Congressional hearings on crime	Crime rate
The public's punitiveness	–	0.023	0.086
Congressional hearings	0.286	–	0.599
Crime rate	0.000	0.012	–

Note: Table cells indicate the probability that lagged values of the predictor variable do *not* influence the dependent variable (thus, values <0.05 indicate a significant relationship). Results are based on a Granger test following a VAR model.

which appear in Table A-4.2, are nearly identical, indicating that the early period is not driving the findings. Together, the results in Tables A-4.1 and A-4.2 strongly support this chapter's conclusions about the public's response to criminal activity and the lack of public response to political elites.

5

Democracy at work? Public opinion and mass incarceration

> It's clear – as we come together today – that too many Americans go to too many prisons for far too long, and for no truly good law enforcement reason.
>
> Attorney General Eric H. Holder Jr. (August 12, 2013)[1]

The incarceration rate has gone up. Way up. And the consequences have been stark. As we saw in Chapter 1, between the early 1970s and 2000, the US incarceration rate increased by 400 percent. Although the United States comprises less than 5 percent of the world's population, almost 25 percent of the world's prison population now resides in US jails and prisons.[2] We also saw that the growing incarceration rate spawned massive economic, social, and political costs, while offering limited and contingent benefits (at best) for crime reduction. Equally important, the social and political costs of mass incarceration have been disproportionately borne by racial minorities and those with the lowest income and education levels.

To gain a sense of the concentrated effects of the carceral state, Figure 5.1 reproduces an image generated by Eric Cadora and Laura Kurgan (2006).[3]

Sections 2.4 and 5.2 include material previously published in Enns, Peter K. 2014. "The Public's Increasing Punitiveness and Its Influence on Mass Incarceration in the United States." *American Journal of Political Science* 58(4):857–872. Reprinted with permission.

[1] Remarks to the Annual Meeting of the American Bar Association's House of Delegates (www .justice.gov/iso/opa/ag/speeches/2013/ag-speech-130812.html).

[2] Prison population data from Walmsley (2009). World population data from *The World Factbook 2013-14*. Washington, DC: Central Intelligence Agency, 2013 (www.cia.gov/library/ publications/the-world-factbook/index.html).

[3] Also see the Justice Mapping Center (www.justicemapping.org/), where Cadora and Charles Swartz document the geographic patterns of incarceration and criminal justice in the United States. Cadora developed "Justice Mapping" in 1998 while working with the Center for Alternative Sentencing and Employment Services under a Community Justice grant of the Open Society Institute.

This figure presents a white dot for each individual from Brooklyn, New York, who was admitted to prison in 2003. Before examining this figure, it is worth considering that in 2000, 29.1 percent of Brooklyn families with children were below the poverty line. The corresponding percentage in poverty for families with a female householder (no husband present) was 44.2 percent. Also of note, 36.4 percent of Brooklyn residents were black or African American and 19.8 percent of residents were Latino.[4] These demographic characteristics matter because, as noted earlier, the rise of mass incarceration has occurred unevenly. Even after controlling for actual crime rates, racial minorities and individuals of low socioeconomic position are disproportionately imprisoned.

Figure 5.1 illustrates these patterns in striking fashion. Not only were Brooklyn residents sentenced to prison at a high rate in 2003, but even within Brooklyn, the patterns of incarceration are concentrated. The dots are clustered in neighborhoods like Bushwick, Bedford Stuyvesant, East New York, Brownsville, Crown Heights, and Flatbush, which also have the highest concentration of black residents and residents in poverty (Cadora, Gordon, and Swartz 2002). If we were to zoom in farther, the concentration of the homes where someone had been incarcerated would appear even more shocking. In one *two-block* area, Cadora and Kurgan found that thirty-one men were currently imprisoned at a cost of $4.4 million per year. Cadora and Kurgan have identified these "million dollar blocks" – single blocks in urban neighborhoods where at least $1 million is spent each year to imprison its residents – concentrated in Brooklyn as well as in cities throughout the country.

Chapter 1 showed how rising incarceration rates have been linked to reduced financial support for higher education, strains on the health care system, and even the outcome of the 2000 presidential campaign. Thus, the fiscal, social, and political consequences of mass incarceration affect all Americans. Yet, despite these broad effects, the focus on Brooklyn and its neighborhoods reminds us that the costs of mass incarceration are not distributed equally. Some individuals, families, and neighborhoods are much more likely than others to experience the carceral state and its consequences. If we want to understand the costs of mass incarceration – especially the social costs – it is crucial to focus on the local level. However, to understand the *causes* of mass incarceration, this chapter takes a step back to the macro perspective. Specifically, I examine changes in the *overall* federal and state incarceration rates. From this macro perspective, the goal is to understand why the United States has become the world's most prolific imprisoner.

As this chapter begins to answer this question, the following pages make several important contributions to the criminal justice literature. First, I explain that in order to understand the incarceration rate, we must study *changes* in the rate of incarcerations. While this may seem like a relatively straightforward

---

4   Data from the US Census Bureau (http://factfinder.census.gov/faces/nav/jsf/pages/index.xhtml).

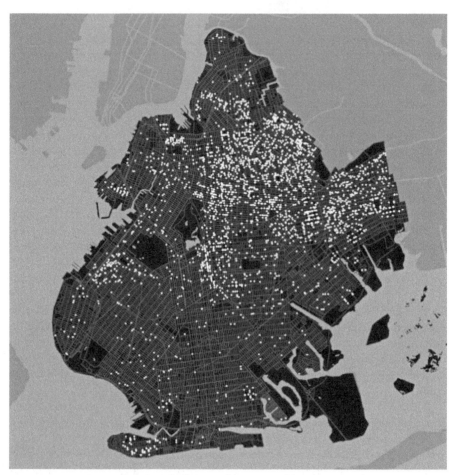

FIGURE 5.1. Prison admissions by home address, Brooklyn, New York, 2003.

Source: The Spatial Information Design Lab, Columbia University Graduate School of Architecture, Planning, and Preservation (www.spatialinformationdesignlab.org/ MEDIA/PDF_04.pdf).

proposition, this approach radically shifts our understanding of how criminal activity relates to criminal justice outcomes. Second, I offer new evidence that during the early 1970s, illegal drug use was a serious concern facing politicians and the country. Third, this chapter offers a direct test of this book's central argument: that public support for being tough on crime has been a driving force in the rise of mass incarceration. In Chapter 4 we learned *why* the public's punitiveness has shifted over time and in Chapter 3 we saw how politicians responded to these punitive shifts. Here, we learn how these attitudes influenced the overall US incarceration rate. Chapter 6 will then narrow the geographic focus to examine the relationship between the public's punitiveness, criminal justice policy, and incarceration rates in the fifty states.

5.1   THE IMPORTANCE OF ANALYZING *CHANGES* IN THE INCARCERATION RATE

A central puzzle in criminal justice research is the seemingly weak relationship between the crime rate and the incarceration rate. As economist Glenn Loury (2010, p. 135) writes, "For two generations, crime rates have fluctuated with no apparent relationship to a steady climb in the extent of imprisonment." Figure 5.2 demonstrates this weak relationship by plotting the crime rate analyzed in the previous chapter and the total state and federal incarceration rate.[5] Notice how the crime rate (dashed line) began to rise in the early 1960s, well over a decade before the incarceration rate (solid line) began to increase. Furthermore, although the crime rate began to drop in the early 1990s, the incarceration rate continued to rise for almost fifteen more years.[6]

Although scholars have typically concluded that the patterns in Figure 5.2 indicate a weak relationship (at best) between the crime rate and the incarceration rate, focusing on the overall incarceration rate in this way can lead to misleading conclusions about the causes of mass incarceration. There are two reasons why focusing on the overall incarceration rate can lead to incorrect inferences. First, we must recognize that a primary way social and political factors influence the incarceration rate is through new admittances (Wacquant 2010).

Suppose, for example, that the crime rate *does* influence the incarceration rate. We would expect an increase (decrease) in crime to correspond with more (fewer) new incarcerations. Similarly, if – as hypothesized – the incarceration rate reflects shifts in the public's support for being tough on crime, whether through increased criminal justice budgets, tougher sentencing laws, or prosecutors and judges paying attention to their political environment, an increase (decrease) in the public's punitiveness should correspond with more (fewer) new incarcerations. The problem with analyzing the incarceration rate is that the overall incarceration rate can move in the *opposite* direction as the rate of new incarcerations.

The disconnect between the incarceration rate and the rate of new incarcerations results because the prison system admitted more individuals than it released every year since the 1970s.[7] Even if the rate of *new* incarcerations remained the same or *declined*, the *total* incarceration rate would still *increase*

---

5   See Clear and Frost (2014, pp. 34–35), Gottschalk (2006, p. 24), Lerman (2013, p. 25), Shannon and Uggen (2013), Travis, Western, and Redburn (2014), Western (2006), and Zimring and Hawkins (1991) for similar evidence of this weak relationship.

6   To facilitate comparison, the two series have been standardized to a common range.

7   In fact, this is the case every year from 1978 to 2008 (Carson and Golinelli 2013). Admissions data before this period are not directly comparable (Statistical Abstract of the United States 1980, p. 200).

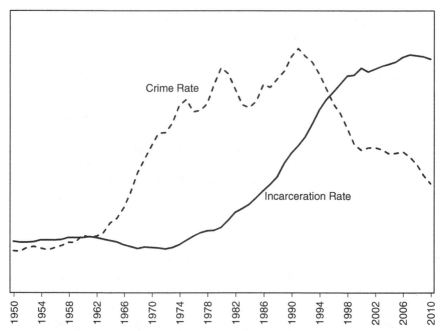

FIGURE 5.2. The crime rate and the incarceration rate from 1950 to 2010.

Source: Crime Rate: Social Indicators, 1973 and Sourcebook of Criminal Justice Statistics, Table 3.106.2011; Incarceration Rate: Sourcebook of Criminal Justice Statistics Online, Table 6.28.10.

because the system admitted more inmates than it let go. Table 5.1 demonstrates this point empirically by analyzing the incarceration rate from 1978 to 2000. In Column 1 we see that after controlling for a linear time trend, no empirical relationship exists between the rate of new admissions and the overall incarceration rate. The coefficient is near zero (−0.04) and imprecisely estimated (the 95 percent confidence interval ranges from −0.34 to 0.26). Of course, new admissions influence the incarceration rate, but we do not observe such a relationship because regardless of whether the rate of new incarcerations increased, decreased, or remained the same, the incarceration rate increased each year.

We can obviate this problem, however, by analyzing changes in the incarceration rate. *Changes* in the incarceration rate will reflect new incarcerations, as more (fewer) admissions will correspond with larger (smaller) changes in the incarceration rate. Indeed, Column 2 in Table 5.1 shows that a strong and significant relationship exists between the rate of new admittances and changes in the incarceration rate, even when controlling for a linear time trend. As expected, the magnitude of this relationship is quite substantial. These results reflect the fact that more (fewer) admissions correspond with a larger (smaller)

TABLE 5.1. *The relationship between prison admissions, the incarceration rate, and the change in the incarceration rate from 1978 to 2000*

	(1) Incarceration rate	(2) Δ Incarceration rate
Admission rate	−0.04	2.85*
	(0.14)	(0.74)
Year	0.13*	−0.33*
	(0.02)	(0.10)
Constant	−2.00*	5.38*
	(0.28)	(1.48)
R^2	0.98	0.51
N	23	22

Note: Ordinary least squares (OLS) coefficients with standard errors in parentheses * = $p < .05$, two-tailed significance levels. To facilitate comparison, incarceration variables have been scaled to a standard deviation of one.

increase in the incarceration rate. In sum, to understand the determinants of mass incarceration, we must analyze *changes* in the incarceration rate.[8]

Analyzing changes in the incarceration rate also addresses another important consideration. Just like the overall incarceration rate can increase even if the rate of new prison admissions declines, the rate of *new admissions* can increase even if the crime rate (or other factors related to the incarceration rate) declines. The return to prison for parole violations is one mechanism that can produce this result. Consider that in 1978, 15.7 percent of the 152,039 admissions to state and federal prisons were parole violations. By contrast, in 1998, out of 603,510 new admissions, the percent of parole violations constituted 34.8 percent of these admissions. This represents a shift in admissions from parole violations from 23,870 to 210,021 in a twenty-year period (Carson and Golinelli 2013).

Many of these reentries to prison were for technical violations, *not* for new crimes committed. Technical violations of parole occur when a parolee does not comply with his or her supervision conditions, such as being employed,

---

[8] If all (or most) sentences were for a year or less, analyzing change would not be necessary. A decline in the rate of new admissions would correspond with a decline in the overall incarceration rate. This, of course, is not the case in the United States. This is the case, however, in Canada, where in 2010/11 more than 90 percent of custodial sentences were for one year or less (Dauvergne 2012, p. 12). For this reason, Figure 2.7, in Chapter 2, examined the incarceration rate, not the change in incarcerations.

attending parole officer meetings, attending substance abuse or other treatment sessions, fulfilling community service requirements, or paying fines. Technical violations account for a substantial proportion of parolee returns to prison. For example, a 2004 report by the North Carolina Sentencing and Policy Advisory Commission found that among those released from prison, 26.1 percent were returned to prison within four years for a technical revocation (Ebron et al. 2004). A 2006 report commissioned by the Kansas Department of Corrections found that among those returned to prison during parole, 93 percent were for technical revocations (Bryl and Fabelo 2006). During sustained increases in the incarceration rate, the number of recent parolees who could be re-incarcerated for technical violations will increase. Because technical violations do not involve a new crime, the rate of new admissions could increase independently of the crime rate.

The increase in guilty pleas during the past several decades offers another example of how admission rates do not necessarily reflect the amount of criminal activity. Figure 5.3 shows how the percent of individuals pleading guilty in US district courts increased from 77 percent in 1980 to 97 percent in 2010.[9] The rise of strict sentencing is one reason for this increase. Defendants have learned that if they go to trial and are found guilty they are very likely to receive the maximum possible sentence. Another reason to plead guilty is that prosecutors will sometimes prosecute for a more severe crime if the case goes to trial. The insufficient number of public defenders also increases the proportion of guilty pleas. Importantly, as the proportion of guilty pleas increases, even if the arrest rate holds constant or declines, the rate of new prison admissions can increase because a higher proportion of those arrested are pleading guilty and serving time.

Parole revocations and guilty please are important components of the criminal justice system and they are clearly related to the overall incarceration rate. However, the over-time dynamics described earlier would conceal the potential relationship between prison admissions and the crime rate or the public's punitive attitudes. Again, analyzing changes in the incarceration rate can obviate this problem. To understand why, consider the previously discussed scenario. I have proposed that new admissions, which influence the incarceration rate, reflect factors such as the number of parolees and the proportion of guilty pleas, as well as the crime rate and the public's punitiveness. The rising frequency of guilty pleas and the increasing number of parolees led to a growing rate of admissions during most of the period of analysis. If the crime rate and the public's punitiveness also increased, the rate of admissions (and the overall incarceration rate) would increase even more. The change in the incarceration rate would correctly capture this pattern. Now suppose the crime

---

9 Data are from Table 5.22.2010 of the *Sourcebook of Criminal Justice Statistics Online*. Percentages do not include cases that were dismissed, which constituted 8 percent of all cases in 2010.

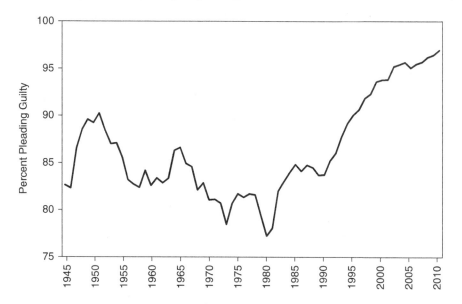

FIGURE 5.3. The percent of guilty pleas in US district courts from 1945 to 2010.

Source: Sourcebook of Criminal Justice Statistics Online, Table 5.22.2010.

rate and the public's punitiveness declined. The admissions rate and the overall incarceration rate would still increase, just to a lesser extent, still moving in the opposite direction of the crime rate and the public's preferences. However, the *change* in the incarceration rate would be less than the previous year, again reflecting the influence of crime and public opinion.[10]

These arguments suggest that if we want to understand the determinants of mass incarceration, we must analyze changes to the incarceration rate. Figure 5.4 revisits the relationship between the crime rate and the incarceration rate, this time plotting the *change* in the incarceration rate. A close correspondence emerges. The correlation between the crime rate and the incarceration rate in Figure 5.2 was $r = 0.31$. The correlation between the crime rate and changes in the incarceration rate in Figure 5.4 is a notable $r = 0.72$. This strong relationship significantly revises conventional wisdom, which maintains that the relationship between crime and incarcerations is weak, at best. Despite the emergence of this relationship, we know that the crime rate is not the whole story. In Chapter 1 we saw that the number of prisoners per crime committed

[10] Interestingly, there is little cost to relying on the change in the incarceration rate. Suppose the crime rate was the only factor that influenced the incarceration rate. Increases (decreases) in crime would correspond with increases (decreases) in the incarceration rate. Thus, changes in the incarceration rate would reflect the crime rate. In other words, analyzing the annual change in the incarceration rate instead of the overall incarceration rate addresses the concerns detailed earlier without compromising the analysis if those concerns are less severe than anticipated.

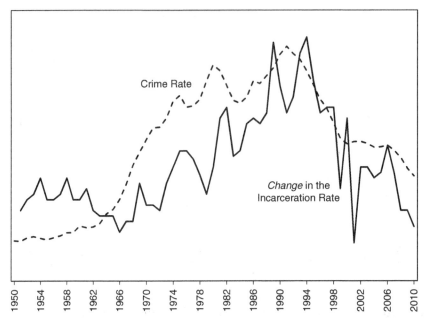

FIGURE 5.4. The crime rate and the *change* in the incarceration rate from 1950 to 2010.

Source: Crime Rate: Social Indicators, 1973 and Sourcebook of Criminal Justice Statistics, Table 3.106.2011; Incarceration Rate: Sourcebook of Criminal Justice Statistics Online, Table 6.28.10.

increased during the 1980s, 1990s, and 2000s (Figure 1.3). Additionally, in Chapter 3 we saw that politicians did not appear to focus on crime until the public became concerned with crime. Nevertheless, Figure 5.4 shows that it is too early to completely discount the potential influence of the crime rate.

Figure 5.4 also offers strong face validity for the argument that we must analyze changes in the incarceration rate. One of the central puzzles of criminal justice research has been the lack of relationship between crime rates and incarceration rates. Consistent with the expectations developed earlier, focusing on changes in the incarceration rate appears to have resolved this puzzle. To understand the determinants of incarceration in the United States, we must examine changes in the incarceration rate. The next step is to evaluate whether the public's attitudes have influenced these changes.

5.2 THE PUBLIC'S PUNITIVENESS AND CHANGES IN THE INCARCERATION RATE

Figure 5.5 offers a first look at the relationship between the public's punitiveness and changes in the incarceration rate. The two series, which are plotted on separate axes, appear to move virtually in tandem. Between 1953 and 2010,

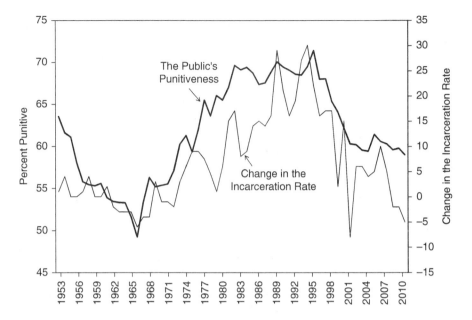

FIGURE 5.5. The public's punitiveness and change in the incarceration rate from 1953 to 2010.

Source: Incarceration Rate: Sourcebook of Criminal Justice Statistics Online, Table 6.28.10. The opinion data were described in Chapter 2.

the correlation is an impressive $r = 0.82$. This close relationship stands in contrast to decades of criminal justice research, which suggests that the public's attitudes have not influenced the growth of the carceral state.[11] The next step is to evaluate whether this relationship holds when controlling for other factors thought to influence the incarceration rate.

5.2.1 Control variables

In order to test the relationship between public support for being tough on crime and changes in the incarceration rate, we need to control for a variety of factors thought to influence the incarceration rate. Controlling for these factors helps ensure that any relationship between the public's attitudes and the

[11] See, for example, Beckett (1997, p. 108), Brown (2006), Cullen, Clark, and Wozniak (1985), Gottschalk (2008, pp. 251–252), Smith (2004, p. 935), Tonry (2009, p. 377), Yates and Fording (2005, p. 1118), Zimring and Hawkins (1991, pp. 125–130), and Zimring and Johnson (2006, p. 266).

incarceration rate is not the result of variables that correlate with the public's punitiveness and changes in the incarceration rate.

The analysis uses two measures to control for the influence of crime. The first measure is the overall crime rate (based on the common over-time variance in the violent and property crime rates) discussed in Chapter 4. The analysis also controls for the rate of illegal drug use, which has long been a concern in the United States. Already in 1950, headlines such as "Youth Narcotic Use Growing" and "Heroin Addicts Mount" drew attention to illegal drug use.[12] Of course, illegal drug use (and the associated penalties) has increased since the 1950s. Today, drug offenses account for 17.4 percent of all prisoners under the jurisdiction of state correctional facilities.[13] In federal prisons (which account for about 10 percent of the overall prison population), drug offenses account for more than 50 percent of the prison population.[14]

Because no direct measures of illegal drug use exist for the entire period of interest, I compiled data on the annual mortality rate where illegal drug use was the cause of death.[15] The idea behind this measure is that when illegal drug use increases (decreases), we would expect the rate of fatalities due to illegal drug use to also increase (decrease). To gain a sense of this measure, and the justice system's response to illegal drug use, Figure 5.6 plots the drug mortality rate and the rate of drug arrests from 1964 to 1988 (to aid comparison, the series have been scaled to a common range). I focus on this period in order to highlight drug activity during the presidencies of Richard Nixon and Ronald Reagan. These presidencies offer an important focal point because President Nixon was the first president to formally declare war on drugs and President Reagan is credited with rejuvenating the drug war (e.g., Alexander 2010, pp. 46–53; Beckett 1997, pp. 52–58; Whitford and Yates 2003, p. 998).

Several important patterns emerge in Figure 5.6. First, the drug arrest rate and the rate of drug mortalities move roughly in tandem during this time period. This result reinforces the validity of using drug mortality data to proxy illegal drug use. If more (fewer) drug deaths correspond with more (less) drug use, it is not surprising that the drug arrest rate corresponds with the drug mortality rate during these years. Second, notice that President Nixon's declaration of war on drugs in 1971 corresponds with a substantial rise in drug mortalities.[16] In fact, the drug mortality rate almost quadrupled between 1969, when Nixon

---

12 These headlines come from the *New York Times*, November 5 and December 3, 1950.
13 www.albany.edu/sourcebook/pdf/t600012010.pdf
14 www.albany.edu/sourcebook/pdf/t62.pdf
15 The data come from the Centers for Disease Control Compressed Mortality Database (http://wonder.cdc.gov/mortSQL.html) and the Vital Statistics of the United States (www.cdc.gov/nchs/products/vsus.htm). Although this is the first complete time series, scholars agree that the annual drug mortality rate offers the best measure of over-time drug use for the period of interest (Hewitt and Milner 1974, Paulozzi and Xi 2008, Samkoff and Baker 1982). See Appendix A-5.1 for full details on the variable coding.
16 Nixon formally declared war on drugs in June 1971, with the announcement, "America's public enemy number one in the United States is drug abuse. In order to fight and defeat this

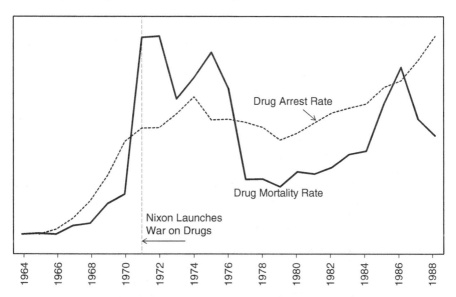

FIGURE 5.6. The drug mortality rate and the drug arrest rate from 1964 to 1988.

Source: The drug mortality data come from the Centers for Disease Control Compressed Mortality Database and the Vital Statistics of the United States. The population data come from the US Census Bureau Statistical Abstract of the United States: 2003 and the US Census Bureau Resident Population by Race, Hispanic Origin, and Age. The drug arrest data come from FBI's Uniform Crime Reports, "Age-Specific Arrest Rates and Race-Specific Arrest Rates for Selected Offenses, 1965–1992."

took office, and 1971. Also note that after declining during the mid 1970s, drug mortality rates began to climb again during Reagan's presidency.

The unequal consequences of the war on drugs are now well known (Provine 2007, 2011). Consider, for example, the 1986 federal Anti-Drug Abuse Act, which punished defendants with five grams of crack cocaine with the same five-year mandatory minimum penalty imposed on defendants in possession of 100 times that amount of powder cocaine. This sentencing disparity carried major racial implications because powder cocaine is much more common among white offenders and crack cocaine is much more common among black offenders.[17] In fact, between 1992 and 2009, 85 percent of those sentenced for crack cocaine offenses under these guidelines were African American. Just 5.7

enemy, it is necessary to wage a new, all-out offensive" (www.presidency.ucsb.edu/ws/index .php?pid=3047&st=public+enemy&st1=#ixzz2gTXSO6r6).

[17] The 2010 Fair Sentencing Act reduced this disparity at the federal level. However, disparate sentencing practices continue to exist in many state laws (Porter and Wright 2011).

percent were white.[18] The war on drugs has been unfair, inefficient, and costly (e.g., Baum 1997; Mauer and King 2007). Nevertheless, Figure 5.6 highlights another important consideration. Both the start of the war on drugs and its rejuvenation correspond with periods of real increases in dangerous drug use. Although some evidence suggests that the racial sentencing disparities may have been intentional (e.g., Alexander 2010, pp. 43–49), we cannot fully understand the roots of the policy without understanding these objective conditions and the public's potential reaction to these conditions.

A final point of note is the disconnect between the drug mortality rate and the drug arrest rate at the far right of Figure 5.6. If we extended the figure, we would see this pattern continue, with the drug arrest rate rising steadily, despite the fact that drug use was declining. Thus, even if Nixon's war on drugs and Reagan's revitalization of this war coincided with actual increases in illegal drug use, the pace of the war on drugs has far outstripped actual drug use (see also Mauer and King 2007, p. 4).

The level of economic inequality is the third control variable in the statistical analysis. A long research history suggests that incarceration is a form of social control and as the level of inequality in society increases, the pressure for this type of social control also increases.[19] As Chambliss and Seidman (1971, p. 33) explain, "The more economically stratified a society becomes, the more it becomes necessary for the dominant groups in that society to enforce through coercion the norms of conduct which guarantee their supremacy." To measure the level of inequality in society, I divide the family income share received by the top 5 percent of families by the share received by the bottom 20 percent.[20] Support for the social control hypothesis will emerge if higher (lower) levels of inequality correspond with increases (decreases) in the incarceration rate.

---

[18] US Sentencing Commission, Office of Research and Data, *Analysis of the Impact of Amendment to the Statutory Penalties for Crack Cocaine Offenses Made by the Fair Sentencing Act of 2010*, January 28, 2011, available at www.ussc.gov/sites/default/files/pdf/research/retroactivity-analyses/fair-sentencing-act/20110128_Crack_Retroactivity_Analysis.pdf. Percentages based on those in prison for crack offenses on October 1, 2010.

[19] See, for example, Chambliss and Seidman (1971), Garland (1990), Gordon (1994), Rusche and Kirchheimer (1939).

[20] I compare the highest available income category to the lowest because when the opinions of different income groups diverge, policy makers are most likely to follow the opinions of those in the highest income decile (Gilens 2005, 2011). This evidence of unequal representation (see also Bartels 2008, Gilens 2012) does *not* call the public opinion hypothesis into question (Enns 2015). Recall that different groups – including different income groups – tend to update their policy preferences in parallel (Kelly and Enns 2010, Page and Shapiro 1992, Ramirez 2013, Soroka and Wlezien 2010), which means that criminal justice policy (and resulting incarcerations) would move in the same direction regardless of whether political actors consider the preferences of a particular group or the overall public (Enns and Wlezien 2011). The income inequality data come from Table F-2 of the US Census Bureau, Current Population Survey, Annual Social and Economic Supplements (www.census.gov/hhes/www/income/data/historical/families/index.html).

It is important to note that the statistical model does *not* directly control for racial attitudes. As discussed in Chapter 2, given the connection between racial attitudes and attitudes toward the criminal justice system (e.g., Hurwitz and Peffley 1997, 2005), by including questions that ask directly about support for the death penalty, spending on police, and other aspects of the criminal justice system, the measure of the public's punitiveness already incorporates any race-based considerations that influence punitive attitudes. After including the measure of public support for being tough on crime, there is no reason to expect racial attitudes or biases to have an independent effect on the incarceration rate. Thus, the absence of a measure of racial bias does not imply that racial attitudes do not matter. Instead, to the extent that racial attitudes influence punitiveness, the measure of the public's support for being tough on crime already incorporates these considerations.[21]

5.2.2 Time series analysis

In order to estimate the relationship between the public's punitiveness and changes in the incarceration rate (while controlling for the crime rate, illegal drug use, and inequality), I utilize a single-equation error correction model (ECM). The ECM is a common statistical approach used with time series data, which is particularly useful in the current context. One advantage of the ECM is that prison populations do not necessarily reflect an immediate response to input variables. For example, if the crime rate increases or the public becomes more punitive, it may take time for these shifts to influence the incarceration rate. The ECM accounts for such considerations by estimating both contemporaneous and long-term relationships between the predictors and the dependent variable (Murray 2009, Spelman 2009). Additionally, given the time series properties of the variables (i.e., the variables contain a unit root and are cointegrated), the ECM is the appropriate statistical approach to hedge against estimating spurious relationships.[22]

---

[21]   Consistent with this expectation, Table A-5.1 in the Appendix shows that the results are robust to controlling for the public's level of racial conservatism.

[22]   See Banerjee et al. (1993), De Boef and Keele (2008), Enns, Masaki, and Kelly (2014), and Esarey (2016). Augmented Dickey Fuller tests indicate that we cannot reject the null hypothesis of a unit root for change in the incarceration rate and the predictors, Crime rate, Drug use, and Inequality. Thus, spurious correlation is of particular concern (e.g., Granger and Newbold 1974). However, when the series are cointegrated – as is the case here – the ECM overcomes the concern of estimating a spurious relationship. Cointegration is established with an augmented Engle-Granger test (Davidson and MacKinnon 1993, pp. 720–721), which requires regressing the change in the incarceration rate on the predictors, then performing an augmented Dickey Fuller test on the residuals, and finally comparing the resulting test statistic (-5.6) to the corresponding critical value in Davidson and MacKinnon (1993, p. 722). Weak exogeneity, another assumption that must be met for an appropriate application of the ECM, is established following Charemza and Deadman (1992, pp. 231–232); that is, the error correction mechanism is insignificant when included in models of each of the predictor variables.

Because the ECM estimates the first difference of the dependent variable, which is change in the incarceration rate, the model analyzes the second difference of the incarceration rate. The second difference means subtracting each observation from the next (which produces the *change* in the incarceration rate) and then subtracting these differences. In addition to being appropriate theoretically and statistically (as described earlier), analyzing the second difference is consistent with previous time series analyses of the incarceration rate (Jacobs and Carmichael 2001).

In an ECM, the coefficients on the differenced predictor variables should be interpreted as the contemporaneous relationship between the predictor and the dependent variable. For example, a positive and significant coefficient on the differenced crime rate (i.e., "Δ Crime rate" in Table 5.2) would suggest that a change in the crime rate produces an immediate change in the incarceration rate. The coefficients for the lagged predictor variables indicate a long-term effect. A long-term effect implies that the predictor and dependent variable move in equilibrium. For example, a positive and significant coefficient on the lagged crime rate (i.e., "Crime rate$_{t-1}$") would suggest that when the crime rate changes, the long-term connection between the crime rate and the incarceration rate would manifest itself through changes in the incarceration rate in future time periods. The total effect of the predictor variables (distributed over future time periods), referred to as the long-run multiplier (LRM), is estimated by dividing the coefficient on the lagged predictor variable by the coefficient on the lagged dependent variable (i.e., "Error correction rate" in Table 5.2). The table refers to the "Error correction rate" because the coefficient on the lagged dependent variable also provides information about the error correction rate; that is, how fast the total effect occurs. Specifically, this coefficient indicates what percentage of the total effect is incorporated into the dependent variable at each future time point.[23]

Table 5.2 reports three models of the relationship between the public's punitiveness and changes in the incarceration rate. Column 1 provides a baseline estimate of the relationship between public opinion and the incarceration rate. Both the short- and long-term coefficients imply a positive and significant relationship between tough-on-crime attitudes and changes in the incarceration rate. Furthermore, the R^2 indicates that support for being tough on crime explains more than 30 percent of the changes in the incarceration rate. The error correction rate (0.68) suggests that shifts in the public's punitiveness influence the incarceration rate relatively quickly. Specifically, the data suggest that approximately 95 percent of the effect of a shift in public opinion on changes in the incarceration rate will be realized four years later.

Column 2 adds controls for the crime rate, illegal drug use, and inequality. The lagged value of public opinion is again positive and significant. Even controlling for the other determinants of incarceration, public opinion matters.

---

[23]   See Banerjee et al. (1993) and De Boef and Keele (2008) for a full discussion of the ECM.

TABLE 5.2. *The relationship between the public's punitiveness and changes in the incarceration rate, controlling for social and political factors from 1953 to 2010*

	(1)	(2)	(3)
Error correction rate	−0.68*	−0.68*	−0.68*
	(0.13)	(0.15)	(0.15)
Δ The public's punitiveness	0.78*	0.42	0.37
	(0.36)	(0.48)	(0.50)
The public's punitiveness$_{t-1}$	0.79*	0.57*	0.53*
	(0.18)	(0.25)	(0.26)
Δ Crime rate		0.77	0.71
		(2.51)	(2.53)
Crime rate$_{t-1}$		0.70	0.91
		(0.74)	(0.83)
Δ Drug use		−0.35	−0.44
		(0.55)	(0.57)
Drug use$_{t-1}$		−0.10	−0.22
		(0.39)	(0.45)
Δ Inequality		5.37	4.64
		(3.67)	(3.90)
Inequality$_{t-1}$		−0.16	−0.39
		(1.07)	(1.14)
Republican strength$_{t-1}$			0.94
			(1.61)
Constant	−45.29*	−30.67	−28.12
	(10.78)	(15.97)	(16.67)
Long-run multipliers			
The public's punitiveness	1.16*	0.83*	0.77*
	(0.15)	(0.32)	(0.34)
Crime rate		1.03	1.33
		(1.06)	(1.17)
Drug use		−0.14	−0.33
		(0.56)	(0.64)
Inequality		−0.23	−0.57
		(1.56)	(1.67)
Republican strength			1.37
			(2.36)
R^2	0.35	0.40	0.41
N	57	57	57

Note: Single-equation error correction model. OLS coefficients with standard errors in parentheses. * $= p < .05$, two-tailed significance levels.

Perhaps not surprisingly, when we add these control variables, we find no evidence of an immediate relationship between the public's attitudes and changes in the incarceration rate. That is, with a fully specified model, it appears that it takes time for the system to respond to the public's attitudes.

The short- and long-term coefficients for the violent and property crime rate are positive but imprecisely estimated, so we cannot conclude that the relationship is statistically different from zero. The lack of evidence for a relationship between the crime rate and changes in the incarceration rate is somewhat surprising, given the strong bivariate relationship observed in Figure 5.4. To further evaluate this relationship, I re-estimated the model *omitting* the measure of the public's punitiveness (this analysis is reported in Column 1 of Table A-5.1 in the Appendix). The observed relationship between the lagged crime rate and changes in the incarceration rate increases substantially (the coefficient becomes 1.97) and is statistically significant ($p < 0.05$). The larger and significant coefficient that emerges when the model does not include the public's punitiveness is consistent with the public's attitudes mediating the relationship between the crime rate and changes in the incarceration rate. This result is also consistent with the statistical results in Chapter 4 and the archival findings in Chapter 3, which together showed that crime rates influence the public's attitudes, which in turn influence politicians (and perhaps others) that influence the incarceration rate. Yet the state-level analysis reported in Chapter 6 will find evidence of a relationship between state crime rates and state incarceration rates, so we should not completely rule out the possibility that crime rates directly influence the incarceration rate.

The relationship between changes in the incarceration rate and the rate of illegal drug use is negative and not statistically significant under any specification. The lack of relationship is consistent with the previous discussion, which pointed out that despite the initial connection between the war on drugs and the rate of illegal drug use, drug arrests (and resulting incarcerations) have far outpaced actual drug use since the late 1980s (Mauer and King 2007). The short-term coefficient for inequality is positive, which would correspond with the expectations of the social control hypothesis, but we cannot conclude that this relationship is significantly different from zero.

The bottom section of the table reports the long-run multipliers (LRMs), which represent the total expected effect (over future time periods) of a unit shift in a predictor variable on change in the incarceration rate.[24] To assess the magnitude of these relationships, I calculate the expected change in the number of incarcerations for a standard deviation shift in the public's punitiveness and in the crime rate. These calculations indicate that the expected effect of public opinion is important in both absolute and relative terms. A standard deviation increase (decrease) in the public's preferences for being tough on

---

[24] I use the Bewley transformation to estimate the standard error and confidence intervals of the LRM (De Boef and Keele 2008).

crime corresponds with an expected increase (decrease) of 5.5 people per 100,000 in the annual change in the incarceration rate. This means that we would expect the incarceration rate to increase by approximately 13,000 additional inmates (with a 95 percent confidence interval of 3,000 to 22,800) for a standard deviation shift in the public's punitiveness. The corresponding value for the crime rate is an expected shift of 5,100 inmates, although the 95 percent confidence interval overlaps zero, ranging from −5,500 to 15,800.

Column 3 adds a measure of the strength of the Republican Party in the federal government. Controlling for the strength of the Republican Party provides information about whether the influence of public opinion we have observed is mediated by who is in office. Although at the federal level both Democrats and Republicans have advanced more punitive criminal justice policies (e.g., Mauer 2006, ch.4), research at the state level suggests that Republican legislators are more likely to implement harsher criminal justice policies (Jacobs and Helms 2001, Smith 2004). To measure Republican influence in government, I generate a summary measure of Republican strength based on whether the president was a Republican or Democrat and the proportion of Republicans in Congress. The measure codes Republican presidents as a 1 (and Democratic presidents as a 0) and then adds this number to the proportion of Republicans (among Republicans and Democrats) in the House and the Senate. This variable ranges from 0.64 in 1964 and 1965 when the Democrats held an overwhelming majority in the House and the Senate and Lyndon Johnson was president to 2.09 in 2005 and 2006 when George W. Bush was president and Republicans held a majority in the House and the Senate. Although the measure does not include state-level officeholders, this variable offers a general indication of the national-level strength of the Republican Party. As Abramowitz (2010, p. 1) explains, "state legislative elections are influenced by the same forces that influence congressional elections." Thus, if Republicans are more likely to legislate more punitive criminal justice policies, higher values of Republican strength should correspond with changes in the incarceration rate.

An augmented Dickey Fuller test indicates that this series is stationary, so only values in levels are entered into the model (including the differenced values does not alter the results). Both the lagged value and the LRM for the public's punitiveness are again significant and of similar magnitude. Additionally, although positive, the coefficient for Republican strength is not significant, which suggests that the public's influence on the incarceration rate is not mediated by who is in office. The roughly equivalent R^2 values across models 2 and 3 also suggest that Republican strength does not add to the explanatory power of the model. By some accounts, the lack of significance for Republican strength is surprising. Yet this null result is consistent with evidence that, especially at the federal level, the differences between Republicans and Democrats' criminal justice policies may not be that large (Beckett 1997; Garland 2001, pp. 13–14; Mauer 2006, ch.4; Nicholson-Crotty, Peterson, and Ramirez 2009). Of course, we must also remember that this is just a proxy for

Republican strength in government. The state-level analysis in Chapter 6 will offer an opportunity to scrutinize how Republicans and Democrats in state government influence state incarceration rates.[25]

Across various model specifications, we see that the public's punitiveness matters both statistically and substantively.[26] To gain further insight into the magnitude of the public's influence on the incarceration rate, it is possible to compare the actual incarceration rate with the rate that would be predicted if the public's support for being tough on crime was held constant at its 1974 level. Evaluating constant public punitiveness is an important counterfactual since some scholars have suggested that the public's attitudes have remained relatively constant (e.g., Roberts et al. 2003, pp. 27–28). I select 1974 because the public's punitiveness had begun to increase by this point, reaching the average level of punitiveness for the entire period of analysis. The results of this comparison (based on Column 3 of Table 5.2) appear in Figure 5.7. The figure reports three series. The solid black line reflects the actual state and federal incarceration rate from 1954 to 2010.[27] The thin dashed line reflects the predicted incarceration rate based on the statistical results in Column 3 of Table 5.2. The statistical model slightly under-predicts the incarceration rate around 1970 and around 2000, but the overall close relationship between the actual and predicted values indicates that the statistical model fits the data very well.[28]

The thick dashed line reflects the predicted incarceration rate based on the statistical results in Column 3, holding the public's punitiveness at its 1974 level. Specifically, this line provides an estimate of what the incarceration rate would have been if the influence of the public's punitiveness (and the other variables) remained the same, but the public's punitiveness had stopped

[25] I also estimated (not shown) the model lagging Republican strength by two years, in case the null result reflects the time it takes electoral shifts to influence policy outcomes. The findings remain unchanged. Of course, this result does not rule out all possible channels of partisan influence. For example, federal judges and prosecutors can potentially influence the incarceration rate long after the politicians who appointed and confirmed them leave office. Nevertheless, we can conclude that knowing which party occupies the White House and knowing the party strength in Congress does not substantially improve our predictions of changes in the incarceration rate.

[26] Table A-5.1 in the Appendix shows that these results are also robust to controls for the public's political ideology, racial conservatism, the rate of unauthorized immigration, and the unemployment rate.

[27] Recall that this series, while representing the best available time series data, actually understates the overall US incarceration rate because it includes only sentences greater than one year.

[28] When a statistical model includes the lagged value of the dependent variable, the relationship between predicted values and the actual values can be inflated because past values are being used to predict current values. That is *not* the case here. The actual value of the lagged dependent variable only enters the 1954 prediction. I then generated the predicted values iteratively, including prior predicted values for the estimate of the lagged dependent variable (not the actual lagged dependent variable). This process ensures that the predicted values in Figure 5.7 are not inflated.

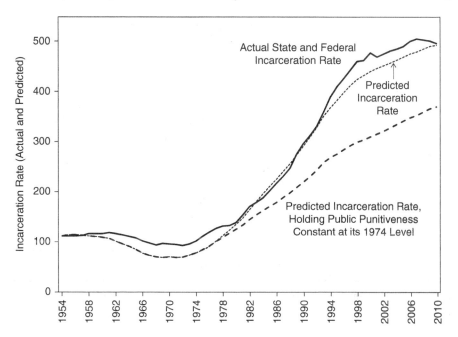

FIGURE 5.7. The incarceration rate and the predicted incarceration rate, holding the public's punitiveness constant at its 1974 level.

Source: The predicted values are based on the results of Column 3 in Table 5.2.

increasing in 1974 (even though all other variables took on their actual values). Subtracting the predicted incarceration rate based on this hypothetical scenario from the predicted values when the public's punitiveness takes on its actual values offers an estimate of the public's influence. The difference between these two predicted values suggests that there would have been an average of approximately 185,000 fewer state and federal incarcerations each year if the public's punitiveness remained at its 1974 level. This represents about 20 percent of the average number of state and federal incarcerations during this period. In other words, this simulation suggests that rising public punitiveness since the mid 1970s accounts for approximately one-fifth of all state and federal incarcerations.[29] In 2010, the total correctional population (including prisons and jails) was 2,363,600 (Glaze and Kaeble 2014, p. 6). These results suggest that rising public punitiveness accounts for about 470,000 of those individuals. While striking, these results may actually be conservative estimates. If we

[29]   Of course, uncertainty exists around these estimates, and these estimates will fluctuate some based on the precise model specification. The key point, however, is that these simulations suggest a substantial public opinion effect.

assumed the public's punitiveness had stopped increasing before the mid 1970s, the estimated effect of public opinion would be even greater.

We have also seen, however, that the public's attitudes have become less punitive since the late 1990s. This pattern is equally important. If the public's punitiveness had remained at its peak, we would expect substantially *more* incarcerations than have occurred. Indeed, the public's declining punitiveness is critical to understanding recent shifts in criminal justice policy and political rhetoric. For example, in recent years we have seen the decriminalization of certain low-level drug offenses, the closing of prisons, and a decline in the overall prison population. Politicians of both parties have also shifted their tone on crime. For example, in 2014 Democratic Senator Corey Booker and Republican Senator Rand Paul issued a joint statement calling for prison reform (O'Keefe 2014). Standard accounts of the rise of mass incarceration cannot explain these changes.[30] Explanations that focus on fiscal restraints following the Great Recession also cannot fully account for these patterns. As we saw in Figure 5.5, the rate of change in the incarceration rate has been declining for well over a decade (also see Clear and Frost 2014, Enns and Shanks-Booth 2015). The current focus on public opinion helps us understand both the rise of mass incarceration and the growing shift in the criminal justice climate.

5.3 CONCLUSION

Marie Gottschalk (2006, p. 236) has explained, "The emergence and consolidation of the US carceral state were a major milestone in American political development that arguably rivals in significance the expansion and contraction of the welfare state in the postwar period." This chapter has begun to analyze the role of the public in this critical aspect of American political development. We have seen that the public's rising punitiveness has been a fundamental determinant of changes in the incarceration rate. This result holds controlling for the crime rate, the level of inequality in society, and a host of other factors (see, for example, Appendix A-5.2). Furthermore, the mass public's influence appears quite substantial. The analysis suggests that if the public had not become more punitive, *millions* of incarcerated individuals would not have been locked up.

The results for the crime rate were less clear. A strong bivariate relationship emerged between the crime rate and changes in the incarceration rate in Figure 5.4. Additionally, the statistical analysis estimates the direct influence of the crime rate to be about 40 percent of the magnitude of the public's

---

[30] For example, Simon's important book *Governing Through Crime* offers an account of the punitive shift of the criminal justice system but not its decline. As Simon notes, "Mass imprisonment is a *stable* solution to the highly competitive political logic established by governing through crime … executives (especially governors and presidents), lawmakers, and courts attempting to play to their strengths in the era of governing through crime *must* embrace mass imprisonment" (2007, p. 159; italics mine).

preferences. We cannot, however, conclude that this relationship is statistically different from zero. The state-level analysis in the following chapter helps clarify the influence of criminal activity.

We have also learned other lessons. If we want to understand what influences the incarceration rate, we must study change. Both the overall rate of incarceration as well as the admissions rate can increase, even if factors that influence the prison population decline. By examining changes in the incarceration rate, we address this concern. Examining the drug mortality rate also offered an important lesson. The war on drugs has largely been deemed a failure that has produced especially negative consequences for African Americans (Provine 2011). While these dismal outcomes are real, it is also important to recognize that the war on drugs may have been a reaction to objective conditions. Finally, while the macro analytical approach I employ is ideally suited for studying changes in the overall incarceration rate, the analysis of Brooklyn illustrated how the rise of mass incarceration – and the resulting consequences – have been unevenly distributed. Thus, when public opinion influences the criminal justice system – whether through sentencing requirements, budgetary allocations, or prosecutorial zeal – we must keep in mind that not all individuals, families, and neighborhoods are affected equally.

A-5 APPENDICES TO CHAPTER 5

A-5.1 Drug mortality data coding

The annual drug mortality rate offers the best measure of over-time drug use for the period of interest (Hewitt and Milner 1974, Paulozzi and Xi 2008, Samkoff and Baker 1982). The data used to generate the annual rate of drug mortalities come from the Centers for Disease Control Compressed Mortality Database (wonder.cdc.gov/mortSQL.html) and the Vital Statistics of the United States (www.cdc.gov/nchs/products/vsus.htm). Drug mortality was identified by the following International Classification of Diseases and Health Problems (ICD) categories: "Other Drug Addiction" (prior to 1968), "Drug Dependence" (between 1968 and 1998), and "Dependence Syndrome" (1999 to the present). Alcohol and tobacco dependence were not incorporated in the estimate of "Dependence Syndrome" (i.e., years 1999–2006) because the previous ICD categories of "Other Drug Addiction" and "Drug Dependence" did not include alcohol or tobacco use. These categories were selected to maximize consistency and comparability in the over-time drug use estimates (see, e.g., recommendations from the World Health Organization (www.who.int/substance_abuse/terminology/definition1/en/), the Centers for Disease Control (www.cdc.gov/nchs/icd/icd9.htm), and Room (1998)). The drug mortality rate is calculated based on the adult population, ages fourteen to sixty-five. The population data come from the US Census Bureau Statistical Abstract of the United States: 2003 (www

.census.gov/compendia/statab/hist_stats.html) and the US Census Bureau Resident Population by Race, Hispanic Origin, and Age (www.census.gov/ compendia/statab/cats/population/estimates_and_projections_by_age_sex_ raceethnicity.html).

A-5.2 Additional robustness checks

The results reported in Table 5.2 in the text show that the relationship between the public's punitiveness and the incarceration rate is robust to a variety of important control variables and model specifications. To further assess the robustness of this relationship, Table A-5.1 reports results with additional controls for the public's general political ideology, the public's racial conservatism, the rate of unauthorized immigration and border enforcement, and the unemployment rate. Not surprisingly, no short-term (i.e., immediate) relationships emerged in Table 5.2. Thus, all models in Table A-5.1 only estimate long-term relationships. Column 1 in Table A-5.1 *omits* the measure of the public's punitiveness. The magnitude of the coefficient for the crime rate increases to 1.97 and the estimate is now statistically different from zero. This increase is consistent with the statistical results in Chapter 4 and the archival findings in Chapter 3, which suggested that the public's attitudes mediated the relationship between the crime rate and political action.

Column 2 of Table A-5.1 replaces the measure of public punitiveness used in the text with an alternate measure (described in footnote 25 of Chapter 2) that adds three questions about the public's perceptions of the crime rate. This alternate measure includes thirty-six distinct opinion questions asked 450 different times. The results are nearly equivalent to those reported in this chapter, offering further evidence that the estimate of the public's punitiveness and the overall results are not sensitive to the specific questions included in the opinion measure. Column 3 lags all variables by three years. The model fit declines slightly, suggesting the one-year lag reported in this chapter is the appropriate model specification. However, the statistical results are roughly equivalent, which indicates that the findings are not sensitive to the lag length selected.

Column 4 adds a control for the public's political ideology. For theoretical reasons, the main analysis focused on the public's punitiveness instead of this general measure of political ideology. For example, Druckman and Jacobs (2006) show that on issues important to the public, policy makers typically rely on policy-specific opinion. Given the prominence of crime issues in the media (Beckett 1997, Mauer 2006) and the salience of the issue to the public (Simon 2007), we should expect policy-specific (not general ideological) responsiveness (Druckman and Jacobs 2006). Nevertheless, to ensure that the previously observed relationship between tough-on-crime attitudes and the incarceration rate does not reflect a response to increases in general ideological conservatism, Column 4 adds Ellis and Stimson's (2009) measure of the public's

TABLE A-5.1. *The relationship between the public's punitiveness and the incarceration rate, controlling for conservative ideology, racial conservatism, the rate of unauthorized immigration and border enforcement, and unemployment*

	(1) No public opinion	(2) W/ Crime perceptions	(3) Three-year lag	(4) Conservative ideology	(5) Racial conservatism	(6) Border enforcement	(7) Unemployment rate
Incarceration rate$_{t-1}$	-0.53*	-0.69*	-0.66*	-0.83*	-0.68*	-1.13*	-0.72*
	(0.12)	(0.14)	(0.14)	(0.15)	(0.14)	(0.15)	(0.14)
The public's punitiveness$_{t-1}$		0.49*	0.417*	0.47*	0.48*	0.54*	0.48*
		(0.22)	(0.207)	(0.22)	(0.24)	(0.26)	(0.23)
Crime rate$_{t-1}$	1.97*	1.26	1.27	2.08*	1.11	2.86*	1.54*
	(0.57)	(0.64)	(0.72)	(0.82)	(0.79)	(0.66)	(0.70)
Drug use$_{t-1}$	-0.35	-0.23	-0.09	-0.31	-0.21	-0.02	-0.28
	(0.39)	(0.38)	(0.40)	(0.38)	(0.39)	(0.38)	(0.42)
Inequality$_{t-1}$	-0.64	-0.31	-1.76	0.87	-0.99	8.18*	-0.90
	(0.99)	(0.97)	(1.03)	(1.16)	(1.47)	(2.11)	(0.99)
Republican strength$_{t-1}$	2.17	1.40	1.20	1.32	1.36	2.08	2.02
	(1.45)	(1.45)	(1.56)	(1.50)	(1.48)	(1.52)	(1.60)
Conservative ideology$_{t-1}$				-0.39			
				(0.32)			
Racial conservatism$_{t-1}$					-0.10		
					(0.29)		

(continued)

123

TABLE A-5.1 (continued)

	(1) No public opinion	(2) W/ Crime perceptions	(3) Three-year lag	(4) Conservative ideology	(5) Racial conservatism	(6) Border enforcement	(7) Unemployment rate
INS apprehensions$_{t-1}$						-0.12 (0.13)	
INS border patrol$_{t-1}$						-17.92* (6.10)	
Δ Unemployment rate							-0.82 (0.78)
Unemployment rate$_{t-1}$							-0.62 (0.59)
Constant	3.35 (4.33)	-27.95 (14.87)	-17.18 (12.89)	-4.50 (22.21)	-17.59 (21.43)	-52.17* (15.06)	-20.95 (13.94)
R^2	0.31	0.37	0.35	0.43	0.37	0.59	0.39
N	57	57	55	54	57	52	57

Note: OLS coefficients with standard errors in parentheses. * = $p < .05$, two-tailed significance levels.
All predictors in Column 3 are lagged three years.

political ideology (recoded in the conservative direction) to the model. Ellis and Stimson's (2009) over-time measure of the public's political ideology is based on all available survey questions that have asked whether respondents identify as political liberals or conservatives.[31] The measure of public punitiveness does not include this type of political ideology question so the two measures do *not* include any common question items. The results indicate that the influence of the public's support for being tough on crime is independent of the public's political ideology. When we control for ideology, the coefficient for tough on crime remains roughly equivalent.[32] The relationship between the incarceration rate and the public's general political ideology is not statistically different from zero.

To control for the public's racial attitudes, Column 5 adds an updated measure of Kellstedt's (2000, 2003) index of the public's racial policy liberalism (recoded in the conservative direction). The previous results should be robust to this control. Despite the disproportionate incarceration of racial minorities and the link between racial predispositions and criminal justice attitudes (Hurwitz and Peffley 1997, 2005), when controlling for tough-on-crime attitudes, there is no reason to expect racial attitudes to directly influence the incarceration rate. To the extent that racial attitudes influence criminal justice attitudes, the inclusion of the public's punitiveness should already account for this relationship. The results in Column 5 are consistent with this expectation. The effect of the public's support for being tough-on-crime remains significant and the coefficient for racial conservatism is negative and not statistically different from zero. Although this negative coefficient is surprising, Nicholson-Crotty, Peterson, and Ramirez (2009) report a negative relationship between racial conservatism and federal criminal justice outcomes. It may be that social desirability bias has led to increasingly liberal responses to racial policy questions, even as support for more punitive policy outcomes increased. This possibility offers further support for utilizing the measure of tough-on-crime attitudes.

Column 6 controls for the rate of unauthorized immigration to the United States and the level of US border enforcement. Although the majority of incarcerations measured by the dependent variable reflect state incarcerations, this model helps ensure that factors that influence federal incarcerations are included in the model. In 1994, just 5.3 percent of new federal incarcerations stemmed from immigration offenses. By 2004, this percentage had increased to

---

[31] The question wording typically follows the format, "How would you describe yourself on most political matters? Generally, do you consider yourself as liberal, moderate, or conservative?" The data are available at www.unc.edu/~jstimson/Data.html. To recode their series in the conservative direction, I subtracted the series from 100.

[32] Although not shown, the results are also robust to adding Stimson's (1999) policy mood to the model; $\beta = 0.93$, s.e.$=.28$ for tough-on-crime opinion.

20.5 percent.[33] The influence of the public's punitiveness remains statistically significant and of similar magnitude to the previous models. Although this model offers a rigorous robustness check, the unauthorized immigration variables introduce some collinearity to the model (for example, Inequality and INS Border Patrol correlate at $r = 0.82$), so we should be cautious about drawing strong inferences from the control variables in this model. Column 7 adds the unemployment rate to the model. Some incarceration research focuses on unemployment levels instead of income inequality. The influence of the public's punitiveness remains virtually unchanged.

---

[33] These statistics come from the Compendium of Federal Justice Statistics http://bjs.ojp.usdoj .gov/content/pub/pdf/cfjso405.pdf and http://bjs.ojp.usdoj.gov/content/pub/pdf/cfjs9404.pdf. The immigration and border enforcement data come from Gordon Hanson (Hanson 2006, Hanson and Spilimbergo 1999), who has used data from the US Immigration and Naturalization Service to construct the best available estimates of unauthorized immigration and immigration enforcement. INS Apprehensions reflects the total number of apprehensions of unauthorized immigrants at US borders. I divide this measure by the total US population to estimate the rate of unauthorized immigration. INS Border Patrol captures immigration enforcement with the number of person hours the US Border Patrol spends policing US borders. Not surprisingly, the two measures are positively correlated ($r = 0.60$). The data were accessed from irps.ucsd.edu/faculty/faculty-directory/gordon-hanson.htm. The data are monthly and extend from July 1963 to September 2004. To generate annual data, for each year, I assigned the average monthly value from the immigration data series. Because the data from 1963 are incomplete and because there are no data prior to 1963, all years prior to 1964 were assigned the value from 1964. Assuming constant immigration prior to 1964 is unproblematic because, as noted earlier, the spike in federal immigration incarcerations is relatively recent. For ease of presentation, I recoded the Border Patrol Hours variable to range from 0 to 1.

6

Punitive politics in the states

The Commissioner of the Massachusetts Department of Correction "is concerned with the 'hardening public attitudes' which, he feels, threaten any humane approach to correction."

(*The Boston Globe*, December 8, 1976)

The United States has the highest incarceration rate in the world – unless we consider the individual states. In 2013, sixteen states ranked *above* the overall US incarceration rate. Louisiana topped the list with an incarceration rate more than one-and-a-half times the US rate. One out of every thirty-one Louisianans was incarcerated, on probation, or on parole.[1] These numbers show that to fully understand the rise of mass incarceration in the United States, we must also look to the states. Not only do the states house the lion's share of the prison population – around 90 percent of all inmates – but state governments have played a crucial role in the growth of the carceral state. And as this chapter's opening quote from Frank A. Hall (the former commissioner of the Massachusetts Department of Correction) implies, public opinion in the states was a major contributing factor.

Perhaps the most important way political actors influenced the incarceration rate (at both the state and federal levels) has been through changes in sentencing laws, such as the adoption of determinate sentencing and mandatory minimum

---

[1] These values, which come from Glaze and Kaeble (2014), actually understate the total scope of the correctional system because they do not include individuals in federal prison. The Pew Center on the States estimates that in 2007 an astonishing one in thirteen adults in Georgia was under some form of correctional supervision (www.convictcriminology.org/pdf/pew/onein31.pdf). The sixteen states with higher incarceration rates than the United States were Louisiana, Oklahoma, Mississippi, Alabama, Georgia, Texas, Arizona, Arkansas, Florida, New Mexico, Delaware, Tennessee, Kentucky, Missouri, Alaska, and Nevada.

sentences.[2] New York's "Rockefeller Drug Laws," which Governor Nelson Rockefeller signed into law on May 8, 1973, illustrate the two ways that sentencing laws can influence the incarceration rate. First, these laws increased the number of people going to prison by legislating mandatory prison sentences for crimes that previously did not result in prison time. For example, prior to the Rockefeller Drug Laws, possession of a small amount of LSD or methamphetamines was a misdemeanor crime. The maximum punishment was one year in a local jail, but probation, conditional discharge (no imprisonment or probation, conditional on meeting court-ordered requirements, such as drug treatment), or unconditional discharge (no imprisonment or probation) was more likely. However, after the Rockefeller Drug Laws, the possession of a tab of LSD carried a mandatory sentence of one year to life and possession of two ounces of methamphetamines carried a mandatory sentence of one to fifteen years.[3]

In addition to increasing the number of people going to jail, changes in sentencing laws increased the incarceration rate by extending the length of sentences. The Rockefeller Drug Laws, for example, increased the sale of an ounce of heroine or cocaine to a Class A-1 Felony – the same classification as first degree murder. This meant that a college kid, like Thomas Eddy, who was convicted of selling two ounces of cocaine to his friends, was sentenced to *fifteen years to life* (Struck 1989).

Although Governor Rockefeller proclaimed his legislation "the toughest antidrug program in the nation" (Markham and Farrell 1973), New York was by no means the only state to revise its sentencing laws. In fact, through the 1970s and 1980s, more punitive sentencing became the norm across states. Consistent with the argument of this book, the timing of these punitive sentencing laws followed the rise in the public's punitiveness observed in previous chapters. Also consistent with expectations, legislation to (*somewhat*) reduce the punitiveness of these laws has followed the more recent decline in public punitiveness that we have observed. For example, in 2004 new legislation in New York reduced the mandatory minimum prison sentences for nonviolent and first time felony drug offenders.[4] Further changes occurred in 2009, when mandatory prison sentences for some drug offenses were eliminated and some minimum sentence lengths were also reduced. Judicial discretion to offer drug court alternatives to certain addicted nonviolent

---

[2] Indeterminate sentences specify a minimum and maximum sentence length and then the parole board determines the actual time to release. Although indeterminate sentences have been criticized for introducing disparity in sentences, determinate sentencing laws, which specify a fixed sentence for particular crimes, have led to much longer average sentence lengths.

[3] The LSD sentence is based on possession of 5.25 mg of LSD. An average tab of LSD weighs 8 mg (Dal Cason and Franzosa 2003, p. 45). For additional information on sentence lengths before and after the Rockefeller Drug Laws, see the "Final Report of the Joint Committee on New York Drug Law Evaluation" (1978). Also see Kohler-Hausmann's (2010) article on "The Attila the Hun Law': New York's Rockefeller Drug Laws and the Making of a Punitive State."

[4] The 2004 Drug Law Reform Act also doubled the weight thresholds for the two most serious possession offenses (A-I and A-II), and those serving life sentences were permitted to apply for re-sentencing (www.criminaljustice.ny.gov/legalservices/ch738_druglaw_reform_2004.htm).

offenders was also established.[5] New York drug laws are by no means lenient today, but these changes are important. If Thomas Eddy was sentenced in 2004 instead of 1981, the minimum sentence would have been eight years instead of fifteen years to life.

Budgetary appropriations are another type of legislative decision that has an important influence on the incarceration rate. Not only does government spending allow and sustain prison growth, but it provides resources to police, prosecutors, and judges. In 2012, state governments spent more than $48.4 *billion* on corrections alone. This is more than $10 billion more than the federal government spent on housing assistance for those in need of income security and more than double the amount the federal government spent on international development and humanitarian assistance. As striking as these statistics are, these numbers actually *understate* the costs of corrections. In many states, costs such as corrections employees' health insurance, retiree health care benefits, pension contributions, capital projects, and state administrative support are paid by central funds, not through the corrections budget. In 2010, for example, an average of 14 percent of prison costs – or approximately $5.4 billion in additional prison-related spending – occurred outside corrections budgets (Henrichson and Delaney 2012). These numbers also do not include budgetary support for police, prosecutors, and judges or indirect costs that result from high incarceration rates, such as an increased need for social services, child welfare support, health care, and education. In sum, it costs extraordinary sums of money to maintain the world's highest incarceration rate and states foot most of this bill.

Given their desire for reelection and political advancement, legislators and governors face a clear incentive to consider the public's punitiveness when deciding on sentencing laws and budgetary allocations. Those more directly involved in the criminal justice system, such as police, prosecutors, and judges, also face incentives to consider the public's attitudes. Research shows that the police pay attention to their public image (Gallagher et al. 2001, Gibson 1997, Tooley et al. 2009). Furthermore, as we have seen, forty-seven states elect their chief prosecutors (Perry 2006), creating a direct incentive for these individuals to consider the public's preferences. The same expectation holds for the thirty-eight states that elect their Supreme Court justices. Indeed, Brace and Boyea (2008) find that in these states, public attitudes toward the death penalty influence both the composition of the state Supreme Court and the votes of these justices.

Even when not elected, judges are unlikely to completely ignore the public's preferences.[6] Consider Judge H. Lawrence Jodrey. In the 1970s,

---

5   http://dcjs.ny.gov/drug-law-reform/index.html
6   Those looking at the US Supreme Court have found that despite enjoying life tenure, a strong relationship exists between the public's policy preferences and Supreme Court outcomes (e.g., Casillas, Enns, and Wohlfarth 2011, Enns and Wohlfarth 2013, McGuire and Stimson 2004).

Judge Jodrey was the Massachusetts District Court Judge in Gloucester, a Democratic-leaning fishing town in the northeastern part of the state.[7] Like all Massachusetts judges, Jodrey enjoyed a lifetime appointment (with mandatory retirement at age seventy). Yet, in a 1976 interview, the judge described how a meeting with town officials alerted him to the public's will. He explained, "They felt that the permissiveness and leniency of recent years is not solving the problems of violence and delinquency. They feel I have been too lenient, although I never thought I was. I think the feelings of the community will have more of an effect now" (Chamberlin 1976).

Judge Jodrey's attention to the public is by no means an anomaly. In fact, in 1978 the National Center for State Courts sponsored a national conference that examined "The Public Image of the Courts." As Edward B. McConnell, the director of the National Center for State Courts, explained:

> Public opinion can, of course, change quite rapidly, and is only one of a number of factors relevant to development of court improvement strategies. But its importance should not be underestimated, for in the long run courts must have public acceptance and support if they are to be strong and effective institutions. (McConnell 1978, p. i)

Whether we consider the police, prosecutors, judges, or legislators, there is good reason to expect public attitudes to influence state incarceration rates. As Garland (2001, p. 203) explains, "To be out of touch with public sentiment on this issue is to invite negative headlines and political disaster." Yet existing research has often failed to find such a relationship (e.g., Smith 2004, Yates and Fording 2005). To more fully test the expected influence of the public's preferences, the following analysis brings three important innovations to the study of state incarceration rates. Previous analyses have typically focused on the 1970s through the 1990s.[8] This chapter, by contrast, utilizes Department of Justice data from the 1950s through 2010. Including the 1950s and 1960s is particularly important because this allows an analysis of years prior to the rise of mass incarceration. The second innovation involves the construction of a dynamic state-level measure of the public's punitiveness from 1953 to 2010. Finally, in addition to analyzing incarceration rates, I analyze states' fiscal support for corrections. The results help illustrate the important influence of public opinion on criminal justice outcomes in the states.

---

[7]   According to the 1976 Election Statistics of the Commonwealth of Massachusetts, in 1976, 55 percent of Gloucester voters supported Jimmy Carter, the Democratic candidate.

[8]   See, for example, Jacobs and Carmichael (2001), Smith (2004), Soss, Fording, and Schram (2011), Yates and Fording (2005).

6.1 STATE INCARCERATION RATES

The goal of this chapter is to understand the rise of state incarceration rates. Figure 6.1 offers a glimpse of how these rates have changed during the past sixty years. The figure plots the incarceration rate per one hundred thousand individuals for each state in 1950 (hollow dots), 1980 (gray dots), and 2010 (solid dots). These data reflect all inmates sentenced to a state prison for more than one year (data on prison sentences of one year or less and individuals serving time in jails are not available for the entire time period). Thus,

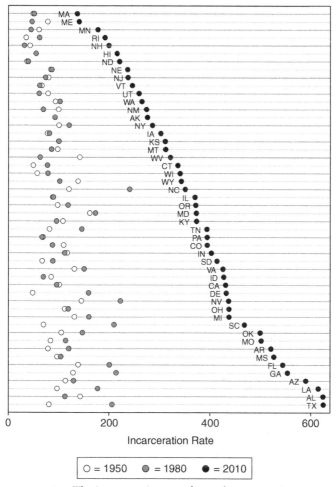

FIGURE 6.1. The incarceration rate for each state, 1950, 1980, and 2010.

Source: *Historical Statistics on Prisoners in State and Federal Institutions, Yearend 1925–1986* and the National Prisoner Statistics data series.

it is important to remember that these numbers, while ideal for over-time comparisons, actually *understate* the total incarceration rate in each state.[9]

Several important patterns emerge in Figure 6.1. The most obvious result is the fact that the incarceration rate increased – and increased substantially – in every state between 1980 (gray dots) and 2010 (solid dots). Even Massachusetts, which had the lowest incarceration rate in the country in 2010, saw the rate of individuals behind bars nearly triple between 1980 and 2010. Equally as important as the overall increase in state incarceration rates is the fact that the amount of this increase varied substantially across states. Texas' incarceration rate grew almost five times more than Massachusetts' during this period.

Looking at state incarceration rates in 1950 (hollow dots) and 1980 (gray dots) shows that the rate of incarceration was not only much less than recent decades but there was much less variation across state incarceration rates. There was variation, however, in whether states increased or decreased the proportion of individuals behind bars. Although most states saw an increase in their incarceration rates, between 1950 and 1980, seventeen states experienced a decline in their rates of incarceration.

Figure 6.2 offers another look at how state incarceration rates have shifted. Here, I plot the incarceration rate from 1925 to 2011 for the states with the three highest incarceration rates in 2010 (Texas, Alabama, and Louisiana), the three lowest incarceration rates (Massachusetts, Maine, and Minnesota), and the overall incarceration rate for the United States.[10] Again, we should remember that these values understate the total incarceration rates because they only include those sentenced to more than a year in a state prison.

Examining these states over the entire period for which data are available reinforces the patterns observed earlier. Although all states increased their incarceration rates through most of the 1970s and 1980s, we see substantial

---

[9] The data from 1950 through 1986 come from *Historical Statistics on Prisoners in State and Federal Institutions, Yearend 1925–1986* (Langan et al. 1988). The remaining data come from the National Prisoner Statistics data series (1987 through 2004 are available at www.bjs.gov/content/dtdata.cfm#corrections and 2005 through 2010 are available at http://bjs.ojp.usdoj .gov/content/pub/pdf/p10.pdf, where p10 corresponds with 2010). During these final twelve years, the incarceration data are based on jurisdiction, which includes all inmates the state has authority over (even in other states). The earlier years were based on custody, which includes all inmates in the state's facilities (including from other states). The coding change does not alter the over-time trajectory of state incarceration rates. From 1977 to 1998, when we have data for both of these measures (i.e., custody and jurisdiction), the lowest over-time correlation, which comes from Alaska, is $r = 0.91$. The next lowest correlation (Oregon) is $r = 0.95$. The over-time patterns of both custody and jurisdiction are nearly identical, but we need to account for the slight difference in total number of inmates these different measures can produce. To do this, I shift the jurisdiction data by the average difference between each state's custody and jurisdiction numbers from 1996 to 1998 (the last three years of both measures). Incarceration data for Hawaii prior to 1951 and Alaska prior to 1971 are not available.

[10] Data for Alabama are not available for 1925, 1926, and 1929 through 1938.

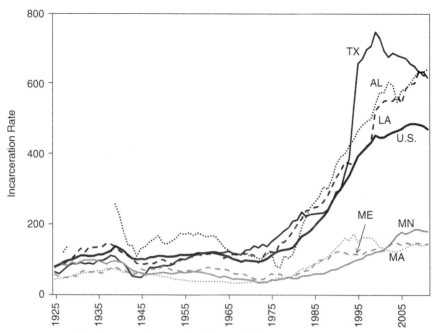

FIGURE 6.2. The incarceration rate for Texas, Alabama, Louisiana, Minnesota, Maine, Massachusetts, and the United States 1925 to 2011.

Source: Historical Statistics on Prisoners in State and Federal Institutions, Yearend 1925–1986 and the National Prisoner Statistics data series.

variation in the rate and duration of this increase. We also see that even considering Alabama's outlier status in the late 1930s and early 1940s, from the mid 1920s through the mid 1960s, the incarceration rates in these states were much closer together and much more consistent than in recent decades. Finally, it is worth noting that the overall US incarceration rate is much closer to the three states with the highest incarceration rates than the states with the three lowest incarceration rates. In order to test whether these patterns followed the public's preferences, the following section develops state-level measures of the public's punitiveness.

6.2 MEASURING STATE PUNITIVENESS

Chapter 2 combined thirty-three different public opinion questions asked 381 different times into a single over-time measure of the public's punitiveness. The challenge for state-level analysis is that these questions come from national surveys, which are not meant to measure opinion within each state. Fortunately, recent research has developed a method to circumvent this problem. Park,

Gelman, and Bafumi (2004) and Lax and Phillips (2009) have shown that national surveys can produce valid and reliable estimates of state opinion with a technique called multilevel regression and poststratification (MRP). MRP is a statistical technique that can produce valid measures of state public opinion by re-weighting national survey data to correspond with each state's population characteristics.

I build on this approach to generate over-time state-level estimates of the public's punitiveness. The individual-level data were available for twenty-nine out of the thirty-three survey question series used to generate the measure of punitive opinion analyzed in previous chapters. For each of these questions, I used a multilevel regression model to estimate the relationship between whether or not the respondent offered the punitive response to the survey question and the respondent's gender (female or male), race (black, white, or other), age (18–29, 30–44, 45–64, or 65+), education (less than high school, high school, some college, college graduate or more), state, and region (Northeast, Midwest, South, West, or DC).[11] The individual demographic variables were selected because they have been shown to correlate strongly with punitive attitudes. The state of the respondent is used to estimate state-level effects, which themselves are modeled as a function of region and state vote in the previous presidential election. Presidential vote share offers a state-level measure of the political environment. Thus, the model of individual survey response incorporates individual and regional characteristics.

Based on this model, I then predict, for each demographic-geographic respondent (e.g., African American females, age 18 to 29, with a college degree in California or white males, age 45 to 64, with less than a high school education in New York), the probability of a punitive response. The result is a predicted response for each demographic-geographic respondent type to each question each year it was asked. Finally, I weight (i.e., poststratify) each demographic-geographic respondent type by the percentage of each type in the state population. These weights allow an estimate of the percentage of respondents within each state who support the punitive position on each of the questions for each year the question was asked.[12]

MRP thus produces a measure of the percent punitive in each state for each of the twenty-nine question series (227 total survey questions) described earlier.

---

[11] When identical survey questions come from more than one poll, the model also includes an indicator to account for each poll in the model. The decision to treat Washington, DC, as a separate region follows Park, Gelman, and Bafumi (2006, p. 377). All models were estimated with the glmer in R.

[12] The state population estimates come from the Integrated Public Use Microdata Series (IPUMS) at the University of Minnesota, which includes 1 percent census samples for 1950, 1960, and 1970, 5 percent samples for 1980, 1990, and 2000, and 1 percent American Community Survey (ACS) samples for 2005–2010. I relied on 1 percent samples when those were the only ones available. Between census years, linear interpolation is used to estimate state population characteristics.

For each state, I then follow the strategy used in Chapter 2 to generate an over-time measure of state punitiveness. That is, for each state, I use Stimson's (1999) Wcalc algorithm to combine these series into an over-time measure of state support for being tough on crime.[13] As mentioned earlier, past research has validated the MRP approach as a method of generating state-level opinion measures from national surveys (Lax and Phillips 2009, Park, Gelman, and Bafumi 2006). Applying MRP to multiple questions asked at repeated time points to generate an over-time measure of the public's policy preferences further reduces measurement error to provide valid estimates of state public opinion (Enns and Koch 2013, 2015). Thus, the large number of surveys combined with MRP offers an ideal strategy to measure public punitiveness in each state.

The California Field Poll offers an opportunity to validate the resulting state-level measures of punitiveness. In almost every year from 1956 through 2006 the California Field Poll has asked Californians whether they support the death penalty. Although the measure of state punitiveness I constructed contains more indicators than just support for the death penalty, given the results in Chapter 2 we would expect that shifts in support for the death penalty would correspond with shifts in punitiveness in general. Furthermore, because the California Field Poll is based on a probability sample of Californians, this poll offers an ideal benchmark for whether we recover valid state-level estimates.

Figure 6.3 reports support for the death penalty based on the California Field Poll and support for being tough on crime based on the MRP methods described earlier. The two series (which are plotted on separate axes to aid comparison) track closely. For most of the past fifty years, both measures overlap and move together. In the 1990s, support for the death penalty declines at a slightly slower pace than the overall measure of punitiveness, but overall the commonalties are impressive. The California Field Poll offers an important validation of the measurement strategy. The next step is to evaluate whether public punitiveness in each state corresponds with state incarceration rates.

6.3 WHAT EXPLAINS CHANGES IN STATE INCARCERATION RATES?

Prior to analyzing the relationship between the public's punitiveness and incarceration rates across *all* the states, I continue with a specific focus on California. In 2013, California had the third largest prison population (behind Texas and Georgia) and California's punitive policies have long been of interest to criminal justice scholars (e.g., Auerhahn 2003, Zimring and Hawkins 1992, Zimring, Hawkins, and Kamin 2001).

Figure 6.3 reported and validated an over-time measure of public punitiveness in California. Figure 6.4(a) plots this measure of Californians' punitiveness

---

[13] See Chapter 2 for a discussion of this methodology and its many advantages.

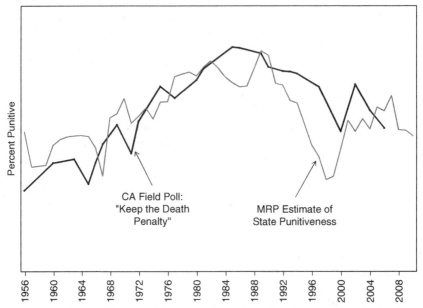

FIGURE 6.3. The public's punitivenss (MRP Estimate) and support for the death penalty (CA Field Poll) in California.

Source: Survey data obtained from the Roper Center for Public Opinion Research, the General Social Survey, the American National Election Study, and the California Field Poll.

alongside changes in California's incarceration rate from 1953 to 2010 (the series are plotted on separate axes to aid comparison). I rely on the change in the incarceration rate because, as discussed in Chapter 5, analyzing the total incarceration rate can produce invalid conclusions about the causes of incarceration rates. In particular, analyzing the change in the incarceration rate avoids the problem that the rate of total incarcerations and the rate of new admissions can increase even when the determinants of incarcerations remain constant or decrease. Importantly, although Figure 6.4(a) indicates that while the change in the incarceration rate was lower in 2010 than in 1953, the *total* incarceration rate in California was *much* higher in 2010. Thus, we must remember that change is ideal for understanding relationships but it does not directly signal how many people are incarcerated.

Looking at Figure 6.4(a), we see that changes in California's incarceration rate appear to closely track shifts in the public's punitiveness. Californians' punitivenesss began to increase in the 1960s and continued to rise until 1990. Changes in the prison population appear to follow a few years behind, with increases in the incarceration rate occurring through the 1970s and 1980s. Through most of the 1990s, punitive attitudes receded in California.

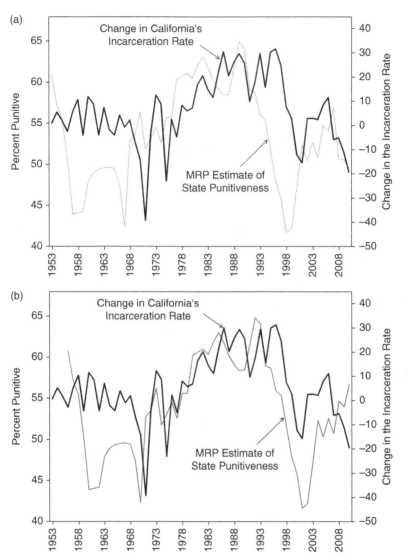

FIGURE 6.4. The California public's punitiveness (MRP Estimate) and changes in California's incarceration rate from 1953 to 2010. (a) No Lags. (b) Punitiveness Lagged three Years.

Source: Incarceration data: *Historical Statistics on Prisoners in State and Federal Institutions, Yearend 1925–1986* and the National Prisoner Statistics data series. Survey data obtained from the Roper Center for Public Opinion Research, the General Social Survey, and the American National Election Study.

Again, with a lag of a few years, changes in the prison rate also began to decline.

Figure 6.4(b) plots the same data, this time lagging punitive attitudes by three years. When police, prosecutors, or judges notice shifting public attitudes, we might expect a relatively quick response. However, the public's shifting preferences may not always be immediately noticeable to these individuals. Thus, it seems reasonable that it could take some time for changing public attitudes to influence the incarceration rate. Politicians, by contrast, should be more attentive to their constituents' preferences. However, changes to sentencing laws and budget allocations take time to trickle through the system. For the national-level analysis in Chapter 5 we saw evidence of a one-year lag (although Appendix A-5.2 showed the results were robust to a three-year lag). Figure 6.4(b) suggests that a three-year lag best approximates the time between shifts in punitiveness and shifts in California's incarceration rate. In fact, with this lag, the year-to-year similarity between Californians' punitiveness and the state's incarceration rate is striking.[14]

In addition to signaling the important influence of public opinion, this year-to-year correspondence suggests that ballot initiatives (when voters in California directly vote on legislation) do not fully account for the public opinion-incarceration rate relationship. Although California is known for ballot initiatives that dramatically affected sentencing outcomes, such as the infamous "three-strikes and you're out law" in 1994, many years typically transpired between successful ballot initiatives related to criminal justice sentencing. Given the length of time between successful initiatives, if these laws were the only factor at work, we would not expect such a strong year-to-year correspondence between the two series. Political actors must also have considered the public's shifting preferences. The following statistical analysis tests whether this year-to-year correspondence applies when all fifty states are analyzed.

6.3.1 Control variables

As with the analysis in Chapter 5, in order to test the relationship between the public's punitiveness and changes in state incarceration rates, we need to control for the other factors thought to influence the incarceration rate.

---

[14] The different lag length for the national-level analysis and this state analysis should not come as a surprise. First, as the subsequent analysis shows, the results are not sensitive to the lag structure. Thus, the differences are not as great as they may seem. Second, the national-level analysis in the previous chapter incorporates state-level incarcerations. Even if it takes an average of three years for state incarceration rates to reflect shifts in public opinion, punitiveness in some states may shift before it shifts in other states. Because these shifts can vary across states, when we look at national public opinion, a one-year lag may best approximate the overall process.

To control for the crime rate, I utilize data from the FBI's Uniform Crime Reporting (UCR) statistics, which are available for each state from 1960 to 2010. Chapter 4 demonstrated that the national violent and property crime rates are highly correlated. The same pattern appears in the states. The average correlation of the state property and violent crime rates is $r = 0.77$, and in twelve states, the correlation is $r = 0.9$ or above. Given the commonalities across measures, the models include the rate of violent crime as a measure of criminal activity.[15]

To control for the social control hypothesis, which predicts that increased inequality will increase the pressure for higher rates of incarceration (e.g., Chambliss and Seidman 1971), the models include a measure of the proportion of income received by the top 1 percent of each state.[16] Because the US prison population shifted from majority white to majority African American and Latino during the period of analysis, and because African Americans have been particularly affected by mass incarceration (e.g., Alexander 2010), the analyses that follow control for the proportion of African Americans in each state. If punitive policies were a reaction to the racial composition of the state, this variable should capture that relationship. As with Chapter 5, the models do not directly control for the public's racial attitudes. To the extent that racial attitudes influence punitive attitudes, the survey questions used to generate the measure of public punitiveness already incorporate relevant racial considerations.

The analysis also controls for the economic climate in each state.[17] Predictions for this variable are mixed. Some research suggests that economic conditions can influence the rate of property and violent crime, with economic

---

[15] Table A-6.1 in the Appendix shows the results are robust to including the rate of property crime in the model. The crime data are available from www.ucrdatatool.gov/index.cfm. Of course, given evidence that the public's punitiveness mediates some of the effect of shifting crime rates, controlling for the crime rate somewhat attenuates the observed effect of public opinion.

[16] The data come from Frank (2009) and are available from www.shsu.edu/eco_mwf/inequality .html. Table A-6.1 in the Appendix shows that the results are robust to including the state Gini coefficient as a measure of inequality. Here, I rely on the income from the top 1 percent because past research shows that when unequal representation exists, it is the preferences of the highest income earners that most closely align with policy outcomes (Gilens 2005, 2011). As mentioned in Chapter 5, the unequal representation research does *not* challenge the public opinion hypothesis because different groups – including different income groups – tend to update their policy preferences in parallel, which means that criminal justice policy (and resulting incarcerations) would move in the same direction regardless of whether political actors consider the preferences of a particular group or the overall public (Enns and Wlezien 2011, Kelly and Enns 2010, Page and Shapiro 1992, Ramirez 2013, Soroka and Wlezien 2010).

[17] Given the much smaller sample size for the national-level analysis in Chapter 5, that analysis did not include as many control variables as the state-level analysis. However, Table A-5.1 in Appendix A-5.2 demonstrated that the results were robust to the inclusion of a variety of additional control variables, including the unemployment rate as a measure of the national economy.

hard times leading to higher crime rates (e.g., Rosenfeld 2009, Rosenfeld and Fornango 2007). From this perspective, if the measure of violent crime in the model does not fully capture all criminal activity, we would expect improving economic conditions to correspond with decreases in criminal activity and thus a declining incarceration rate. However, we have also seen the enormous fiscal costs of increases in the prison population. Thus, we might expect a growing state economy to correspond with increases in the incarceration rate, as increased government revenue may transfer to more support for police, prosecutors, and prisons. Although the expected influence of the economy is unclear, I use per capita state gross domestic product (GDP) to measure state economic conditions. State GDP is the best available measure of each state's economic climate for the period of analysis.

Finally, I control for the partisan composition of state government. The models include a dichotomous variable to indicate whether the governor was a Republican and a measure of the proportion of the lower legislative chamber controlled by the Republican Party. The data come from Klarner (2003).[18]

In contrast to the changes in the overall US incarceration rate analyzed in the previous chapter, changes in each state's incarceration rate are stationary time series.[19] Thus, I estimate an autoregressive distributed lag (ADL) model that includes the lagged value of the dependent variable (Keele and Kelly 2006). Because of the clustered nature of the state panel data, I follow the recommendation of Harden (2011, 2012) and estimate "bootstrap cluster standard errors" (BCSE). An F-test does not reject the null hypothesis that the combined influence of state fixed effects equals zero ($p = 0.51$), so the model does not include state fixed effects.[20] I do, however, include three regional dichotomous variables, with the South as the baseline category, to control for specific regional factors that may have influenced incarceration rates.

6.3.2 Incarceration rate results

Table 6.1 presents the results. Column 1 includes only lagged values of the public's support for being tough on crime. Consistent with Figure 6.4(b), lagging the public's punitiveness by three years produces the best-fitting model so I report this specification (although all results are consistent with punitiveness lagged between one and four periods). As expected, the coefficient that corresponds with past values of the public's punitiveness is positive

---

[18] The Klarner data are available here: https://thedata.harvard.edu/dvn/dv/cklarner.
[19] Augmented Dicker Fuller tests indicate that we reject the null hypothesis of a unit root for changes in every state's incarceration rate.
[20] As reported in Table A-6.1 in the Appendix, the results are robust to including state fixed effects and to alternate lag specifications.

TABLE 6.1. *The relationship between the public's punitiveness and state incarceration rates, controlling for social and political factors from 1953 to 2010*

	(1)	(2)	(3)
ΔIncarceration rate$_{t-1}$	0.17*	0.126	0.125
	(0.08)	(0.077)	(0.081)
Public punitiveness$_{t-3}$	0.35*	0.23*	0.24*
	(0.06)	(0.06)	(0.06)
Violent crime rate$_{t-1}$		0.013*	0.013*
		(0.002)	(0.002)
State GDP$_{t-1}$		−0.05	−0.06
		(0.05)	(0.05)
Top 1% income share$_{t-1}$		4.47	3.29
		(16.61)	(17.01)
% African American$_{t-1}$		−0.08	−0.06
		(0.09)	(0.09)
Republican governor$_{t-1}$			−0.29
			(0.70)
% Rep. in legislature$_{t-1}$			3.99
			(2.75)
Northeast		−2.52	−2.66
		(1.42)	(1.40)
Midwest		−1.06	−1.48
		(1.19)	(1.31)
West		−1.89	−2.25
		(1.54)	(1.62)
Constant	−14.45*	−10.04*	−11.82*
	(3.08)	(3.57)	(4.15)
Adj. R^2	0.06	0.08	0.08
N	2,760	2,373	2,325
No. of states	50	50	49

Notes: The dependent variable is the change in state incarceration rates. OLS coefficients with bootstrap cluster standard errors in parentheses. * $= p < 0.05$; two-tailed tests. Column 3 includes only forty-nine states because Nebraska has a nonpartisan legislature.

and statistically significant. Column 2 adds controls for the crime rate, state economic conditions, inequality, the proportion of the state that is African American, and regional controls. To allow a more contemporaneous relationship between these control variables and changes in the incarceration rate, these variables are lagged one year. Appendix A-6.1 shows, however, that the results remain unchanged with longer lag lengths. Because data for some of the control variables do not exist prior to 1964, the sample size decreases slightly. In this model, past values of the public's punitiveness are again positive and significant. The substantive magnitude of the public opinion effect (which I discuss next) is quite impressive. The relationship between the crime rate and the prison population is also positive and statistically significant. In the previous chapter, in the multivariate analysis, we did not observe a significant relationship between the crime rate and changes in the incarceration rate. However, in the state-level analysis this relationship emerges. This result suggests that crime rates have had a more consistent influence on incarceration rates than previously thought.

Column 3 controls for Republican political strength in the state. Controlling for state party strength offers a test of whether the previously observed relationship between the public's support for being tough on crime and the incarceration rate is mediated by who is in office. The relationship between the public's preferences and state incarcerations continues to be significant and of similar magnitude, suggesting that this relationship is not mediated by the party in power. Although the proportion of the legislature that is Republican is positively correlated with state incarcerations, the estimate is imprecisely estimated. Researchers analyzing the 1970s, 1980s, and 1990s have consistently found a positive relationship between Republican officeholders and rising incarceration rates (Jacobs and Carmichael 2001, Smith 2004, Yates and Fording 2005). Upon replicating Column 3 for the period from 1970 to 2000, the estimated effect of the public's preferences remains significant ($\beta = 0.31$, s.e. $= 0.09$) and the proportion Republican also emerges as significant (one-tailed test, $\beta = 5.71$, s.e. $= 3.25$). Thus, it appears that the relationship between the partisanship of state governments and incarceration rates is most evident during this thirty-year period. Prior to the 1970s as well as in more recent years, state criminal justice policy does not appear to be driven by which party is in office.

To assess the magnitude of the public's influence, I use the results from Column 3 to estimate the expected average incarceration rate, (across all states) each year under various counterfactual scenarios. First, I estimated the predicted incarceration rate allowing all variables to take their actual values *except* for the public's punitiveness and the crime rate in each state, which were held constant at their 1964 value (the first time point in the Column 3 analysis).[21] The dashed gray line in Figure 6.5 depicts these predicted values, which suggest that if the crime rate and the public's punitiveness had held constant at their 1964 level, the trajectory of the average state incarceration rate would have been relatively flat in subsequent decades. The solid gray line presents the expected incarceration rate if all variables *except* for the public's

---

[21]   As with Chapter 5, to ensure that the fit between predicted values and actual values in Figure 6.5 is not inflated, the actual value of the lagged dependent variable influences only the estimate of the first predicted value (i.e., 1964). The values for all subsequent years are estimated iteratively, using the previous year's predicted value in place of the lagged value of the dependent variable to generate that year's predicted value.

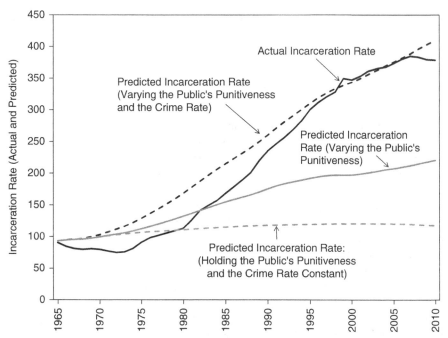

FIGURE 6.5. The average state incarceration rate and the predicted incarceration rate for various counterfactual scenarios.

Source: The predicted values are based on the results of Column 3 in Table 6.1.

punitiveness are held constant at their 1964 level. The upward trajectory of this gray line suggests that shifts in the public's punitiveness had a substantial influence on state incarceration rates. In fact, these estimates suggest that changes in the public's punitiveness accounted for more than three hundred forty thousand additional state incarcerations *in 2010 alone*.

The dashed black line corresponds with the predicted incarceration rate holding all variables constant *except* the crime rate *and* the public's punitiveness. Thus, this line captures the predicted incarceration rate if we allow only crime and public punitiveness to vary. We have seen in previous chapters that increases in the crime rate strongly influence the public's punitive attitudes and that politicians tend to focus on rising crime when the public expresses concern with criminal activity. Given the reinforcing relationship between these two variables, the expected incarceration rate when only the crime rate and the public's punitiveness vary may be the most informative counterfactual. We see that the expected values correspond closely with the actual average state incarceration rate (solid black line). Knowing the crime rate and public support for being tough on crime in the states almost fully accounts for the observed rise in state incarceration rates.[22] Considering the minimal influence previous research assigns to public opinion and the crime rate, this is a crucial result.[23]

6.4 A SECOND TEST: STATE EXPENDITURES ON CORRECTIONS

We have seen a strong relationship between the public's punitiveness and state incarceration rates. As mentioned earlier, police, judges, prosecutors, legislators, and governors could all contribute to this relationship. Given the visibility of their decisions and their electoral incentives, we would especially expect legislators and governors to play a role in this process. If this is the case, we should also observe a relationship between the public's attitudes and specific legislative outputs that relate to criminal justice outcomes. To test this expectation, I examine the percent of each state's budget that is devoted to corrections (i.e., spending on prisons, jails, and parole offices).

This measure is advantageous because the proportion of the budget devoted to corrections offers a direct indication of political support for prisons and incarceration. Increased funding for corrections relative to other policy areas suggests more political support. Of course, one might worry that in some instances, *decreased* funding could signal more punitive political support if more individuals are locked up but *less* is spent on each inmate. In practice, this turns out not to be the case. Organizations want to grow. As Pfeffer and Salancik (1978, p. 139) explain, "Growth enhances an organization's survival potential because it provides additional stability and reduces uncertainty and also provides leverage for the organization in managing interorganizational relationships." The implication is that even if punitive policies lead to less direct spending on each inmate, organizational leaders will still want to grow the corrections budget.

This logic is evident in the behavior of Sheriff Joe Arpaio, the sheriff of Maricopa County, Arizona. Sheriff Arpaio has become known for offering the cheapest prison meals in the United States. The sheriff's office website boasts, "The average meal costs between 15 and 40 cents, and inmates are fed only twice daily, to cut the labor costs of meal delivery. He even stopped serving them salt and pepper to save tax payers $20,000 a year."[24] Despite this cost-saving approach, in 2013 Sheriff Arpaio tried to *double* his budget,

---

[22] Given the relatively small value of the adjusted R^2 reported in Table 6.1, the fit between the predicted values and the change in state incarceration rates may seem surprising. Notice, however, that the predicted values capture the broad trajectory of incarcerations but not the specific ups and downs. This explains part of the low R^2. Also, Figure 6.5 reports the expected and actual incarceration rate across all states. The focus on all states smooths out some of the unexplained variance that the low R^2 reflects in the statistical analysis.

[23] See, for example, Beckett (1997, p. 108), Gottschalk (2008, pp. 252–252), and Zimring and Hawkins (1991, pp. 125–130) on the public's lack of influence on the incarceration rate and see Gottschalk (2006), Loury (2010), Shannon and Uggen (2013), and Western (2006) on the lack of relationship between the crime rate and the incarceration rate.

[24] See www.mcso.org/About/Sheriff.aspx.

"requesting an additional \$274 million on top of his \$280 million budget to pay for a new jail, additional staff and an overhaul of the agency's aircraft, vehicles and technology equipment" (Ye Hee Lee 2013). Even when meals cost less than a quarter, resources matter.

In order to analyze the relationship between punitive public attitudes and the proportion of state budgets devoted to corrections, I again estimate three separate models, controlling for the same social, economic, and political factors analyzed earlier. Augmented Dickey Fuller tests indicate that the percent of the budget devoted to corrections is an integrated time series.[25] A cointegration test indicates that state punitive attitudes are cointegrated with the percent of the budget going to corrections, so I estimate a single-equation Error Correction Model.[26] As mentioned earlier, given the clustered nature of the state panel data, I estimate "bootstrap cluster standard errors" (BCSE) (Harden 2011, 2012). An F-test does not reject the null hypothesis that the combined influence of state fixed effects equals zero ($p = 0.39$), so the model does not include state fixed effects.[27] However, as with the incarceration analysis, I do control for potential regional differences. The budget data are available through 2012, so the analysis ends in that year.

6.4.1 Corrections expenditure results

Table 6.2 reports the relationship between the public's punitiveness in each state and the proportion of each state's budget devoted to corrections. As with the previous model, public opinion is lagged three years (again, the results are not sensitive to lag length). Since we would expect factors like the partisan composition of the legislature and economic conditions to have a more contemporaneous effect on budget decisions, other variables are lagged one year, but these results are also not sensitive to lag length (see Appendix A-6.2).

In Column 1, we see the expected positive and significant relationship between the public's attitudes and corrections spending.[28] Column 2 adds

---

[25] The augmented Dickey Fuller test fails to reject the null hypothesis of a unit root for every state except Vermont and Minnesota.

[26] See Chapter 5 for a full discussion of ECMs. Based on MacKinnon's critical values, the t-statistic associated with the lagged dependent variable provides evidence of a cointegrating relationship between the public's punitiveness and the proportion of spending on corrections. Although the single-equation ECM is simply an alternate parameterization of the general ADL model, the ECM specification is advantageous because it offers a test of cointegration, which is a necessary requirement when estimating this type of model with integrated data (Enns, Masaki, and Kelly 2014).

[27] As shown in Table A-6.2 the results are robust to the inclusion of fixed effects.

[28] I also estimated these models including changes in the predictor variables to allow for short-term effects (see Table A-6.2 in Appendix A-6.2). The results reported in the following text were unchanged with this specification. Interestingly, with that specification, a short-term relationship emerges between the percent of African Americans in the state and the percent of the budget devoted to corrections. However, this result is sensitive to alternate lag specifications, so it should be interpreted with caution.

TABLE 6.2. *The relationship between the public's punitiveness and the proportion of state spending on corrections, controlling for social and political factors from 1953 to 2012*

	(1)	(2)	(3)
% Corrections spending$_{t-1}$	−0.044*	−0.07*	−0.08*
	(0.006)	(0.01)	(0.01)
Public punitiveness$_{t-3}$	0.004*	0.003*	0.003*
	(0.001)	(0.001)	(0.001)
Violent crime rate$_{t-1}$		0.0002*	0.0002*
		(0.0000)	(0.0000)
State GDP$_{t-1}$		−0.001	−0.001
		(0.001)	(0.001)
Top 1% income share$_{t-1}$		0.34	0.31
		(0.26)	(0.26)
% African American$_{t-1}$		−0.001	−0.001
		(0.001)	(0.001)
Republican governor$_{t-1}$			0.005
			(0.012)
% Rep. in legislature$_{t-1}$			0.073
			(0.042)
Northeast		−0.04*	−0.05*
		(0.02)	(0.02)
Midwest		−0.04	−0.05*
		(0.02)	(0.02)
West		−0.03	−0.03
		(0.01)	(0.02)
Constant	−0.10*	−0.05	−0.09*
	(0.03)	(0.04)	(0.04)
Adj. R^2	0.03	0.05	0.05
N	2,836	2,448	2,399
No. of states	50	50	49

Notes: Single-equation error correction model. The dependent variable is the change in the proportion of state spending devoted to corrections. OLS coefficients with bootstrap cluster standard errors in parentheses. * = $p < 0.05$; two-tailed tests. Column 3 includes only forty-nine states because Nebraska has a nonpartisan legislature.

controls for the crime rate, state economic conditions, inequality, the proportion of African Americans in the state, and regional controls. The public's punitiveness and the crime rate are both significant. The negative and significant coefficients for the Northeast and Midwest indicate that, on average, these regions devoted less of their budgets to corrections than Southern states. The final model (Column 3) includes an indicator for Republican governors and the proportion of the lower legislative chamber that is Republican. The latter variable is statistically significant at the 0.10 level ($p = 0.084$), offering some evidence that more Republican legislators corresponds with a greater percent of the budget devoted to corrections. As with the incarceration rate analysis, this relationship becomes stronger and statistically significant when the analysis is restricted to 1970 to 2000 (see Appendix A-6.2).[29] The estimated effects of other variables in the model are relatively unchanged by the time period of analysis.

To gain a sense of the magnitude of these relationships, I repeated the previous counterfactual scenarios. These results appear in Figure 6.6. The dashed gray line reports the predicted percent of state budgets devoted to corrections when all variables take their actual value *except* for the public's punitiveness and the crime rate in each state, which were held constant at their 1964 value. The relatively flat trajectory of the dashed gray line suggests that if the crime rate and the public's punitiveness had held constant at their 1964 level, the average proportion of state spending on corrections would have been relatively flat in subsequent decades. The solid gray line presents the expected percent spent on corrections if all variables *except* for the public's punitiveness are held constant at their 1964 level. We see that during the 1980s and 1990s, the public's punitiveness corresponded with increased financial support for corrections. The percentage increase is relatively minor (less than one-half a percent of the total average state budget), but this still amounts to a total of almost $5 billion (adjusted for inflation) each year during the early 1990s. The dashed black line corresponds with the predicted budget holding all variables constant *except* the crime rate *and* the public's punitiveness. As noted earlier, considering the reinforcing relationship between these two variables, the combined effect of these two variables is probably the most informative counterfactual. We see that the expected values correspond closely with the actual average percent devoted to corrections (solid black line). As with the incarceration rate, the crime rate and the public's punitiveness are critical to understanding state budget priorities.[30]

---

[29] The relationships between state GDP and the percent of the budget devoted to corrections also emerges as significant in the truncated analysis.

[30] As mentioned in Footnote 22, given the small value of the adjusted R^2 reported in Table 6.2, the fit between the predicted values and the actual percent of state budgets devoted to corrections may seem surprising. This pattern occurs for two reasons. First, the predicted values capture the broad trajectory of the corrections budgets but not the specific ups and downs. Second, Figure 6.6 reports the expected and actual percent of the budget devoted to corrections across all states. The focus on all states smooths out some of the unexplained variance that the low R^2 reflects in the statistical analysis.

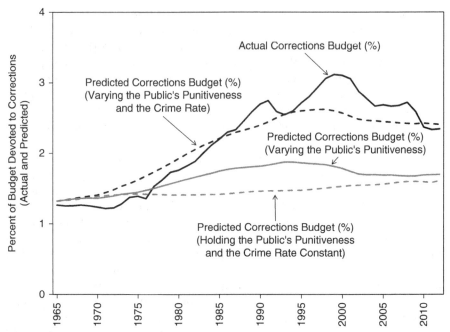

FIGURE 6.6. The percent of state budgets devoted to corrections and the predicted budget for various counterfactual scenarios.

Source: The predicted values are based on the results of Column 3 in Table 6.2.

6.5 CONCLUSION

On January 22, 2014, in his annual State of the State Address, California Governor "Jerry" Brown explained, "The Federal courts, backed up by the United States Supreme Court, have ordered major reductions in our prison population and dramatic improvements in the medical and mental health programs that the state makes available."[31] Previously, Governor Brown had proclaimed, "Our prisons are dangerously overcrowded."[32] What makes this second statement incredible is that it was spoken by a different Governor Brown – Jerry Brown's father, "Pat" Brown Sr. – *fifty-five years earlier.*

Governor Pat Brown drew attention to California's overcrowded prisons in his inaugural address in January 1959. At that time, 19,299 individuals were serving time in California with a sentence of at least a year. Almost half a century later, California reached its peak prison population of 173,421. We have seen that to varying degrees, this expansion occurred in every US state.

31 http://governors.library.ca.gov/addresses/s_39-JBrown4.html
32 http://governors.library.ca.gov/addresses/32-Pbrown01.html

But mass incarceration was not a foregone conclusion. In 1959, Governor Brown's inaugural address went on to propose that:

> We should also determine whether some prisoners are now kept confined after punishment has served its purpose ... we should establish new forestry camps and industrial training programs so that after release, every man can offer society an effective skill and regular work habits ... we must press forward in the prevention of delinquency ... If we can find a way to reach the promise and the core of goodness in our emotionally disturbed children, we strike at the roots of crime.

Pat Brown, who had served as district attorney for San Francisco and state attorney general, was not soft on crime. Yet Brown's policy recommendations in 1959 illustrate that mass incarceration in the United States was far from an inevitable political outcome. It took the public's punitive turn to produce this result. Politicians and those directly involved in the criminal justice system also chose to follow the public. Without the public's increasing punitiveness through the 1960s, 1970s and 1980s, or without political actors following the public, criminal justice policy and the incarceration rate would look very different in the United States.

Of course, the public's punitiveness did not materialize inexplicably. Chapter 4 showed the close connection between the crime rate, news coverage of crime, and the public's punitiveness. Consistent with these findings, the analyses in this chapter indicate that when we examine the average changes across states, the crime rate and the public's punitiveness can account for most of the variation in state incarceration rates and the proportion of state budgets devoted to corrections. The next, and concluding, chapter considers these findings and their implications for the future of incarceration in the United States.

A-6 APPENDICES TO CHAPTER 6

A-6.1 Incarceration rate analysis: additional robustness checks

Table A-6.1 reports various robustness checks related to the incarceration rate analysis reported in Chapter 6. The first column replicates Column 1 of Table 6.1 to provide a baseline comparison for the specifications described below. Column 2 controls for the violent and property crime rates. The main analyses in Chapter 6 include only the violent crime rate because the violent and property crime rates are highly correlated in most states. These high correlations become especially problematic when additional control variables are added and the period available for analysis is reduced. In Column 2, we see, however, that the effect of the public's punitiveness remains significant when controlling for both measures of the crime rate. The magnitude of the public opinion coefficient decreases, but this is not surprising given the previous evidence of the relationship between crime rates and the public's punitiveness.

TABLE A-6.1. *Robustness checks: the relationship between the public's punitiveness and state incarceration rates, controlling for social and political factors from 1953 to 2010*

	(1) Table 6.1 Col. 1	(2) Violent & prop. crime	(3) Two-year lags	(4) One lag	(5) Four lags	(6) State F.E.	(7) Gini coef.	(8) 1970 to 2000
ΔIncarceration rate$_{t-1}$	0.17* (0.08)	0.12 (0.08)	0.12 (0.08)	0.13 (0.08)	0.12 (0.08)	0.08* (0.02)	0.12 (0.08)	0.05 (0.09)
Public punitiveness$_{t-3}$	0.35* (0.06)	0.16* (0.05)	0.22* (0.06)					
Public punitiveness$_{t-1}$				0.20* (0.06)		0.122* (0.060)	0.21* (0.06)	0.31* (0.09)
Public punitiveness$_{t-4}$					0.35* (0.06)			
Violent crime rate$_{t-1}$		0.005* (0.002)	0.013* (0.003)	0.014* (0.003)	0.012* (0.002)	0.033* (0.003)	0.013* (0.002)	0.006* (0.003)
Property crime rate$_{t-1}$		0.002* (0.000)						
State GDP$_{t-1}$			-0.02 (0.05)	-0.04 (0.04)	-0.05 (0.04)	-0.09 (0.06)	-0.17* (0.04)	0.20* (0.09)

Top 1% income share$_{t-1}$			−13.58 (15.58)	2.07 (16.33)	6.06 (15.86)	3.46 (17.33)		27.69 (36.38)
% African American$_{t-1}$			−0.06 (0.09)	−0.09 (0.09)	−0.05 (0.09)	−0.43 (0.37)	−0.07 (0.08)	0.18 (0.12)
Republican governor$_{t-1}$			−0.71 (0.78)			−0.19 (0.68)		−0.54 (1.04)
% Rep. in legislature$_{t-1}$			3.43 (2.73)			−3.05 (3.28)		5.72 (3.23)
Gini coefficient$_{t-1}$							41.12* (10.71)	
Constant	−14.45* (3.08)	−12.78* (2.98)	−8.52* (3.66)	−8.50* (3.76)	−16.36* (3.93)	−13.95* (4.55)	−27.90* (5.12)	−20.44* (7.04)
Adj. R^2	0.06	0.10	0.07	0.08	0.09	0.12	0.08	0.07
N	2,760	2,515	2,277	2,373	2,373	2,325	2,373	1,508
No. of states	50	50	49	50	50	49	50	49

Note: The dependent variable is the change in state incarceration rates. OLS coefficients with bootstrap cluster standard errors in parentheses. * = $p < 0.05$; two-tailed tests. Regional controls are included in Columns 3, 4, 5, 7, and 8. All control variables lagged two years in Column 3.

We also see that the coefficient for the violent crime rate drops by more than half, which further illustrates the similarities between the two crime measures.

Since it could take additional time for some of the control variables to influence changes in the incarceration rate, Column 3 replicates the analysis lagging all control variables by two years. The roughly equivalent results indicate that the findings in this chapter are not sensitive to the lag length of the control variables. Columns 4 and 5 show that the estimated effect of the public's punitiveness is robust to various lag lengths. Column 6 adds state fixed effects in addition to the other control variables in the model. The main analyses in the text did not include state fixed effects because an F-test did not reject the null hypothesis that the combined influence of state fixed effects equals zero. Consistent with this result, adding state fixed effects does not substantively alter the results. The coefficient for public punitiveness does decline some, however, and the adjusted R^2 increases. The fixed effects could be picking up on cross-sectional differences in public punitiveness across states, or other differences across states, such as historical factors, cultural considerations, or unmeasured demographic considerations. Column 7 uses the state Gini coefficient as an alternate measure of state inequality. Again the main results hold. The last column restricts the analysis to the period 1970 to 2000. Given past research, the negative coefficient for percent of Republicans in the state legislature in Table 6.1 was surprising. Previous research, however, has focused on the period between 1970 and 2000. In Column 8 we see that the coefficient for percent Republican in the state legislature is positive and significant with a one-tailed test ($p = 0.04$). This result suggests that previous research on the relationship between partisanship of state governments and incarceration rates may be period specific.

A-6.2 Corrections expenditures analysis: additional robustness checks

Table A-6.2 reports various robustness checks related to the corrections expenditure analysis reported in Chapter 6. The first column replicates Column 1 of Table 6.2. The positive and significant relationship for the public's punitiveness offers a baseline comparison for the specifications described below. The second column is based on an error correction model that includes short-term effects. Including short-term effects is the standard approach to ECMs, but given the theoretical expectation of long-term effects and the lack of evidence of short-term effects in chapter 5, the ECMs reported in this Chapter only estimated long-term effects. Column 2 shows that this decision did not influence the key findings. As noted in the text (see Footnote 28), we do see evidence of a short-term relationship between the percent of African Americans in the state and the percent of the budget devoted to corrections, but this result is sensitive to model specification.

Column 3 lags all of the control variables by two years. Stimson, MacKuen, and Erikson (1995) argue that politicians rationally anticipate future conditions

TABLE A-6.2. *Robustness checks: the relationship between the public's punitiveness and the proportion of state spending on corrections, controlling for social and political factors from 1953 to 2012*

	(1) Table 6.2 Col. 1	(2) Short-term relationships◇	(3) Two-year lag	(4) One lag	(5) Four lags	(6) State F.E.	(7) 1970–2000 with F.E.
% Corrections spending$_{t-1}$	−0.044* (0.006)	−0.08* (0.01)	−0.07* (0.01)	−0.07* (0.01)	−0.08* (0.01)	−0.14* (0.01)	−0.19* (0.02)
Public punitiveness$_{t-3}$	0.004* (0.001)	0.003* (0.001)	0.0024* (0.0008)			0.003* (0.001)	0.003* (0.001)
Public punitiveness$_{t-1}$				0.0024* (0.0011)			
Public punitiveness$_{t-4}$					0.005* (0.001)		
Violent crime rate$_{t-1}$		0.0002* (0.0001)	0.0002* (0.0001)	0.0002* (0.0001)	0.0002* (0.0000)	0.0004* (0.0000)	0.0001 (0.0001)
State GDP$_{t-1}$		−0.001 (0.001)	−0.000 (0.001)	−0.001 (0.001)	−0.001 (0.001)	−0.001 (0.001)	0.008* (0.002)
Top 1% income share$_{t-1}$		0.40 (0.31)	−0.12 (0.27)	0.26 (0.27)	0.35 (0.27)	1.03* (0.28)	0.80 (0.51)
Δ% African American$_{t-1}$		0.14* (0.04)					
% African American$_{t-1}$		−0.000 (0.001)	−0.001 (0.001)	−0.001 (0.001)	−0.000 (0.001)	−0.001 (0.001)	0.03* (0.01)

(continued)

TABLE A-6.2 (*continued*)

	(1) Table 6.2 Col. 1	(2) Short-term relationships◇	(3) Two-year lag	(4) One lag	(5) Four lags	(6) State F.E.	(7) 1970–2000 with F.E.
Republican governor$_{t-1}$		0.004	−0.004	0.004	0.006	0.01	0.01
		(0.013)	(0.011)	(0.012)	(0.012)	(0.01)	(0.02)
% Rep. in legislature$_{t-1}$		0.07	0.084	0.07	0.080	0.03	0.22*
		(0.04)	(0.046)	(0.04)	(0.043)	(0.05)	(0.09)
Northeast		−0.056*	−0.05*	−0.05*	−0.043*		
		(0.026)	(0.02)	(0.02)	(0.021)		
Midwest		−0.060*	−0.06*	−0.05*	−0.051*		
		(0.026)	(0.02)	(0.02)	(0.022)		
West		−0.023	−0.037	−0.03	−0.02		
		(0.026)	(0.021)	(0.02)	(0.02)		
Constant	−0.10*	−0.09	−0.01	−0.04	−0.20*	−0.11	−0.35*
	(0.03)	(0.06)	(0.04)	(0.06)	(0.05)	(0.09)	(0.15)
Adj. R^2	0.03	0.06	0.05	0.05	0.06	0.05	0.01
N	2,836	2,350	2,350	2,399	2,399	2,399	1,519
No. of states	50	49	49	49	49	49	49

Note: Single-equation error correction models. The dependent variable is the change in the proportion of state spending devoted to corrections. OLS coefficients with bootstrap cluster standard errors in parentheses. * = $p < 0.05$; two-tailed tests. ◇ Only significant short-term effects are shown. All control variables lagged two years in Column 3.

in order to maximize the chance of winning future elections. Others argue that politicians react to current or even past conditions. Thus, it is not clear what lag structure best represents political processes. Since budget allocations follow the fiscal year and budget decisions are made the prior year, the lag structure reported in this chapter roughly corresponds to the middle perspective. To ensure this decision did not alter the results, Column 3 lags all control variables by two years, allowing more time for these variables to influence budget outcomes. The results are virtually unchanged. Columns 4 and 5 ensure that the results for public opinion do not depend on the lag associated with the public's punitiveness. The results are robust for a one-year and four-year lag.

The main analyses in the text did not include state fixed effects because an F-test did not reject the null hypothesis that the combined influence of state fixed effects equals zero. Consistent with this result, Column 6 shows that adding state fixed effects does not substantively alter the results. Finally, Column 7 replicates Column 6 from 1970 to 2000. As with the incarceration rate analysis, the relationship between the percent of Republicans in the legislature is larger and statistically significant for this time period. We also see a statistically significant relationship between state GDP and the percent of the budget devoted to corrections during this period. The result for the public's punitiveness remains the same.

7

Conclusion

> In ones and twos, men got out of the cars. Shadows became substance as lights revealed solid shapes moving toward the jail door. Atticus remained where he was. The men hid him from view. "He in there, Mr. Finch?" a man said … "You know what we want," another man said. "Get aside from the door, Mr. Finch."

Of course, Atticus did not budge. Atticus Finch – Tom Robinson's lawyer in *To Kill a Mockingbird* – reflects an important ideal of the US legal system. Standing between his jailed client and an angry mob, Atticus Finch represents a legal system that offers protection from the public's punitive whims.[1]

Scholars and legal practitioners have long embraced the idea that the US criminal justice system is insulated from public opinion. Based on his travels throughout America in 1831, Alexis de Tocqueville (p. 268) observed:

> In the United States it is easy to discover how well adapted the legal spirit is, both by its qualities and, I would say, even by its defects, to neutralize the vices inherent in popular government. When the American people let themselves get intoxicated by their passions or carried away by their ideas, the lawyers apply an almost invisible brake which slows them down and halts them.

The previous chapters call this ideal into question. If an "invisible brake" was applied during the past half-century, it appears to have been no match for the accelerating force of public opinion. We have seen that the public became increasingly punitive during much of the 1960s, 1970s, 1980s, and 1990s and these punitive attitudes exerted a major influence on criminal justice policy and the incarceration rate. If the public had not become so punitive, there is no reason to expect that the United States would have become the world's most aggressive imprisoner.

[1] The quote that opens this chapter comes from Harper Lee's *To Kill a Mockingbird* (1960, p. 151).

We saw in Chapter 3, for example, that the politicians most associated with tough-on-crime stances, such as Barry Goldwater and Richard Nixon, appeared to follow – not lead – the public. Indeed, internal memos from Nixon's 1968 presidential campaign suggest that his focus on crime was a direct response to public concern expressed in opinion polls. The analyses in Chapter 4, which showed that presidential rhetoric and congressional hearings followed the public's punitiveness, further illustrate political reactions to the mass public. And in Chapters 5 and 6, we saw that changes in the overall US incarceration rate and changes in state incarceration rates reflected changes in the public's punitiveness. Of course, politicians and political rhetoric can influence the public, but the public's punitiveness has been a driving force in the rise of mass incarceration.

Importantly, the public's influence works both ways. In recent years, it appears that the public has finally applied a brake on criminal justice, leading to a deceleration of the prison boom. Changes to the criminal justice system that seemed unimaginable twenty years ago – such as the closing of some prisons, the decriminalization of certain low-level drug offenses, and even conservative interest groups calling for a change in criminal justice policy – make sense in light of the declining public punitiveness evident in Chapter 2.[2]

7.1 THE IMPORTANCE OF STUDYING CHANGE

The theory and analyses in this book stem from a simple concept. If we want to understand why the incarceration rate in the US has *changed* so dramatically, we must consider *over-time* processes. Although the over-time approach is intuitive, focusing on over-time dynamics has yielded crucial insights for understanding the incarceration rate, the public's punitiveness, the crime rate, and news coverage of crime.

Chapter 2 demonstrated that while public opinion can look "mushy" when analyzed at a single time point, a focus on opinion change provides a meaningful signal of public support for being tough on crime. For example, even when public support for both the death penalty *and* the rehabilitation of prisoners seems incompatible, attitudes towards these two issues tend to change in tandem. Thus, regardless of which survey question we focus on, we get the same message about the public's shifting punitiveness. We also saw that whether political actors strategically consider the public's preferences or simply try to avoid highly controversial decisions, changes in public opinion offer the most meaningful information. Equally important, consistent with past research (e.g., Page and Shapiro 1992, Ramirez 2013), we saw that different segments of the

---

[2] For example, the group Right on Crime, which has been endorsed by numerous conservative politicians (http://rightoncrime.com/statement-of-principles/), draws attention to "overcriminalization," highlights the high costs of prisons, and questions the use of incarceration for nonviolent drug offenders (http://rightoncrime.com/priority-issues/).

public appear to become more or less punitive in tandem. Thus, regardless of which constituent groups political actors pay attention to, they are likely to get the same message.

The over-time focus in Chapter 4 highlighted important patterns related to crime and news coverage of crime. First, we saw that the rate of property and violent crime tends to shift in unison in the United States. Furthermore, the crime rate shifts in similar ways across the country. Important differences can and do emerge, but the similar over-time trajectories hold implications for how we understand the causes of crime and the public's reaction to crime. Scholars and pundits often look to the particular policies of a city to explain shifts in local crime rates. However, when crime declines in tandem across most urban areas and states, this pattern suggests that broad social phenomena, not localized policies, are more likely to account for the changes.

In terms of the public reaction to crime, when crime rates shift in similar ways, regardless of whether individuals notice reporting on local crime, national crime, violent crime, or property crime, the messages about whether crime is increasing or decreasing will be roughly the same. This pattern is reinforced by the fact that media consistently over-report violent crime and crimes committed by minorities. This reporting bias means the public consistently overestimates the amount of violent crime and the proportion of crimes committed by minorities. However, because this bias is relatively constant, the public's punitiveness reacts to the crime rate in systematic ways. Of course, a systematic response does not necessarily imply a fully informed or rational response. Indeed, current bipartisan calls for criminal justice reform highlight the fact that the public's reaction to rising crime rates and the criminal justice system's response to the public were wildly disproportionate.

Chapter 5 explained the importance of analyzing changes in the incarceration rate. This focus on change resolved one of the most enduring puzzles of criminal justice research: the fact that the overall incarceration rate appears only weakly related (at best) to the crime rate. When we analyze the change in the incarceration rate instead of the total incarceration rate, the expected relationship emerges. The over-time focus also demonstrated a statistically significant and substantively important relationship between the public's punitiveness and changes in the incarceration rate. Without an over-time focus, these relationships would not have emerged.

7.2 WHAT MIGHT HAVE BEEN

The tough-on-crime rhetoric of prominent Republican politicians like Barry Goldwater, Richard Nixon, and Ronald Reagan has led many scholars to focus attention on the role these individuals may have played in the rise of mass incarceration in the United States. Yet the analysis of Lyndon Johnson's shift on crime in Chapter 3 suggests that Johnson – a liberal Democrat – deserves careful attention. Johnson's approach on crime switched from "improvements in schools, vocational training, employment services, [and] crime prevention" to the view that "crime will not wait while we pull it up by the roots. We must arrest and reverse the trend toward lawlessness."[3] Considering the rising punitiveness in public attitudes at the time, in retrospect Johnson's switch is not surprising. Some would even say that, as president, following the public's preferences was his duty. However, since prominent Republicans were already in step with the public's shifting preferences, once Johnson reversed course on criminal justice, the public was even more likely to have its way. Johnson's failure to hold firm on addressing the roots of crime – despite his strong approval ratings – was a critical juncture in the rise of mass incarceration.

Johnson's switch on crime also highlights an important aspect of a two-party political system like in the United States. Prior to the rise in the public's punitiveness, Democrats like Johnson and California Governor Pat Brown Sr. could emphasize long-term solutions to crime, like investing in education and job training. However, when the public's preferences shifted in the direction of more support for being tough on crime, both Republicans and Democrats faced an incentive to focus on *immediate* responses, like advocating more police, more arrests, stricter sentences, and more imprisonments. As Garland (2001, p. 200) explains, punitive responses "are immediate, easy to implement, and can claim to 'work' as a punitive end in themselves even when they fail in all other respects." Once one party followed the public in this direction, the other party was not able to appease the public with a focus on long-term crime prevention goals like improving schools or increasing vocational training. Both parties converged on the most immediate response to the public's concerns.

As discussed in Chapter 4, racial prejudice and historical conditions, such as urban riots, also matter. These factors likely strengthened the relationship between the crime rate and the public's punitiveness. Furthermore, different media frames might have led to a different outcome. On one hand, the strength of the relationship between the amount of news coverage of crime and the crime rate is quite impressive. On the other hand, the specific news frames employed by the media appear to heavily influence the public's attitudes. If news media consistently emphasized thematic frames, focusing on the social factors that influence criminal activity or flaws in the criminal justice system, instead of offering episodic frames with a particular focus on violent crime and crime committed by racial minorities, the public's punitiveness may have shifted in different ways. Although it is hard to imagine the media framing crime differently, in *The Decline of the Death Penalty*, Baumgartner, De Boef, and Boydstun (2008) show that in the mid 1990s media coverage of the death penalty changed substantially and public support for the death penalty

---

3 Lyndon B. Johnson. May 9, 1964: Remarks in New York City Before the 50th Anniversary and March 8, 1965: Special Message to the Congress on Law Enforcement and the Administration of Justice.

declined as a result. If such a switch in crime reporting had occurred in the 1970s, the history of incarceration in the United States would have looked very different.

7.3   THE HUMAN TOLL OF MASS INCARCERATION

In order to understand the rise of mass incarceration, the analyses have taken a macro-level approach. I have focused on the overall national and state incarceration rates, national and state-level public punitiveness, aggregate crime statistics, and a national measure of news coverage of crime. This macro approach is the appropriate level of analysis to understand why the United States has become the world's incarceration leader. However, throughout the pages of this book, I have also aimed to remind readers that it is individuals, families, and neighborhoods who experience the consequences of the criminal justice system.

The individuals include Robert Riley, who we learned received a life sentence with no possibility of parole because of his two previous drug arrests outside of Grateful Dead shows. We also learned of the judge in Riley's case, Ronald E. Longstaff, who lamented, "It gives me no satisfaction that a gentle person such as Mr. Riley will remain in prison the rest of his life." Stephanie George was another individual who appeared in Chapter 1. She received a sentence of life without parole when her boyfriend testified that he had paid her to store drugs in her home. Bernard Noble, a forty-nine-year-old father of seven, was recently in the news because he is serving a thirteen-year sentence for possessing the equivalent of two marijuana joints.[4]

Of course, there are literally tens of millions of additional stories. As Marie Gottschalk (2015) highlights, the 2.2 million individuals in jail or prison actually understates the scope of the carceral state. When we consider those under some form of government supervision (e.g., jail, prison, probation, or parole), the number jumps to 7 million. Even this number does not capture the 11.6 million jail admissions each year or the approximately 7 percent of all working-age adults who are felons or ex-felons (Gottschalk 2015, Minton 2012, Schmitt and Warner 2010). Each of these individuals has a story. Many of these stories are heartbreaking. Others inspire anger and punitive thoughts. The key, however, is to remember that the aggregate numbers reflect individuals.

We must also remember that the individuals involved extend well beyond those under the direct supervision of the carceral state. As we have seen, families and communities struggle with the consequences of the criminal justice system. In addition to the adverse fiscal and health effects that families and communities endure, these individuals must also deal with the family separation that incarceration causes. Thus, mass incarceration holds especially dire consequences for the children of those who are incarcerated. In addition

4   See, e.g., Westcott (2015).

to numerous educational, health, and economic disadvantages that often result from having a parent incarcerated, Wakefield and Wildeman (2013) find that recent parental incarceration doubles the risk of child homelessness and is associated with a 40 percent increase in infant mortality.

Those who work in the criminal justice system must also be considered. Research on correctional officers offers a particularly salient indication of the potential effects of the criminal justice system on those it employs. For example, numerous studies document the challenging aspects of working in a prison and the elevated physical and mental health risks among corrections officers. As Finn (2000, p. 11) explains, "The available empirical and anecdotal evidence convincingly documents that stress among correctional officers is widespread and, in many cases, severe." Furthermore, as the prison system has expanded and prisons have become more crowded, these mental and physical risks have intensified.

In sum, when we focus on the criminal justice *system* and *mass* incarceration, we must pause and remember that there are individual names, faces, and stories behind the aggregate statistics. These individuals include inmates, prosecutors, judges, and corrections officers, as well as their children, parents, and friends. We must also remember that by influencing the criminal justice system, public punitiveness has affected each of these individuals.

7.4 PUBLIC OPINION AS A UNIFYING FRAMEWORK

Political decisions created mass incarceration. There is little scholarly disagreement on this point. As Travis, Western, and Redburn (2014, p. 342) explain, "The growth of the prison population can be traced to policies expanding the use of imprisonment for felony convictions, imposing longer sentences on those committed to prison, and intensifying punishment for the sale and use of drugs." Yet substantial debate exists regarding *why* these political decisions were made.

This book has argued that we cannot understand these choices without considering public opinion. The policy makers who have legislated mandatory minimum sentences, reclassified drug offenses, and allocated criminal justice budgets face electoral incentives to follow the public's preferences. The previous chapters have also highlighted the fact that the many judges and prosecutors who are elected in the United States also face incentives to consider the public's will. Furthermore, even those directly involved in the criminal justice system who are not elected may consider the public's preferences. As Chapter 2 detailed, whether political actors strategically follow the public's preferences or simply try to avoid decisions that would stir the public's ire, these choices should reflect changes in the public's punitiveness – and the evidence strongly supports this expectation.

While I have argued that insufficient scholarly attention has been devoted to understanding the mass public's influence on the incarceration rate, this book should be viewed as an affirmation of the past work of criminologists, legal scholars, historians, sociologists, and political scientists who study the criminal justice system. The current focus on public opinion does not necessarily challenge existing perspectives. By contrast, the emphasis on the public's attitudes offers a theoretical framework for understanding previous research. Bringing public opinion to the study of mass incarceration provides a theoretical account of why US political elites have advanced some of the most punitive criminal justice policies in the world.

In addition to helping us understand the incarceration rate and the political decisions that produced it, the focus on public opinion builds on a growing literature that emphasizes the importance of public opinion for understanding the overall judicial system. Baumgartner, De Boef, and Boydstun (2008) and Brace and Boyea (2008), for example, document the important influence of public opinion on death penalty decisions. Substantial research has also found a relationship between public opinion and Supreme Court decisions (Casillas, Enns, and Wohlfarth 2011, Epstein and Martin 2011, McGuire and Stimson 2004). Increasingly, the evidence suggests that in order to fully understand the US legal system, we must consider the public's preferences.

The focus on public opinion also offers an important consideration for those working to reform the criminal justice system. We have seen strong empirical support for Garland's (1990, p. 62) claim that "penal reformers will have to address themselves directly to popular feelings if they intend to produce real change." The vast size of the criminal justice system and the fact that it is spread across federal, state, and local levels can make reform seem like a daunting task. The evidence that the organized interest group system is dominated by those directly connected to the criminal justice system (Miller 2008) can make reform seem even more difficult. Yet this broad system responds to the public. The public played a prominent role in the rise of mass incarceration and it will play a central role if mass incarceration is to end. Equally important, the public has been moving in a less punitive direction for more than a decade and policies have begun to change. The time is right for reform.

7.5 THE FUTURE OF THE US PRISON SYSTEM

We have seen that since the 1990s, the crime rate has dropped, news coverage of crime has dropped, and the public's punitiveness has dropped. Consistent with these patterns, important changes in the criminal justice system are happening. As noted earlier, sentences for certain drug crimes have been reduced, the overall prison population has decreased, some prisons have closed, and death penalty sentences have declined.[5] Additionally, California voters have scaled back their Three Strikes law and voters in four states have legalized marijuana for recreational use. Perhaps most noteworthy, prominent politicians of both parties,

5   See, for example, Apuzzo (2014), Baumgartner, De Boef, and Boydstun (2008), and Porter (2012).

such as Democratic Senator Corey Booker and Republican Senator Rand Paul, have come together in favor of bipartisan reform of the criminal justice system.

Despite these changes, we remain a punitive society. The public still holds punitive attitudes and our policies are still punitive – just less so than in the 1990s. One example comes from New York Governor Cuomo's failed attempt to support college education in prisons. Governor Cuomo proposed to spend $1 million on college education programs in prison to help reduce recidivism. This would amount to 0.036 of a percent of New York's $2.8 billion corrections budget. Yet, the proposal was so politically controversial that Cuomo abandoned it after six weeks.[6] The maximum punishment that can be applied to juveniles also illustrates the fact that declining punitiveness can still produce highly punitive outcomes. In 2005, the US Supreme Court banned the death penalty for juveniles. The Court then banned juvenile life without parole for non-homicides in 2010 and in 2012 ruled that juveniles convicted of murder cannot be subjected to a *mandatory* sentence of life imprisonment without the possibility of parole. Despite this trend in a less punitive direction, approximately twenty-five hundred individuals are still serving life without parole for crimes committed as teenagers and juveniles in thirty-four states can still be sentenced to life without parole. In other words, given the extreme level of punitiveness that the criminal justice system reached, a shift in a less punitive direction can still result in punitive policies, such as life without parole for juveniles (recall that even adults in Canada cannot be sentenced to life without parole).[7]

Nevertheless, the current move in a less punitive direction can continue. We have seen that how much the public's and the criminal justice system's punitiveness declines will likely depend on the crime rate and how the news covers criminal activity. Although the determinants of crime are not well understood, various types of crime tend to move in similar ways across the country. At least during the past sixty years, as crime goes, so goes the news, and the public, and the criminal justice system. The crime rate and media's coverage of crime and the criminal justice system will be an important barometer of future public opinion and policy.

Given these relationships, what should we expect from the public and the criminal justice system in the coming years? Clear and Frost argue that criminal justice in the United States has reached "the end of an era" (2014, p. 7) and that "a new agenda is about to arise" (p. 188). Clear and Frost's chapter 7 also details a concrete agenda for greatly reducing the number imprisoned (also see, Gottschalk 2015; Tonry 2011, ch. 6). In particular, they highlight the importance of repealing mandatory sentences (especially for drug-related crimes), reducing the length of prison sentences, and reducing

---

6 See, for example, Kaplan (2014).
7 The recently decided *Montgomery v. Louisiana* (2016) states that the Supreme Court has jurisdiction to decide whether a state supreme court correctly refused to give retroactive effect to the Supreme Court's 2012 decision in *Miller v. Alabama*. Also see, sentencingproject.org/doc/publications/jj_Juvenile_Life_Without_Parole.pdf.

rates of recidivism. In addition to reducing the number imprisoned, criminal justice reform has begun to focus on the conditions inside prisons. As Marie Gottschalk (2015, p. 563) explains, "too many people are serving time in US jails, prisons, and detention centers that are abusive and degrading." Indeed, media has increasingly drawn attention to violence and abuse in prisons, overcrowded conditions, inadequate health care, and extensive use of solitary confinement. These conditions are, of course, devastating to those who are incarcerated. But they also hold implications for those outside the prison system. Most of those currently incarcerated will return to their families and communities. All of society benefits if the criminal justice system helps prepare these individuals for this return.

I agree with Clear and Frost that we could be in the midst of a new era, and the public is ready for – and leading us toward – these types of changes. But the public's level of punitiveness must remain steady or continue to decline for these changes in the criminal justice system to continue. An uptick in crime, followed by the standard media coverage of crime, could push the public back in a more punitive direction.

However, even if crime rates do not continue to fall, media portrayals of crime and the criminal justice system may be different than in the past. The nature of media is changing faster than ever before. Large segments of the public now get their news from comedy shows, podcasts, Twitter, and Facebook. The Web has allowed news and information to target individuals at an unprecedented level. It may be that the relationship between news and punitive attitudes changes in this new media era. Technology also matters in other ways. The filming of police stops (by members of the public and by police departments) has certainly influenced how the criminal justice system is portrayed by the media. Organizations like The Marshall Project – a nonprofit, nonpartisan news organization devoted entirely to covering America's criminal justice system (www.themarshallproject.org) – now also have a voice. Public attitudes will continue to influence the criminal justice system, but the media environment that influences the public is becoming increasingly complex. The implications remain to be seen.

In the final analysis, for the many people who think the United States should relinquish its role as the *Incarceration Nation*, there is reason to be optimistic. Public punitiveness has been on the decline and politicians of both parties have noticed. But many more changes must occur before this title no longer applies.

References

Abramowitz, Alan I. 2010. "All Politics Is National: Using the Generic Ballot to Forecast the 2010 State Legislative Elections." *University of Virginia Center for Politics: Sabato's Crystal Ball.* www.centerforpolitics.org/crystalball/articles/aia20100 72902/ (July 29, 2010).

Alexander, Michelle. 2010. *The New Jim Crow.* New York: The New Press.

Amnesty International. 2012. *Death Sentences and Executions 2011.* London: Amnesty International Publications.

Apuzzo, Matt. 2014. "New Rule Permits Early Release for Thousands of Drug offenenders." *The New York Times* (July 18). www.nytimes.com/2014/07/19/us/new-rule-permits-early-release-for-thousands-of-drug-offenders.html?_r=0.

Arceneaux, Kevin. 2005. "Does Federalism Weaken Democratic Representation in the United States?" *Publius* 35(2):297–311.

Arceneaux, Kevin. 2006. "The Federal Face of Voting: Are Elected Officials Held Accountable for the Functions Relevant to Their Office?" *Political Psychology* 27(5):731–754.

Arts, Wil and John Gelissen. 2002. "Three Worlds of Welfare Capitalism or More? A State-of-the-art Report." *Journal of European Social Policy* 12(2):137–158.

Auerhahn, Kathleen. 2003. *Selective Incapacitation and Public Policy: Evaluating California's Imprisonment Crisis.* Albany State University of New York Press.

Baker, Mary Holland, Barbara C. Nienstedt, Ronald S. Everett, and Richard McCleary. 1983. "The Impact of a Crime Wave: Perceptions, Fear, and Confidence in the Police." *Law and Society Review* 17(2):319–336.

Banerjee, Anindya, Juan Dolado, John W. Galbraith, and David F. Hendry. 1993. *Integration, Error Correction, and the Econometric Analysis of Non-Stationary Data.* Oxford: Oxford University Press.

Barkan, Steven E. and Steven F. Cohn. 1994. "Racial Prejudice and Support for the Death Penalty by Whites." *Criminology & Penology* 31(2):202–209.

Barkan, Steven E. and Steven F. Cohn. 2005. "Why Whites Favor Spending More to Fight Crime: The Role of Racial Prejudice." *Social Problems* 52(2):300–314.

Barker, Vanessa. 2006. "The Politics of Punishing." *Punishment and Society* 8(1):5–32.

Barlow, Melissa Hickman. 1998. "Race and the Problem of Crime in 'Time' and 'Newsweek' Cover Stories, 1946 to 1995." *Social Justice* 25(2):149–183.

Bartels, Larry M. 2008. *Unequal Democracy*. Princeton, NJ: Princeton University Press.

Baum, Dan. 1997. *Smoke and Mirrors: The War on Drugs and the Politics of Failure*. Boston, MA: Back Bay Books.

Baumer, Eric P. and Kevin T. Wolff. 2014. "Evaluating Contemporary Crime Drop(s) in America, New York City, and Many Other Places." *Justice Quarterly* 31(1):5–38.

Baumer, Eric P., Steven F. Messner, and Richard Rosenfeld. 2003. "Explaining Spatial Variation in Support for Capital Punishment: A Multilevel Analysis." *American Journal of Sociology* 108(4):844–875.

Baumgartner, Frank R. and Bryan D. Jones. 1993. *Agendas and Instability in American Politics*. Chicago: University of Chicago Press.

Baumgartner, Frank R., Suzanna De Boef, and Amber Boydstun. 2008. *The Decline of the Death Penalty and the Discovery of Innocence*. New York: Cambridge University Press.

Baumgartner, Frank R., Suzanna Linn, and Amber E. Boydstun. 2010. The Decline of the Death Penalty: How Media Framing Changed Capital Punishment in America. In *Winning with Words: The Origins and Impact of Framing*, eds. Brian F. Schaffner and Patrick J. Sellers. New York: Routledge, chapter 9, pp. 159–184.

Beale, Sara Sun. 2006. "The News Media's Influence on Criminal Justice Policy: How Market-Driven News Promotes Punitiveness." *William and Mary Law Review* 48(2):397–481.

Beale, Sara Sun. 2013. The Story of Ewing v. California: Three Strikes Laws and the Limits of the Eighth Amendment Proportionality Review. In *Criminal Law Stories*, eds. Donna Coker and Robert Weisberg. New York: Foundation Press/Thomas Reuters.

Becker, Theodore L. 1966. "A Survey Study of Hawaiian Judges: The Effects on Decisions of Judicial Role Variations." *American Political Science Review* 60(3):677–680.

Beckett, Katherine. 1997. *Making Crime Pay: Law and Order in Contemporary American Politics*. New York: Oxford University Press.

Beckett, Katherine and Alexes Harris. 2011. "On Cash and Conviction: Money Sanctions as Misguided Policy." *Criminology and Public Policy* 10(3):509–537.

Beckett, Katherine and Theodore Sasson. 2004. *The Politics of Injustice*. 2nd edn. Thousand Oaks, CA: Sage Publications.

Bentley, Arthur F. 2008 [1908]. *The Process of Government*. New Brunswick, NJ: Transaction Publishers.

Berry, Frances Stokes and William D. Berry. 1990. "State Lottery Adoptions as Policy Innovations: An Event History Analysis." *American Political Science Review* 84(2):395–415.

Berstein, Neil. 2005. *All Alone in the World*. New York: The New Press.

Best, Joel. 2011. Locating Moral Panics within the Sociology of Social Problems. In *Moral Panic and the Politics of Anxiety*, ed. Sean Hier. New York: Routledge, chapter 3, pp. 37–52.

Biderman, Albert D. and James P. Lynch. 1991. *Understanding Crime Incidence Statistics: Why the UCR Diverges from the NCS*. New York: Springer.

Blumstein, Alfred, Jacqueline Cohen, and Richard Rosenfeld. 1991. "Trend and Deviation in Crime Rates: A Comparison of UCR and NCS Data for Burglary and Robbery." *Criminology* 29(2):237–263.

Blumstein, Alfred, Jacqueline Cohen, and Richard Rosenfeld. 1992. "The UCR-NCS Relationship Revisited: A Reply to Menard." *Criminology* 30(1):115–124.

Blumstein, Alfred, Michael Tonry, and Asheley Van Ness. 2005. "Cross-National Measures of Punitiveness." *Crime and Justice* 33(1):347–376.

Boyd, James. 1970. "Nixon's Southern Strategy 'It's All in the Charts,'" *New York Times*. www.nytimes.com/packages/html/books/phillips-southern.pdf (May 17, 1970).

Boydstun, Amber E. 2013. *Making the News*. Chicago: University of Chicago Press.

Brace, Paul R. and Brent Boyea. 2008. "State Public Opinion, the Death Penalty and the Practice of Electing Judges." *American Journal of Political Science* 52(2): 360–372.

Brown, Elizabeth K. 2006. "The Dog that Did Not Bark." *Punishment and Society* 8(3):287–312.

Bryl, Jason and Tony Fabelo. 2006. *Final Report: Analysis of Parole Data from 2003-2005*. Washington, DC: The JFA Institute.

Burch, Traci. 2013. *Trading Democracy for Justice*. Chicago: University of Chicago Press.

Cadora, Eric, Mannix Gordon, and Charles Swartz. 2002. *Criminal Justice and Health and Human Services: An Exploration of Overlapping Needs, Resources, and Interests in Brooklyn Neighborhoods*. www.urban.org/research/publication/criminal-justice-and-health-and-human-services/view/full_report. Urban Institute.

Campbell, James E. 2008. *The American Campaign: U.S. Presidential Campaigns and the National Vote*. 2nd edn. College Station: Texas A & M University Press.

Canes-Wrone, Brandice. 2006. *Who Leads Whom?* Chicago: University of Chicago Press.

Carson, E. Ann and Daniela Golinelli. 2013. *Prisoners in 2012, Trends in Admissions and Releases, 1991-2012*. Washington, DC: US Department of Justice.

Casillas, Christopher J., Peter K. Enns, and Patrick C. Wohlfarth. 2011. "How Public Opinion Constrains the U.S. Supreme Court." *American Journal of Political Science* 55(1):74–88.

Chaiken, Shelly and Yaacov Trope. 1999. *Dual Process Theories in Social Psychology*. New York: Guilford Press.

Chamberlin, Tony. 1976. "Public Sending a Message to Judges: Get Tough." *The Boston Globe*. December 8, 1976, pp. 1 and 14.

Chambliss, William J. and Robert B. Seidman. 1971. *Law, Order, and Power*. Reading, MA: Addison-Wesley.

Charemza, Wojciech W. and Derek F. Deadman. 1992. *New Directions in Econometric Practice*. 2nd edn. Northhampton, MA: Edward Elgar.

Chemerinksy, Erwin. 2003. "Cruel and Unusual: The Story of Leandro Andrade." *Drake Law Review* 52(1):1–24.

Chen, Keith M. and Jesse M. Shapiro. 2007. "Do Harsher Prison Conditions Reduce Recidivism? A Discontinuity-based Approach." *American Law and Economics Review* 9(1):1–29.

Chiricos, Ted, Kathy Padgett, Jake Bratton, Justin T. Pickett, and Marc Gertz. 2012. "Racial Threat and Opposition to the Re-enfranchisement of Ex-felons." *International Journal of Criminology and Sociology* 1(1):13–28.

Chiricos, Ted, Kelly Welch, and Marc Gertz. 2004. "Racial Typification of Crime and Support for Punitive Measures." *Criminology* 42(2):358–390.

Chiricos, Theodore G. 1987. "Rates of Crime and Unemployment: An Analysis of Aggregate Research Evidence." *Social Problems* 34(2):187–212.

Christianson, Scott. 1998. *With Liberty for Some: 500 Years of Imprisonment in America*. New York: Northeastern University Press.

Clear, Todd R. 2007. *Imprisoning Communities: How Mass Incarceration Makes Disadvantaged Neighborhoods Worse*. New York: Oxford University Press.

Clear, Todd R. 2009. "Incarceration and Communities." *Criminal Justice Matters* 75(1):26–27.

Clear, Todd R. and Natasha A. Frost. 2014. *The Punishment Imperative*. New York: New York University Press.

Cohen, Stanley. 1972. *Folk Devils and Moral Panics*. New York: St. Martin's Press.

Cook, Beverley B. 1977. "Public Opinion and Federal Judicial Policy." *American Journal of Political Science* 21(3):567–600.

Cowen, Nick. 2010. *Comparisons of Crime in OECD Countries*. London: CIVITAS Institute for the Study of Civil Society.

Cullen, Francis T., Bonnie S. Fisher, and Brandon K. Applegate. 2000. "Public Opinion about Punishment and Corrections." *Crime and Justice* 27(1):1–79.

Cullen, Francis T., Gregory A. Clark, and John F. Wozniak. 1985. "Explaining the Get Tough Movement: Can the Public be Blamed?" *Federal Probation* 16(2): 16–24.

Dal Cason, Terry A. and Edward S. Franzosa. 2003. Occurrences and Forms of the Hallucinogens. In *Hallucinogens: A Forensic Drug Handbook*, ed. Richard Laing. London: Elsevier Science Ltd, chapter 2, pp. 37–65.

Dardis, Frank E., Frank R. Baumgartner, Amber E. Boydstun, Suzanna De Boef, and Fuyuan Shen. 2008. "Media Framing of Capital Punishment and Its Impact on Individuals' Cognitive Responses." *Mass Communication and Society* 11(2): 115–140.

Dauvergne, Mia. 2012. *Adult Criminal Court Statistics in Canada, 2010/2011*. Ottawa: Statistics Canada.

Davidson, Russell and James G. MacKinnon. 1993. *Estimation and Inference in Econometrics*. New York: Oxford University Press.

Davis, James A. 1980. "Conservative Weather in a Liberalizing Climate: Change in Selected NORC General Social Survey Items, 1972-1978." *Social Forces* 58(4):1129–1156.

De Boef, Suzanna and Luke Keele. 2008. "Taking Time Seriously." *American Journal of Political Science* 52(1):184–200.

Delli Carpini, Michael X. and Scott Keeter. 1996. *What Americans Know about Politics and Why it Matters*. New Haven, CT: Yale University Press.

Denhof, Michael D. and Caterina G. Spinaris. 2013. "Depression, PTSD, and Comorbidity in United States Corrections Professionals: Prevalence and Impact on Health and Functioning." *Desert Waters Correctional Outreach*. http://desertwaters.com/wp-content/uploads/2013/09/Comorbidity_Study_09-03-131.pdf.

Ditton, Paula M. and Doris James Wilson. 1999. "Truth in Sentencing in State Prisons." *Bureau of Justice Statistics Special Report*, pp. 1–16. http://bjs.gov/content/pub/pdf/tssp.pdf.

Domanick, Joe. 2004. *Cruel Justice: Three Strikes and the Politics of Crime in America's Golden State*. Los Angeles: University of California Press.

Donohue, John J., III. 2009. Assessing the Relative Benefits of Incarceration: Overall Changes and the Benefits on the Margin. In *Do Prisons Make Us Safer?* eds. Steven Raphael and Michael A. Stoll. New York: Russell Sage Foundation, chapter 9, pp. 269–341.

Donohue, John J. and Justin Wolfers. 2005. "Uses and Abuses of Empirical Evidence in the Death Penalty Debate." *Stanford Law Review* 58(3):791–845.

Downs, Anthony. 1957. *An Economic Theory of Democracy*. New York: Harper and Row.

Druckman, James N. 2001. "The Implications of Framing Effects for Citizen Competence." *Political Behavior* 23(3):225–256.

Druckman, James N. and Lawrence R. Jacobs. 2006. "Lumpers and Splitters: The Public Opinion Information that Politicians Collect and Use." *Public Opinion Quarterly* 70(4):453–476.

Druckman, James N. and Lawrence R. Jacobs. 2011. Segmented Representation: The Reagan White House and Disproportionate Responsiveness. In *Who Gets Represented?* eds. Peter K. Enns and Christopher Wlezien. New York: Russell Sage Foundation, chapter 6, pp. 166–188.

Durham, Alexis M., III. 1993. "Public Opinion Regarding Sentences for Crime: Does it Exist?" *Journal of Criminal Justice* 21(1):1–11.

Easton, David. 1965. *A Systems Analysis of Political Life*. New York: Wiley.

Eberhardt, Jennifer L., Phillip Atiba Goff, Valerie J. Purdie, and Paul G. Davies. 2004. "Seeing Black: Race, Crime, and Visual Processing." *Journal of Personality and Psychology* 87(6):876–893.

Ebron, Rebecca, Tawanda Etheridge, Ginny Hevener, Karen Jones, and Susan Katzenelson. 2004. *Correctional Program Evaluation: Offenders Placed on Probation or Released from Prison*. North Carolina Department of Correction.

Edwards, George C., III. 2003. *On Deaf Ears: The Limits of the Bully Pulpit*. New Haven, CT: Yale University Press.

Ellis, Christopher and James A. Stimson. 2009. "Symbolic Ideology in the American Electorate." *Electoral Studies* 28(3):388–402.

Ellis, Christopher R., Joseph Daniel Ura, and Jenna Ashley Robinson. 2006. "The Dynamic Consequences of Nonvoting in American National Elections." *Political Research Quarterly* 59(2):227–233.

Enns, Peter K. 2010. "The Public's Increasing Punitiveness and Its Influence on Mass Incarceration in the United States." Paper presented at the 2010 Annual Meeting of the American Political Science Association.

Enns, Peter K. 2014a. "The Public's Increasing Punitiveness and Its Influence on Mass Incarceration in the United States." *American Journal of Political Science* 58(4):857–872.

Enns, Peter K. 2014b. "Supplementary/Online Appendix for: The Public's Increasing Punitiveness and Its Influence on Mass Incarceration in the United States." *American Journal of Political Science* 54(4). http://onlinelibrary.wiley.com/doi/10.1111/ajps.12098/suppinfo.

Enns, Peter K. 2015. "Relative Policy Support and Coincidental Representation." *Perspectives on Politics.* 13(4): 1053–1064.

Enns, Peter K. and Paul M. Kellstedt. 2008. "Policy Mood and Political Sophistication: Why Everybody Moves Mood." *British Journal of Political Science* 38(3): 433–454.

Enns, Peter K. and Julianna Koch. 2013. "Public Opinion in the U.S. States: 1956 to 2010." *State Politics and Policy Quarterly* 13(3):349–372.

Enns, Peter K. and Julianna Koch. 2015. "State Policy Mood: The Importance of Over-Time Dynamics." *State Politics and Policy Quarterly* 15(4):436–446.

Enns, Peter K., Takaaki Masaki, and Nathan Kelly. 2014. "Time Series Analysis and Spurious Regression: An Error Correction." Paper presented at the Annual Meeting of the Southern Political Science Association, New Orleans, LA.

Enns, Peter K. and Gregory McAvoy. 2012. "The Role of Partisanship in Aggregate Opinion." *Political Behavior* 34(4):627–651.

Enns, Peter K. and Brian Richman. 2013. "Presidential Campaigns and the Fundamentals Reconsidered." *Journal of Politics* 75(3):803–820.

Enns, Peter K. and Delphia Shanks-Booth. 2015. "The Great Recession and State Criminal Justice Policy: Do Economic Hard Times Matter?" *Russell Sage Foundation Great Recession Brief.*

Enns, Peter K. and Christopher Wlezien. 2011. Group Opinion and the Study of Representation. In *Who Gets Represented?* eds. Peter K. Enns and Christopher Wlezien. New York: Russell Sage Foundation, chapter 1, pp. 1–25.

Enns, Peter K. and Patrick C. Wohlfarth. 2013. "The Swing Justice." *Journal of Politics* 75(4):1089–1107.

Epstein, Lee and Andrew D. Martin. 2011. "Does Public Opinion Influence the Supreme Court? Possibly Yes (But We're Not Sure Why)." *University of Pennsylvania Journal of Constitutional Law* 13(2):263–281.

Epstein, Leon D. and Austin Ranney. 1966. "Who Voted for Goldwater: The Wisconsin Case." *Political Science Quarterly* 81(1):82–94.

Erikson, Robert S., Michael B. MacKuen, and James A. Stimson. 2002. *The Macro Polity.* New York: Cambridge University Press.

Esarey, Justin. 2016. "Fractionally Integrated Data and the Autodistributed Lage Model: Results from a Simulation Study." *Political Analysis.* Forthcoming.

Esping-Anderson, Gøsta. 1990. *The Three Worlds of Welfare Capitalism.* Princeton, NJ: Princeton University Press.

Farrall, Stephen and Will Jennings. 2012. "Policy Feedback and the Criminal Justice Agenda." *Contemporary British History* 26(4):467–488.

Farrell, Graham and Ken Clark. 2004. "What Does the World Spend on Criminal Justice?" The European Institute for Crime Prevention and Control, affiliated with the United Nations. HEUNI Paper No. 20 www.heuni .fi/material/attachments/heuni/papers/6KtlkZMtL/HEUNI_papers_20.pdf.

Fenno, Richard F., Jr. 1977. "U.S. House Members in Their Constituencies: An Exploration." *American Political Science Review* 71(3):883–917.

Fenno, Richard F. 1978. *Home Style: House Members in Their Districts.* Boston, MA: Little, Brown.

Finn, Peter. 2000. "Addressing Correctional Office Stress: Programs and Strategies." U.S. Department of Justice (www.ncjrs.gov/pdffiles1/nij/183474.pdf).

Flamm, Michael W. 2005. *Law and Order: Street Crime, Civil Unrest, and the Crisis of Liberalism in the 1960s.* New York: Columbia University Press.

Forman, James, Jr. 2012. "Racial Critiques of Mass Incarceration: Beyond the New Jim Crow." *New York University Law Review* 87(1):101–146.

Foster, Holly and John Hagan. 2007. "Incarceration and Intergenerational Social Exclusion." *Social Problems* 54(4):399–433.

Frank, Mark W. 2009. "Inequality and Growth in the United States: Evidence from a New State-Level Panel of Income Inequality Measures." *Economic Inquiry* 47(1):55–68.

Frost, Natasha A. 2010. "Beyond Public Opinion Polls: Punitive Public Sentiment & Criminal Justice Policy." *Sociology Compass* 4(3):156–168.

Gaes, Gerald G. and Scott D. Camp. 2009. "Unintended Consequences: Experimental Evidence for the Criminogenic Effect of Prison Security Level Placement on Post-release Recidivism." *Journal of Experimental Criminology* 5(2): 139–162.

Gallagher, Catherine, Edward R. Maguire, Stephen D. Mastrofski, and Michael D. Reisig. 2001. "The Public Image of Police." *Report to International Association of Chiefs of Police*, October 2, 2001. http://dnn9ciwm8.azurewebsites.net/The-Public-Image-of-the-Police.

Gamson, William A. and Andre Modigliani. 1987. The Changing Culture of Affirmative Action. In *Research in Political Sociology, Vol.3*, ed. R. A. Braumgart. Greenwich: JAI Press, pp. 137–177.

Garland, David. 1990. *Punishment and Modern Society*. Chicago: University of Chicago Press.

Garland, David. 2001. *The Culture of Control*. Chicago: University of Chicago Press.

Gelman, Andrew and Gary King. 1993. "Why Are American Presidential Election Campaign Polls so Variable When Votes Are so Predictable?" *British Journal of Political Science* 23(4):409–451.

Gerber, Marisa. June 29, 2015. "L.A. County D.A. Jackie Lacey to Unveil Details on Wrongful-Conviction Unit." *Los Angeles Times* (www.latimes.com/local/lanow/la-me-ln-conviction-integrity-unit-20150629-story.html).

Gibson, Dirk C. 1997. "A Quantitative Description of FBI Public Relations." *Public Relations Review* 23(1):11–30.

Gibson, James L. 1980. "Environmental Constraints on the Behavior of Judges: A Representational Model of Judicial Decision Making." *Law & Society Review* 14(2):343–370.

Gilens, Martin. 2005. "Inequality and and Democratic Responsiveness." *Public Opinion Quarterly* 69(5):778–796.

Gilens, Martin. 2011. Policy Consequences of Representational Inequality. In *Who Gets Represented?* eds. Peter K. Enns and Christopher Wlezien. New York: Russell Sage Foundation.

Gilens, Martin. 2012. *Affluence and Influence: Economic Inequality and Political Power in America*. Princeton, NJ: Princeton University Press and Russell Sage Foundation.

Gilliam, Franklin D., Jr., and Shanto Iyengar. 2000. "Prime Suspects: The Influence of Local Television News on the Viewing Public." *American Journal of Political Science* 44(3):560–573.

Gilliam, Franklin D., Jr., Shanto Iyengar, Adam Simon, and Oliver Wright. 1996. "Crime in Black and White: The Violent, Scary World of Local News." *The Harvard International Journal of Press/Politics* 1(3):6–23.

Gitlin, Todd. 1980. *The Whole World is Watching*. Los Angeles: University of California Press.

Glaze, Lauren E. 2011. "Corrections Populations in the United States, 2010." *Bureau of Justice Statistics, U.S. Department of Justice* 1–9.

Glaze, Lauren E. and Danielle Kaeble. 2014. "Corrections Populations in the United States, 2013." *Bureau of Justice Statistics, U.S. Department of Justice* 1–13.

Gordon, Diana R. 1994. *The Return of the Dangerous Classes: Drug Prohibition and Policy Politics*. New York: Norton.

Gordon, Sanford C. and Gregory A. Huber. 2009. "The Political Economy of Prosecution." *Annual Review of Law and Social Science* 5:135–156.

Gottschalk, Marie. 2006. *The Prison and the Gallows: The Politics of Mass Incarceration in America*. New York: Cambridge University Press.

Gottschalk, Marie. 2008. "Hiding in Plain Sight: American Politics and the Carceral State." *Annual Review of Political Science* 11:235–260.

Gottschalk, Marie. 2015. "Bring it On: The Future of Penal Reform, the Carceral State, and American Politics." *Ohio State Journal of Criminal Law* 12(2):559–603.

Gove, Walter R., Michael Hughes, and Michael Geerken. 1985. "Are Uniform Crime Reports a Valid Indicator of the Index Crimes? An Affirmative Answer with Minor Qualifications." *Criminology* 23(3):451–502.

Graber, Doris Appel. 1980. *Crime News and the Public*. New York: Praeger Press.

Granger, C.W.J. 1969. "Investigating Causal Relations by Econometric Models and Cross-Spectral Methods." *Econometrica* 37(3):424–438.

Granger, Clive W.J. 2004. "Time Series Analysis, Cointegration, and Applications." *American Economic Review* 94(3):421–425.

Granger, Clive W.J. and Paul Newbold. 1974. "Spurious Regressions in Econometrics." *Journal of Econometrics* 26(2):1045–1066.

Grattet, Ryken, David Farabee, Richard McCleary, Susan Turner, and Steven Raphael. 2011. *Expert Panel Study of the Inmate Classification Score System*. Sacramento: California Department of Corrections and Rehabilitation.

Gray, Virginia and David Lowery. 1996. *The Population Ecology of Interest Representation: Lobbying Communities in the American States*. Ann Arbor: University of Michigan Press.

Guzzi, Paul. 1976. *Elections Statistics: Commonwealth of Massachusetts*. Compiled in the Office of Paul Guzzi, Secretary of the Commonwealth.

Hale, Chris. 1998. "Crime and the Business Cycle in Post-war Britain Revisited." *British Journal of Criminology* 38(4): 681–698.

Hall, Peter and Daniel W. Gingerich. 2009. "Varieties of Capitalism and Institutional Complementarities in the Political Economy: An Empirical Analysis." *British Journal of Political Science* 39(3):449–482.

Hall, Stuart, Chas Critcher, Tony Jefferson, John Clarke, and Brian Roberts. 1978. *Policing the Crisis*. London: Palgrave Macmillan.

Hanson, Gordon H. 2006. "Illegal Migration from Mexico to the United States." *Journal of Economic Literature* 44(4):869–924.

Hanson, Gordon H. and Antonio Spilimbergo. 1999. "Illegal Immigration, Border Enforcement and Relative Wages: Evidence from Apprehensions at the U.S.-Mexico Border." *American Economic Review* 89(5):1337–1357.

Harden, Jeffrey J. 2011. "A Bootstrap Method for Conducting Statistical Inference with Clustered Data." *State Politics and Policy Quarterly* 11(2):223–246.

Harden, Jeffrey J. 2012. "Improving Statistical Inference with Clustered Data." *Statistics, Politics, and Policy* 3(1):1–27.

Harris, Frank. 1932. *Presentation of Crime in Newspapers*. Hanover, NH: Sociological Press.

Haskins, Anna R. 2014. "Unintended Consequences: Effects of Paternal Incarceration on Child School Readiness and Later Special Education Placement." *Sociological Science* 1(1):141–158.

Hastie, Reid and Bernadette Park. 1986. "The Relationship between Memory and Judgment Depends on Whether the Task Is Memory-Based or On-Line." *Psychological Review* 93(3):258–268.

Henrichson, Christian and Ruth Delaney. 2012. *The Price of Prisons*. New York: VERA Institute of Justice.

Hetey, Rebecca C. and Jennifer L. Eberhardt. 2014. "Racial Disparities in Incarceration Increase Acceptance of Punitive Policies." *Psychological Science* 25(10):1949–1954.

Hewitt, David and Jean Milner. 1974. "Drug-Related Deaths in the United States – First Decade of an Epidemic." *Health Services Reports* 89(3):211–218.

Ho, Taiping and Jerome McKean. 2004. "Confidence in the Police and Perceptions of Risk." *Western Criminology Review* 5(2):108–118.

Hofstadter, Richard. 2008. *The Paranoid Style in American Politics*. New York: Vintage Books.

Hogan, Michael J., Ted Chiricos, and Marc Getz. 2005. "Economic Insecurity, Blame, and Punitive Attitudes." *Justice Quarterly* 22(3):392–412.

Holbrook, R. Andrew and Timothy G. Hill. 2005. "Agenda-Setting and Priming in Prime Time Television: Crime Dramas as Political Cues." *Political Communication* 22(3):277–295.

Hurwitz, Jon and Mark Peffley. 1997. "Public Perceptions of Race and Crime: The Role of Racial Stereotypes." *American Journal of Political Science* 41(2): 375–401.

Hurwitz, Jon and Mark Peffley. 2005. "Playing the Race Card in the Post–Willie Horton Era." *Public Opinion Quarterly* 69(1):99–112.

Iyengar, Shanto. 1991. *Is Anyone Responsible? How Television Frames Political Issues*. Chicago: Chicago University Press.

Iyengar, Shanto. 2011. *Media Politics*. 2nd edn. New York: W.W. Norton.

Iyengar, Shanto and Donald R. Kinder. 1987. *News that Matters: Television and American Opinion*. Chicago: University of Chicago Press.

Jacobs, David and Jason T. Carmichael. 2001. "The Politics of Punishment across Time and Space: A Pooled Time-Series Analysis of Imprisonment Rates." *Social Forces* 80(1):61–89.

Jacobs, David and Ronald Helms. 2001. "Toward a Political Sociology of Punishment: Politics and Changes in the Incarcerated Population." *Social Science Research* 30(2):171–194.

Jang, Hyunseok, Hee-Jong Joo, and Jihong (Solomon) Zhao. 2010. "Determinants of Public Confidence in Police: An International Perspective." *Journal of Criminal Justice* 38(1):57–68.

Jennings, Will, Stephen Farrall, and Shaun Bevan. 2012. "The Economy, Crime and Time: An Analysis of Recorded Property Crime in England & Wales 1961-2006." *International Journal of Law, Crime, and Justice* 40(3):192–210.

Johnson, Devon. 2008. "Racial Prejudice, Perceived Injustice, and the Black-White Gap in Punitive Attitudes." *Journal of Criminal Justice* 36(2):198–206.

Johnson, Elizabeth I. and Jane Waldfogel. 2002. "Parental Incarceration: Recent Trends and Implications for Child Welfare." *Social Service Review* 76(3):460–479.

Johnson, Rucker and Steven Raphael. 2009. "The Effects of Male Incarceration Dynamics on Acquired Immune Deficiency Syndrome Infection Rates among African American Women and Men." *Journal of Law and Economics* 52(2):251–293.

Johnson, Rucker and Steven Raphael. 2012. "How Much Crime Reduction Does the Marginal Prisoner Buy?" *Journal of Law and Economics* 55(2):275–310.

Joint Committee on New York Drug Law Evaluation. 1978. *The Nation's Toughest Drug Law: Evaluating the New York Experience, Final Report of the Joint Committee on New York Drug Law Evaluation.* New York: The Association of the Bar of the City of New York.

Jones, Bryan D. and Frank R. Baumgartner. 2005. *The Politics of Attention.* Chicago: University of Chicago Press.

Kaplan, Thomas. 2014. "Cuomo Drops Plan to Use State Money to Pay for College for Inmates." *The New York Times.* (April 2). www.nytimes.com/2014/04/03/nyregion/cuomo-drops-plan-to-use-state-money-to-pay-for-college-classes-for-inmates.html?_r=0.

Katzenstein, Mary Fainsod and Mitali Nagrecha. 2011. "A New Punishment Regime." *Criminology and Public Policy* 10(3):555–568.

Katzenstein, Mary Fainson and Maureen R. Waller. 2015 "Taxing the Poor: Incarceration, Poverty, Governance, and the seizure of Family Resources." *Perspectives on Politics* 13(3):638–565.

Keele, Luke and Nathan J. Kelly. 2006. "Dynamic Models for Dynamic Theories: The Ins and Outs of Lagged Dependent Variables." *Political Analysis* 14(2): 186–205.

Kellstedt, Paul M. 2000. "Media Framing and the Dynamics of Racial Policy Preferences." *American Journal of Political Science* 44(2):245–260.

Kellstedt, Paul M. 2003. *The Mass Media and the Dynamics of American Racial Attitudes.* New York: Cambridge University Press.

Kelly, Nathan J. and Peter K. Enns. 2010. "Inequality and the Dynamics of Public Opinion: The Self-Reinforcing Link between Economic Inequality and Mass Preferences." *American Journal of Political Science* 54(4):855–870.

Key, V. O., Jr. 1961. *Public Opinion and American Democracy.* New York: Alfred A Knopf.

King, Anna and Shadd Maruna. 2009. "Is a Conservative Just a Liberal Who Has Been Mugged?" *Punishment & Society* 11(2):147–169.

Kingdon, John W. 1984. *Agendas, Alternatives, and Public Policies.* Boston, MA: Little, Brown.

Klarner, Carl. 2003. "The Measurement of the Partisan Balance of State Government." *State Politics and Policy Quarterly* 3(3):309–319.

Kohler-Hausmann, Juilly. 2010. "'The Attila the Hun Law': New York's Rockefeller Drug Laws and the Making of a Punitive State." *Journal of Social History* 44(1):71–95.

Korpi, Walter and Joakim Palme. 1998. "The Paradox of Redistribution and Strategies of Equality: Welfare State Institutions, Inequality, and Poverty in the Western Countries." *American Sociological Review* 63(5):661–687.

Langan, Patrick A., John V. Fundis, Lawrence A. Greenfield, and Victoria W. Schneider. 1988. *Historical Statistics on Prisoners in State and Federal Institutions, Yearend 1925-86.* U.S. Department of Justice Bureau of Justice Statistics.

Lax, Jeffrey R. and Justin H. Phillips. 2009. "How Should We Estimate Public Opinion in the States?" *American Journal of Political Science* 53(1):107–121.

Lee, Harper. 1960. *To Kill a Mockingbird.* New York: Warner Books, Inc.

Lee, Hedwig, Tyler McCormick, Margaret T. Hicken, and Christopher Wildeman. 2015. "Racial Inequalities in Connectedness to Imprisoned Individuals in the United States." *Du Bois Review* 12(2): 269–282.

Lenz, Gabriel S. 2009. "Learning and Opinion Change, Not Priming: Reconsidering the Priming Hypothesis." *American Journal of Political Science* 53(4):821–837.

Lenz, Gabriel S. 2012. *Follow the Leader?* Chicago: University of Chicago Press.

Lerman, Amy E. 2009. The People Prisons Make: Effects of Incarceration on Criminal Psychology. In *Do Prisons Make Us Safer?* eds. Steven Raphael and Michael A. Stoll. New York: Russell Sage Foundation, chapter 5, pp. 151–176.

Lerman, Amy E. 2013. *The Modern Prison Paradox.* New York: Cambridge University Press.

Lerman, Amy E. and Vesla M. Weaver. 2014a. *Arresting Citizenship: The Democratic Consequences of American Crime Control.* Chicago: University of Chicago Press.

Lerman, Amy E. and Vesla Weaver. 2014b. Race and Crime in American Politics: From Law and Order to Willie Horton and Beyond. In *Oxford Handbook of Race, Ethnicity, Immigration, and Crime*, eds. Sandra M. Bucerius and Michael Tonry. New York: Oxford University Press, chapter 2, pp. 41–69.

Levendusky, Matthew. 2009. *The Partisan Sort.* Chicago: University of Chicago Press.

Levitt, Steven D. 2004. "Understanding Why Crime Fell in the 1990s: Four Factors that Explain the Decline and Six that Do Not." *Journal of Economic Perspectives* 18(1):163–190.

Liebling, Alison and Shadd Maruna. 2011. Introduction: The Effects of Imprisonment Revisited. In *The Effects of Imprisonment*, eds. Alison Liebling and Shadd Maruna. 2nd edn. New York: Routledge, chapter 1, pp. 1–29.

Lodge, Milton, Marco R. Steenbergen, and Shawn Brau. 1995. "The Responsive Voter: Campaign Information and the Dynamics of Candidate Evaluation." *American Political Science Review* 89(2):309–326.

Loo, Dennis D. and Ruth-Ellen M. Grimes. 2004. "Polls, Politics, and Crime: The 'Law and Order' Issue of the 1960s." *Western Criminology Review* 5(1):50–67.

Loury, Glenn C. 2010. "Crime, Inequality, and Social Justice." *Daedalus* 139(3):134–140.

Lyons, Jeffrey, William P. Jaeger, and Jennifer Wolak. 2013. "The Roots of Citizens' Knowledge of State Politics." *State Politics and Policy Quarterly* 13(2):183–202.

Manza, Jeff and Christopher Uggen. 2004. "Punishment and Democracy: Disenfranchisement of Nonincarcerated Felons in the United States." *Perspectives on Politics* 2(3):491–505.

Manza, Jeff and Christopher Uggen. 2006. *Locked Out: Felon Disenfranchisement and American Democracy.* New York: Oxford University Press.

Markham, James M. and William E. Farrell. 1973. "Toughest in the Nation." *The New York Times*, 13 May 1973. Available: http://timesmachine.nytimes.com/timesmachine/1973/05/13/90952714.html [Last accessed: August 8, 2014].

Marsh, Harry L. 1991. "A Comparative Analysis of Crime Coverage in Newspapers in the United States and Other Countries from 1960-1989: A Review of the Literature." *Journal of Criminal Justice* 19(1):67–79.

Marshall, Joshua Micah. 2000. "Death in Venice: Europe's Death-Penalty Elitism." *The New Republic* 223(5):12–14.

Maruna, Shadd and Anna King. 2009. "Once a Criminal, Always a Criminal?: 'Reedemability' and the Psychology of Punitive Public Attitudes." *European Journal on Criminal Justice Policy and Research* 15(1-2):7–24.

Maruna, Shadd, Amanda Matravers, and Anna King. 2004. "Disowning our Shadow: A Psychoanalytic Approach to Understanding Punitive Public Attitudes." *Deviant Behavior* 25(3):277–299.

Massoglia, Michael. 2008*a*. "Incarceration as Exposure: The Prison, Infectious Disease, and Other Stress-Related Illnesses." *Journal of Health and Social Behavior* 49(March):67–71.

Massoglia, Michael. 2008*b*. "Incarceration, Health, and Racial Disparities in Health." *Law and Society Review* 42(2):275–306.

Matthews, Roger. 2005. "The Myth of Punitiveness." *Theoretical Criminology* 9(2):175–201.

Mauer, Marc. 2006. *Race to Incarcerate*. New York: The New Press.

Mauer, Marc. 2011. "Addressing Racial Disparities in Incarceration." *The Prison Journal* 91(3):87S–101S.

Mauer, Marc and Ryan S. King. 2007. *A 25-Year Quagmire: The War on Drugs and Its Impact on American Society*. Washington, DC: The Sentencing Project.

Maxson, Cheryl, Karen Hennigan, and David C. Sloane. 2003. *Factors that Influence Public Opinion of the Police*. Washington, DC: United States Department of Justice, National Institute of Justice.

Mayer, William G. 1992. *The Changing American Mind: How and Why Public Opinion Changed between 1960 and 1988*. Ann Arbor: University of Michigan Press.

Mayhew, David R. 1974. *Congress: The Electoral Connection*. New Haven, CT: Yale University Press.

McAvoy, Gregory E. and Peter K. Enns. 2010. "Using Approval of the President's Handling of the Economy to Understand Who Polarizes and Why." *Presidential Studies Quarterly* 40(3):545–558.

McCarty, Nolan, Keith T. Poole, and Howard Rosenthal. 2006. *Polarized America: The Dance of Ideology and Unequal Riches*. Cambridge, MA: MIT Press.

McConnell, Edward B. 1978. "The Public Image of Courts." Prepared for The National Center for State Courts by Yankelovich, Skelly and White, Inc.

McDowall, David and Colin Loftin. 2005. "Are U.S. Crime Rate Trends Historically Contingent?" *Journal of Research in Crime and Delinquency* 42(4):359–383.

McDowall, David and Colin Loftin. 2007. What Is Convergence, and What Do We Know about It? In *What Is Convergence, and What Do We Know about It?* eds. James P. Lynch and Lynn A. Addington. New York: Oxford University Press, chapter 4, pp. 93–121.

McDowall, David and Colin Loftin. 2009. "Do US City Crime Rates Follow a National Trend? The Influence of Nationwide Conditions on Local Crime Patterns." *Journal of Quantitative Criminology* 25(3):307–324.

McGuire, Kevin T. and James A. Stimson. 2004. "The Least Dangerous Branch Revisited: New Evidence on Supreme Court Responsiveness to Public Preferences." *Journal of Politics* 66(4):1018–1035.

Melossi, Dario. 2008. *Controlling Crime, Controlling Society: Thinking about Crime in Europe and America*. Cambridge, UK: Polity Press.

Metcalfe, Christi, Justin T. Pickett, and Christina Mancini. 2015. "Using Path Analysis to Explain Racialized Support for Punitive Delinquency Policies." *Journal of Quantitative Criminology* 31(4): 699–725.

Middendorf, J. William, II. 2006. *A Glorious Disaster: Barry Goldwater's Presidential Campaign and the Origins of the Conservative Movement*. New York: Basic Books.

Miller, Lisa L. 2008. *The Perils of Federalism*. New York: Oxford University Press.

Minton, Todd D. 2012. *Jail Inmates at Midyear 2012 – Statistical Tables*. Bureau of Justice Statistics, U.S. Department of Justice. www.bjs.gov/content/pub/pdf/jim12st.pdf.

Moravcsik, Andrew. 2001. "The New Abolitionism: Why Does the U.S. Practice the Death Penalty while Europe Does Not?" *European Studies Newsletter* 4(1/2): 1–8.

Morone, James A. 2009. "The Politics of the Death Penalty." *Perspectives on Politics* 7(4):921–922.

Murakawa, Naomi. 2014. *The First Civil Right: How Liberals Built Prison America*. New York: Oxford University Press.

Murray, Michael P. 2009. "Modern Time-Series Methods and the Dynamics of Prison Populations." *Criminology and Public Policy* 8(1):79–86.

Mutz, Diana C. and Lilach Nir. 2010. "Not Necessarily the News: Does Fictional Television Influence Real-World Policy Preferences?" *Mass Communication and Society* 13(2):196–217.

Newell, Walker. 2013. "The Legacy of Nixon, Reagan, and Horton: How the Tough on Crime Movement Enabled a New Regime of Race-Influenced Employment Discrimination." *Berkeley Journal of African-American Law & Policy* 15(1):3–34.

Nicholson-Crotty, Sean and Kenneth J. Meier. 2003. "Crime and Punishment: The Politics of Federal Criminal Justice Sanctions." *Political Research Quarterly* 56(2):119–126.

Nicholson-Crotty, Sean, David A. M. Peterson, and Mark D. Ramirez. 2009. "Dynamic Representation(s): Federal Criminal Justice Policy and an Alternative Dimension of Public Mood." *Political Behavior* 31(4):629–655.

Niemi, Richard G., John Mueller, and Tom W. Smith. 1989. *Trends in Public Opinion: A Compendium of Survey Data*. Westport, CT: Greenwood Press.

O'Keefe, Ed. July 8, 2014. "Cory Booker, Rand Paul Team Up on Sentencing Reform Bill." *The Washington Post* (www.washingtonpost.com/news/post-politics/wp/2014/07/08/cory-booker-rand-paul-team-up-on-sentencing-reform-bill/).

Olson, Mancur. 1965. *The Logic of Collective Action*. Cambridge: Harvard University Press.

Page, Benjamin I. and Robert Y. Shapiro. 1983. "Effects of Public Opinion on Policy." *American Political Science Review* 77(1):175–190.

Page, Benjamin I. and Robert Y. Shapiro. 1992. *The Rational Public: Fifty Years of Trends in Americans' Policy Preferences*. Chicago: University of Chicago Press.

Pager, Devah. 2003. "The Mark of a Criminal Record." *American Journal of Sociology* 108(5):937–975.

Pager, Devah. 2005. "Double Jeopardy: Race, Crime, and Getting a Job." *Wisconsin Law Review* 2005(2):617–660.

Pager, Devah. 2007. *Marked: Race, Crime, and Finding Work in an Era of Mass Incarceration*. Chicago: University of Chicago Press.

Park, David K., Andrew Gelman, and Joseph Bafumi. 2004. "Bayesian Multilevel Estimation with Poststratification: State-Level Estimates from National Polls." *Political Analysis* 12(4):375–385.

Park, David K., Andrew Gelman, and Joseph Bafumi. 2006. State-Level Opinions from National Surveys: Poststratification using Multilevel Logistic Regression. In *Public Opinion in State Politics*, ed. Jeffrey Cohen. Palo Alto, CA: Stanford University Press.

Paulozzi, Leonard J. and Yongli Xi. 2008. "Recent Changes in Drug Poisoning Mortality in the United States by Urban-Rural Status and Drug Type." *Pharmacoepidemiology and Drug Safety* 17(10):997–1005.

Peffley, Mark and Jon Hurwitz. 2010. *Justice in America*. New York: Cambridge University Press.

Perry, Steven W. 2006. "Prosecutors in State Courts, 2005." *Bureau of Justice Statistics Bulletin* pp. 1–12.

Pettit, Becky and Bruce Western. 2004. "Mass Imprisonment and the Life Course: Race and Class Inequality in U.S. Incarceration." *American Sociological Review* 69(2):151–169.

Pfeffer, Jeffrey and Gerald R. Salancik. 1978. *The External Control of Organizations*. New York: Harper & Row.

Phillips, Kevin. 2015 [1969]. *The Emerging Republican Majority*. Princeton, NJ: Princeton University Press.

Pickett, Justin T. and Ted Chiricos. 2012. "Controlling Other People's Children: Racialized Views of Delinquency and Whites' Punitive Attitudes toward Juvenile Offenders." *Criminology* 50(3):673–710.

Pickett, Justin T., Ted Chiricos, Kristin M. Golden, and Marc Gertz. 2012. "Reconsidering the Relationship between Perceived Neighborhood Racial Composition and Whites' Perceptions of Victimization Risk: Do Racial Stereotypes Matter?" *Criminology* 50(1):145–186.

Pollak, Jessica M. and Charis E. Kubrin. 2007. "Crime in the News: How Crimes, Offenders and Victims Are Portrayed in the Media." *Journal of Criminal Justice and Popular Culture* 14(1):59–83.

Porter, Nicole D. 2012. *On the Chopping Block 2012: State Prison Closings*. Washington, DC: The Sentencing Project.

Porter, Nicole D. and Valerie Wright. 2011. *Cracked Justice*. Washington, DC: The Sentencing Project.

Potter, Gary W. and Victor E. Kappeler. 2006. *Constructing Crime: Perspectives on Making News and Social Problems*. 2nd edn. Long Grove, IL: Waveland Press, Inc.

Prior, Markus. 2007. *Post-Broadcast Democracy: How Media Choice Increases Inequality in Political Involvement and Polarizes Elections.* New York: Cambridge University Press.

Provine, Doris Marie. 2007. *Unequal under Law: Race and the War on Drugs.* Chicago: University of Chicago Press.

Provine, Doris Marie. 2011. "Race and Inequality in the War on Drugs." *Annual Review of Law and Social Science* 7:41–60.

Ramirez, Mark D. 2013. "Punitive Sentiment." *Criminology* 51(2):329–364.

Rand, Michael R. and Callie M. Rennison. 2002. "True Crime Stories? Accounting for Differences in Our National Crime Indicators." *Chance* 15(1):47–51.

Raphael, Steven. 2014. *The New Scarlet Letter? Negotiating the U.S. Labor Market with a Criminal Record.* Kalamazoo, MI: W.E. Upjohn Institute for Employment Research.

Raphael, Steven and Michael A. Stoll. 2009. Why Are so Many Americans in Prison? In *Do Prisons Make us Safer?* eds. Steven Raphael and Michael A. Stoll. New York: Russell Sage Foundation, chapter 2, pp. 27–72.

Rasinski, Kenneth A. 1989. "The Effect of Question Wording on Public Support for Government Spending." *Public Opinion Quarterly* 53(3):388–394.

Reiner, Robert. 2002. Media Made Criminality: The Representation of Crime in the Mass Media. In *The Oxford Handbook of Criminology*, 3rd edn., eds. Mike Maguire, Rod Morgan, and Robert Reiner. Oxford: Oxford University Press, pp. 302–340.

Roberts, Julian V. 1997. American Attitudes about Punishment: Myth and Reality. In *Sentencing Reform in Overcrowded Times*, eds. Michael Tonry and Kathleen Hatlestad. New York: Oxford University Press, chapter 5, pp. 250–255.

Roberts, Julian V. and Loretta J. Stalans. 2000. *Public Opinion, Crime, and Criminal Justice.* Boulder, CO: Westview Press.

Roberts, Julian V., Loretta J. Stalans, David Indermaur, and Mike Hough. 2003. *Penal Populism and Public Opinion: Lessons from Five Countries.* Oxford: Oxford University Press.

Room, Robin. 1998. "Alcohol and Drug Disorders in the International Classification of Diseases: A Shifting Kaleidoscope." *Drug and Alcohol Review* 17(3):305–317.

Rogers, John B. 2001. FOCUS I Survey and Final Report: A Summary of the Findings: Families Officers and Corrections Understanding Stress. (www.ncjrs.gov/pdffiles1/nij/grants/188094.pdf).

Rosenfeld, Richard. 2009. "Crime Is the Problem: Homicide, Acquisitive Crime, and Economic Conditions." *Journal of Quantitative Criminology* 25(3):287–306.

Rosenfeld, Richard and Robert Fornango. 2007. "The Impact of Economic Conditions on Robbery and Property Crime: The Role of Consumer Sentiment." *Criminology* 45(4):735–769.

Rosenfeld, Richard, Karen Terry, and Preeti Chauhan. 2014. "New York's Crime Drop Puzzle: Introduction to the Special Issue." *Justice Quarterly* 31(1):1–4.

Rusche, Georg and Otto Kirchheimer. 1939. *Punishment and Social Structure.* New York: Columbia University Press.

Samkoff, Judith S. and Susan P. Baker. 1982. "Recent Trends in Fatal Poisoning by Opiates in the United States." *American Journal of Public Health* 72(11):1251–1256.

Scheufele, Dietram A. 1999. "Framing as a Theory of Media Effects." *Journal of Communications* 49(1):103–122.

Schmitt, John and Kris Warner. 2010. *Ex-offenders and the Labor Market*. Center for Economic and Policy Research. www.cepr.net/documents/publications/ex offenders-2010-11.pdf.

Schneider, Anne Larason. 2006. "Patterns of Change in the Use of Imprisonment in the American States: An Integration of Path Dependence, Punctuated Equilibrium and Policy Design Approaches." *Political Research Quarterly* 59(3):457–470.

Schneider, Sandra K. and William G. Jacoby. 2012. "Are Americans 'Intuitive Federalists'?" Paper prepared for presentation at the Annual Meeting of the Midwest Political Science Association.

Schnittker, Jason and Andrea John. 2007. "Enduring Stigma: The Long-Term Effects of Incarceration on Health." *Journal of Health and Social Behavior* 48(2):115–130.

Schnittker, Jason, Michael Massoglia, and Christopher Uggen. 2011. "Incarceration and the Health of the African American Community." *Du Bois Review* 8(1):1–9.

Schnittker, Jason, Michael Massoglia, and Christopher Uggen. 2012. "Out and Down: Incarceration and Psychiatric Disorders." *Journal of Health and Social Behavior* 53(4):448–464.

Shannon, Sarah and Christopher Uggen. 2013. "Visualizing Punishment." *The Society Pages*. February. http://thesocietypages.org/papers/visualizing-punishment/.

Shaw, Greg M., Roberty Y. Shapiro, Shmuel Lock, and Lawrence R. Jacobs. 1998. "Trends: Crime, the Police, and Civil Liberties." *Public Opinion Quarterly* 62(3):405–426.

Silver, Charles and Robert Shapiro. 1984. "Public Opinion and the Federal Judiciary: Crime, Punishment, and Demographic Constraints." *Population Research and Policy Review* 3(3):255–280.

Simon, Jonathan. 2007. *Governing through Crime*. Oxford: Oxford University Press.

Skogan, Wesley G. 2009. "Concern about Crime and Confidence in the Police." *Police Quarterly* 12(3):301–318.

Smith, Kevin B. 2004. "The Politics of Punishment: Evaluating Political Explanations of Incarceration Rates." *Journal of Politics* 66(3):925–938.

Smith, Tom W. 1987. "That Which We Call Welfare by Any Other Name Would Smell Sweeter: An Analysis of the Impact of Question Wording on Response Patterns." *Public Opinion Quarterly* 51(1):75–83.

Snauffer, Douglas. 2006. *Crime Television*. Westport, CT: Praeger.

Soroka, Stuart N. 2014. *Negativity in Democratic Politics: Causes and Consequences*. New York: Cambridge University Press.

Soroka, Stuart N. and Christopher Wlezien. 2010. *Degrees of Democracy: Politics, Public Opinion, and Policy*. New York: Cambridge University Press.

Soss, Joe, Richard C. Fording, and Sanford F. Schram. 2011. *Disciplining the Poor: Neoliberal Paternalism and the Persistent Power of Race*. Chicago: University of Chicago Press.

Soss, Joe, Laura Langbein, and Alan R. Metelko. 2003. "Why Do White Americans Support the Death Penalty?" *Journal of Politics* 65(2):397–421.

Spelman, William. 2000. The Limited Importance of Prison Expansion. In *The Crime Drop in America*, eds. Alfred Blumstein and Joel Wallman. New York: Cambridge University Press, chapter 4, pp. 97–129.

Spelman, William. 2009. "Crime, Cash, and Limited Options: Explaining the Prison Boom." *Criminology and Public Policy* 8(1):29–77.

Stack, Steven J. and Olga Tsoudis. 1997. "Suicide Risk among Correctional Officers: A Logistic Regression Analysis." *Archives of Suicide Research* 3(3): 183–186.

Stimson, James A. 1991. *Public Opinion in America: Moods, Cycles, and Swings.* Boulder, CO: Westview Press.

Stimson, James A. 1999. *Public Opinion in America: Moods, Cycles, and Swings.* 2nd edn. Boulder, CO: Westview Press.

Stimson, James A., Michael B. MacKuen, and Robert S. Erikson. 1995. "Dynamic Representation." *American Political Science Review* 89(3):543–565.

Stokes, Donald E. 1966. "Some Dynamic Elements of Contests for the Presidency." *The American Political Science Review* 60(1):19–28.

Struck, Doug. 1989. "Got 15 Years to Life for Drug Sale: College Student Does Slow Time." *The Baltimore Sun* (June 4). Available: http://articles.latimes.com/1989-06-04/news/mn-2566_1_drug-sale-maximum-security-prisons-street-corners-selling-heroin [Last accessed: August 8, 2014].

Tierney, John. 2012a. "For Lesser Crimes, Rethinking Life behind Bars." *New York Times* (December 11). www.nytimes.com/2012/12/12/science/mandatory-prison-sentences-face-growing-skepticism.html?_r=0.

Tierney, John. 2012b. "Life without Parole: Four Inmates' Stories." *New York Times* (December 12), 2012. www.nytimes.com/2012/12/12/science/life-without-parole-four-inmates-stories.html.

Tocqueville, Alexis de. 1988. *Democracy in America* (George Lawrence, trans.; J. P. Mayer, ed.; New York: HarperPerennial).

Tonry, Michael. 2004. *Thinking about Crime.* New York: Oxford University Press.

Tonry, Michael. 2009. "Explanations of American Punishment Policies." *Punishment and Society* 11(3):377–394.

Tonry, Michael. 2011. *Punishing Race.* New York: Oxford University Press.

Tooley, Michael, Jeffrey Linkenbach, Brian J. Lande, and Gary M. Lande. 2009. "The Media, the Public, and the Law Enforcement Community: Correcting Misperceptions." *The Police Chief* LXXVI(6). www.policechiefmagazine.org/magazine/index.cfm?fuseaction=display_arch&article_id=1828&issue_id=62009.

Travis, Jeremy, Bruce Western, and Steve Redburn. 2014. *The Growth of Incarceration in the United States.* Washington, DC: The National Academies Press.

Truman, David. 1951. *The Governmental Process.* New York: Alfred A. Knopf.

Tsebelis, George. 2002. *Veto Players: How Political Institutions Work.* New York: Russell Sage Foundation.

Tuchman, Gaye. 1978. *Making News: A Study in the Construction of Reality.* New York: The Free Press.

Uggen, Christopher. 2008. "Editorial Introduction: The Effect of Criminal Background Checks on Hiring Ex-offenders." *Criminology and Public Policy* 7(3): 367–369.

Uggen, Christopher. 2012. *Crime and the Great Recession.* Stanford, CA: Stanford Center on Poverty and Inequality.

Uggen, Christopher, Sarah Shannon, and Jeff Manza. 2012. "State-Level Estimates of Felon Disenfranchisement in the United States, 2010." The Sentencing Project. July 2012. http://sentencingproject.org/doc/publications/fd_State_Level_Estimates_of_Felon_Disen_2010.pdf

Uggen, Christopher, Mike Vuolo, Sarah Lageson, Ebony Ruhland, and Hilary K. Whitman. 2014. "The Edge of Stigma: An Experimental Audit of the Effects of Low-Level Criminal Records on Employment." *Criminology* 52(4): 627–654.

Unah, Isaac and Elizabeth K. Coggins. 2013. "When Governors Speak up for Justice: Punishment Politics and Mass Incarceration in the American States." *Political Sciences & Public Affairs* 1(1):1–12.

Unnever, James D. and Francis T. Cullen. 2010. "The Social Sources of Americans' Punitiveness: A Test of Three Competing Models." *Criminology* 48(1):99–129.

Useem, Bert and Anne Morrison Piehl. 2008. *Prison State: The Challenges of Mass Incarceration*. New York: Cambridge University Press.

Wacquant, Loïc. 2010. "Class, race and Hyperincarceration in Revanchist America." *Daedalus* 139(3):74–90.

Wakefield, Sara and Christopher Uggen. 2010. "Incarceration and Stratification." *Annual Review of Sociology* 36:387–406.

Wakefield, Sara and Chistopher Wildeman. 2011. "Mass Imprisonment and Racial Disparities in Childhood Behavioral Problems." *Criminology and Public Policy* 10(3):793–817.

Wakefield, Sara and Christopher Wildeman. 2013. *Children of the Prison Boom: Mass Incarceration and the Future of American Inequality*. New York: Oxford University Press.

Walmsley, Roy. 2009. *World Prison Population List*. 8th edn. Ann Arbor: University of Michigan Press.

Warr, Mark. 1995. "Poll Trends: Public Opinion on Crime and Punishment." *Public Opinion Quarterly* 59(2):296–310.

Weaver, Kent R., Robert Y. Shapiro, and Lawrence R. Jacobs. 1995. "Trends: Welfare." *Public Opinion Quarterly* 59(4):606–627.

Weaver, Vesla M. 2007. "Frontlash: Race and the Development of Punitive Crime Policy." *Studies in American Political Development* 21(2):230–265.

Weaver, Vesla M. and Amy E. Lerman. 2010. "Political Consequences of the Carceral State." *American Political Science Review* 104(4):817–833.

West Group. 1999. *California Penal Code*. West Group.

Westcott, Lucy. 2015. "America's Drug Laws at Work: Louisiana Man Serving 13 Years for Weed Denied Clemency." *Newsweek* (6/19/15). www.newsweek.com/bernard-noble-weed-marijuana-legalize-marijuana-war-drugs-drug-policy-345061.

Western, Bruce. 2006. *Punishment and Inequality in America*. New York: Russell Sage Foundation.

Western, Bruce, Jeffrey R. Kling, and David F. Weiman. 2001. "The Labor Market Consequences of Incarceration." *Crime and Delinquency* 47(3):410–427.

Whitford, Andrew B. and Jeff Yates. 2003. "Policy Signals and Executive Governance: Presidential Rhetoric in the War on Drugs." *Journal of Politics* 65(4):995–1012.

Wildeman, Christopher, Anna R. Haskins, and Christopher Muller. 2013. Implications of Mass Imprisonment for Inequality among American Children. In *The Punitive Turn: New Approaches to Race and Incarceration*, eds. Deborah E. McDowell, Claudrena Harold, and Juan Battle. Charlottesville, MA: University of Virginia Press, chapter 2, pp. 117–191.

Wildeman, Christopher, Sara Wakefield, and Kristin Turney. 2012. "Misidentifying the Effects of Parental Incarceration? A Comment on Johnson and Easterline (2012)." *Journal of Marriage and Family* 75(1):252–258.

Wilson, James Q. 1975. *Thinking about Crime*. New York: Basic Books.

Wlezien, Christopher. 2005. "On the Salience of Political Issues: The Problem with 'Most Important Problem.'" *Electoral Studies* 24(4):555–579.

Wlezien, Christopher and Stuart Soroka. 2011. Inequality in Policy Responsiveness? In *Who Gets Represented?*, eds. Peter K. Enns and Christopher Wlezien. New York: Russell Sage Foundation, chapter 10, pp. 285–310.

Wlezien, Christopher and Stuart N. Soroka. 2012. "Political Institutions and the Opinion-Policy Link." *West European Politics* 35(6):1407–1432.

Yates, Jeff and Richard Fording. 2005. "Politics and State Punitiveness in Black and White." *Journal of Politics* 67(4):1099–1121.

Ye Hee Lee, Michelle. 2013. "MCSO Sheriff Arpaio seeks to double budget for jail, upgrades." *The Arizona Republic*. February 19, 2013. www.azcentral.com/news/articles/20130219mcso-arpaio-seeks-double-budget-jail-upgrades.html.

Zaller, John R. 1992. *The Nature and Origins of Mass Opinion*. New York: Cambridge University Press.

Zaller, John. 2003. Coming to Grips with V.O. Key's Concept of Latent Opinion. In *Electoral Democracy*, eds. Michael B. MacKuen and George Rabinowitz. Ann Arbor, MI: University of Michigan Press.

Zimring, Franklin E. and Gordon Hawkins. 1991. *The Scale of Imprisonment*. Chicago: University of Chicago Press.

Zimring, Franklin E. and Gordon Hawkins. 1992. "Prison Population and Criminal Justice in California." *CPS Brief* 4(8):1–7.

Zimring, Franklin E., Gordon Hawkins, and Sam Kamin. 2001. *Punishment and Democracy: Three Strikes and You're Out in California*. New York: Oxford University Press.

Zimring, Franklin E. and David T. Johnson. 2006. "Public Opinion and the Governance of Punishment in Democratic Political Systems." *The ANNALS of the American Academy of Political and Social Science* 605(1):266–280.

Zlotnick, David M. 2008. "The Future of Federal Sentencing Policy: Learning Lessons from Republican Judicial Appointees in the Guidelines Era." *University of Colorado Law Review* 79(1):1–76.

Index